D0850282

DISCARDED BY

MACPHÁIDÍN LIBRARY

CUSHING-MARTIN LIBRARY
STONEHILL COLLEGE
NORTH EASTON, MASSACHUSETTS 02357

Managing a Sales Force

Second edition

Other titles from Marketing Improvements Limited

How to Handle Major Customers Profitably

Motivating your Sales Force

Negotiating Profitable Sales

Recruiting and Selecting Successful Salesmen

Running an Effective Sales Office

Training Salesmen on the Job

The Management of Marketing

Managing a Sales Force
Second edition

Mike Wilson
of Marketing Improvements Limited

Gower

© M. T. Wilson 1970, 1983

All rights reserved. No part of this publication may be reproduced, stored in a retrieval system, or transmitted in any form or by any means, electronic, mechanical, photocopying, recording, or otherwise without the prior permission of Gower Publishing Company Limited.

First published 1970 by Gower Press Limited
Reprinted 1971, 1973, 1974, 1979, 1980, 1981

Second edition published 1983 by
Gower Publishing Company Limited
Aldershot, Hants, England
Reprinted 1985

Wilson, M. T.
   Managing a sales force.—2nd ed.
   1. Sales management
   I. Title
   658.8'1   HF5438.4

ISBN 0 566 02377 6

Printed by Nene Litho
Bound by Woolnough Bookbinding
both of Wellingborough, Northamptonshire

TO DANNY
For her love, patience and encouragement

Contents

Part Two: HOW TO MANAGE A SALES FORCE

Illustrations

Preface to the Second Edition

It is now over ten years since *Managing a Sales Force* was first published, a decade which has been traumatic for the world at large and the business community and all associated with it in particular.

The established pattern of world economics has been destroyed by the energy crisis which started in late 1973 and has been an underlying cause of recurring recessions ever since. Inflation and currency fluctuations have caused costs to rise with a rapidity and volatility previously unknown.

No country in the world has been left untouched by these processes. For a few nations who possess oil (or other highly demanded commodities) it has been a period of unprecedented and often uncontrollable growth, bringing great wealth but also almost unbearable pressure on the social and economic fabrics of the countries concerned. Iran and Nigeria in their different ways exemplify the opportunities and problems of coping with such dramatic changes. For the majority of countries, including most of the industrialised world, the energy crisis has forced a total reshaping of their economic and social frameworks. Market after market, industry after industry, have been affected, causing stagnation, decline or even elimination (as in the case of the UK motorcycle industry).

Politically it has been a decade of significance too with Britain joining the EEC and successive governments swinging from interventionist attitudes towards industry (for example, price controls) to virtual "laisser faire" with immense unrelieved economic hardship being suffered by employers and employees alike as the government concentrated its efforts on reducing inflation by controlling the money supply.

The UK of course is not alone in trying to adjust to the "new economics" of more expensive raw materials, notably oil, and the desire of commodity-rich nations to industrialise, thus reducing their traditional imports. Even those nations that had enjoyed considerable economic growth and high and rising standards of living, such as the USA, Sweden, France and West Germany, have been forced to rethink their traditional approaches to managing their economies.

Socially much has changed as well, with strong moves towards employee protection, elimination of sex and race discrimination, consumerism, etc. Technologically it has also been an era of rapid development, notably in computerisation where the microchip has brought significant dataprocessing capability within the reach of every firm and indeed a large number of consumers.

This book, however, is not about the rapidly changing world at large but about what it means to sales management. Most of these great waves of change sweeping through society of course impact the sales manager both directly and indirectly. His own world too has changed radically. The marketplaces in which he deals are no longer likely to be expanding, where sales forecasting could simply mean adding 10% to last year's figures. Market stagnation or decline changes not only the scale of activity but also its very nature. More sales managers than ever before must be concerned with profit or margin protection through mechanisms other than sales increases. Thus "productivity" is more likely to be the name of the game than "growth".

His customers have changed too, particularly for the sales manager selling through distribution networks. There has been a dramatic polarisation in most markets, the big customers getting larger, the small specialising or going to the wall. For example, in the food trade, where a handful of retailers now control the majority of the industry, the whole sales activity of the manufacturer has had to be completely reshaped. Sales forces have been decimated as it needs far fewer sales staff, albeit much more skilled, to handle the tiny number of key accounts. Similar trends towards the concentration of buying power can be observed in most industries and most countries.

The nature of competition has changed too. It is becoming ever more international because of the expansion of the European Economic Community, the dramatic growth of the Japanese economy and the underlying drive of all countries to expand exports to pay for their escalating oil bills. In the UK we are seeing market after market now increasingly occupied by imported products – cars, washing machines, hi-fi equipment, machine tools, etc.

Matching these changes in the external environment, there have been significant developments inside the firm. Recruitment and, particularly, termination of staff have become increasingly governed by legislation. It is now commonplace to find sales forces unionised, an incredible thought for most companies ten years ago.

If not commonplace as yet, it is increasingly usual to find women in the sales force and sales management, doing jobs that ten years ago would have been regarded as exclusively male preserves. The growth of sex equality has great advantages for sales management as it practically doubles the pool from which to select the talents required. (Unfortunately, the English language has not yet evolved an elegant phase to cover "he or she" so whilst certain key descriptions have been changed in this edition, most of the text has been left in the masculine gender. Any such references should be read as being applicable to persons of either sex unless commonsense dictates otherwise.)

Many of the routines of sales activity (eg, order reception and processing, enquiry handling) which depended totally on manual effort are now partially or entirely computerised. Developments in behavioural science and learning technology have changed the way in which many sales forces are trained, transmuting the traditional class-room methods into audio-visual self-learning packages.

In summary, the sales manager of the 1980s is facing a world radically different from the one his predecessor did ten years ago. It is a world characterised by static markets, increasing international competition, fewer larger customers and rising costs, a world in which success demands fewer, more highly skilled sales staff, more precisely focused on the key issue of the business, profits from productivity.

Perhaps most significant of all, these characteristics are found in most industrialised societies (and in many so-called "developing nations" too), suggesting that the economic problems and the social changes they cause have become more internationally common in the last decade. For example, the problems facing the steel industry are remarkably similar in many different countries throughout the world.

If it is a more constrained and challenging environment than a decade ago, at least the sales manager has a few more allies and weapons today with which to fight the battle for profits. A much clearer recognition of the crucial importance of the sales function from society in general and top management in particular has been caused by the desperate need for sales revenue. In the more sophisticated companies at least there tends to be closer harmony between "marketing" (ie, product management, promotion, etc) and "sales", forced by the major customers who demand not only sales, service and negotiation, but also special advertising and promotions and often special products. Advances in computer technology offer significant cost-saving opportunities right across the sales function, while improvements in educational technology can provide more effective ways of developing the knowledge and skills of the sales team.

In preparing the second edition of this book all these major external and internal factors, both positive and negative, have been borne in mind and not surprisingly certain sections have had to be changed radically and all of it updated even where the basic concepts and techniques discussed remain valid. The addition of the third section, "Sales Management in Practice", in many ways is symptomatic of these changes. In a volatile environment it can be difficult to identify clear trends and therefore it is illuminating to review a series of case histories to form a view at least on the range of best current practice and the experiences of others.

Perhaps the sheer rate of change and confusion in the world makes a book like this even more necessary: it should form a sound basis on which the practising sales manager can construct his own sales activity adapted to the individual needs of his situation. The primary intention of this book has not changed in that regard.

It was written originally because the bulk of the literature seemed to be aimed at the student rather than the businessman and to be presented in a way that made it hard for the sales manager to absorb. By the nature of their job, and often of character and education too, most sales managers flinch from the concentrated study that a textbook demands. Even when a manager thoroughly reads a book he too often finds that much of what is said does not apply to his level of experience or to his particular business.

Purpose of this book

This book attempts to overcome these objections. It is written for the practitioner, not the student, although the student may find items of value in it. It is based on experience gained in Europe but which has also been tested in many other parts of the world. It is constructed in a way that enables the practising sales manager to refer to individual sections readily without having to plough through the whole text. Moreover, space has been allocated for the sales manager to write in his own experiences, problems and practices so that the book can be made specific to his own business.

Who should read it

This book is for the sales manager, but this job title covers a multitude of different functions in different companies in different parts of the world. More precisely, therefore, it is intended for those who control field sales forces either internationally, nationally, regionally or at an area level. Obviously some of the broader areas discussed may be of little immediate value to the recently appointed District Manager. Conversely some of the detailed techniques of salesmen management may have been long since delegated by the General Sales Manager of a major corporation. Nevertheless any manager concerned with the performance of a field force should find the vital elements of his job discussed in this book.

This book is designed to cope with the often false distinctions that are drawn between consumer and industrial marketing, and between selling goods and selling services. Examples have been chosen to try and demonstrate that at sales management level at least the differences in technique are far smaller than the conventional wisdom would suggest. Of course each company is unique in terms of its history, personnel, products and practices; the question is how far these characteristics affect the application of fundamental concepts and methods of sales management. This is why space has been left for the reader to write in his particular practice so that he can represent the uniqueness of his business.

Contents

The book is in three sections. The first explores the place of sales management within the marketing function. It identifies the role it must play if it is to be integrated into the total strategy. The job of the sales manager is then analysed against this background to see what it is that he must do as a manager, as a controller of a sales force and as a member of the marketing team. At the end of this section the sales manager should have a clearer picture of his responsibilities both in general and specific terms and be able to define what further knowledge and skills he must develop to discharge those responsibilities fully.

The second part is concerned with how the sales manager does his job and is broken down into the particular functions he performs of planning, organising, staffing, training, motivating and controlling his sales force. This is the "how to" part of the book and concentrates on method and technique rather than concept and academic background. The yardstick for selection of material is the best current practice that is generally applicable and has been chosen mainly from the European scene.

The third part, which is totally new, is designed to demonstrate sales management in practice – to show via a number of case histories how the principles and techniques described earlier can and do work in real life, and how companies are searching for innovations in sales management practice as they are driven relentlessly by their environments to achieve greater efficiency. For many readers, it is this section that will make the whole book "come alive" as they see the concepts and methods that have earlier been discussed sequentially and analytically being synthesised and put into action by companies in a wide variety of industries and situations.

How it should be used

This book is not meant for bedside reading. It is designed for use as a working tool by the practising sales manager. Apart from the early chapters which delineate the area covered by sales management, and the final section, all the material is organised in the following way. Each topic is introduced by a general description showing its relationship with other aspects of sales management, inherent difficulties, common misconceptions and failures of current practice. Techniques that have proved successful are then described with examples from a cross-section of industry to show the practical application of them. Finally working sheets, checklists, analysis forms, planning formats etc are provided for the reader so that he can translate the general methods into specific action in his particular environment.

At the end of each chapter, there is a form headed Action Planning Checklist. This form identifies the major points of the chapter and suggests how the sales manager can turn these items into action. It is recommended that the prescribed action is written on the form (or on a copy of it) and dated so that it can be followed up and evaluated later. Amendments will be needed from time to time in the answers given. Further questions will also probably spring to mind. By planning action in this way the sales manager can keep a continuous record of his decisions and so assess how his performance is progressing.

This checklist is not meant as a self-examination of how much has been learnt from the chapter. It is intended to convert description into practice.

Thus the book will become increasingly personalised as the manager uses it to improve his performance. Obviously the amount of space that has been left is limited and will have to be supplemented in many cases by copies of the working papers but this is generally no problem for the modern manager who has reprographic facilities readily available.

Conclusion

This book is designed to be used. It is not meant to decorate the inevitable bookshelf in the executive suite which is already overcrowded with unopened tomes bought in a flush of managerial enthusiasm. This book should be on the desk, in the briefcase, in the car or wherever the work is done. It is meant to get dirty with handling, to be written in and noted on because this is the only way the descriptions can be translated into applications. Sales management is not an academic discipline, but a dynamic practice aimed at producing profitable results. Therefore the body of knowledge contained in this volume has no value in itself. It only becomes valuable when it is used. The construction of the book is intended to avoid the basic deficiencies of traditional textbooks. But the responsibility still must rest with the user to make it work for him.

This book attempts to bridge the gap between what is known and what is done. The techniques recommended here have been tested sufficiently for it to be stated that they will improve managerial performance if properly applied. However, no book can create a manager. From what little is known, it is clear that a part at least of management ability is innate. This character element will not be significantly changed by reading a book. What this book can do is to improve the sales manager within the limitations of his intrinsic qualities if he cares to use it as a working tool.

Marketing Improvements Limited   Mike Wilson
Ulster House
Ulster Terrace
Regent's Park
London NW1

Acknowledgements

In a book like this which is constructed from the experiences of working with many thousands of managers over many years it is impossible to express individual appreciation to all who deserve it.

Without in any way disregarding the contribution of others, I must mention particularly the staff and external faculty of the College of Marketing who contributed so much to the original content and especially my colleagues in Marketing Improvements and all our clients who for the last eighteen years have been an unfailing source of inspiration, information and advice. Finally my special thanks to Ros Weale for research support and Sue Plummer for once again typing a hieroglyphic manuscript; without them this Second Edition could not have been prepared in time to meet the publishing deadline!

M.T.W.

PART ONE

THE MARKETING FUNCTION AND THE ROLE OF THE SALES MANAGER

CHAPTER 1

Role of the Sales Force Within the Marketing Function

Traditionally, business enterprise has consisted of two major functions: production, which was concerned with making the product or service available; and selling, which distributed the products or services to customers in exchange for money. Obviously there are other important business functions such as finance and research but these cannot exist until the making and selling processes have been at least defined. What money and research are required cannot be identified until what is to be made and sold is specified. In the very small business, for example in that of the village blacksmith, both functions were vested in the one man and he had little difficulty in arranging the relationship between them. His production of horseshoes could be directly determined by the number and types of horses brought to him.

The problems of industry today have been largely created by the move away from this basic situation. As the small business grows, not only does the workload expand but also the market area served gets larger. Thus, very quickly, the one man neither knows all his customers nor can he control all the functions of the business. Initial growth for a company is usually caused by pressure of demand and so the first reaction is to concentrate on expansion of production. This results in a relative underdevelopment of the sales side, which is seen as less important in a demand situation. By concentration on production, however, the scales of demand and supply soon begin to balance and often start to tip in the opposite direction. The company which has been in a demand situation, working towards a goal of what can be made and how it can be sold, is faced, often suddenly, with a supply position. The question now to be asked is – what can be sold and how can it be made?

Every sales manager must appreciate the implications of this simple analysis, for it contains within it the fundamental reasons for the vast changes that are happening within and around the sales function. Selling has changed from a simple process of persuading customers to buy goods or services that have been conceived solely by the producers. It is today a vital part of the larger function which is known as marketing.

What is marketing?

Marketing is a term now commonly used in most companies, although many companies still seem to use it simply as a synonym for selling, or as a grander title for advertising.

The correct application, however, carries the meaning far beyond such limited views. The concept of marketing is not new. It is simply the arrangement of the company so that it can function in much the same way as the village blacksmith did. He had two enormous advantages over today's corporations. He controlled all the functions of the business directly and he had an intimate knowledge of his market. This is all that the marketing concept really demands: that the business should be based on the needs of the consumers and that its functions should be so co-ordinated that the whole company works towards the satisfaction of these needs at a profit.

Definition of marketing

The Institute of Marketing defines marketing as the management function responsible for identifying, anticipating and satisfying customer requirements profitably. The necessity for looking at the business in this way is obvious from the simple analogies of business growth given above. In a supply situation where customers can readily obtain their requirements, the best way that a company has of ensuring that its products are favoured is to arrange production of those products which best meet the customer's needs. Moreover, the greater the need satisfactions offered, the higher the price obtainable. Thus, it will be easier to ensure profitability, which must be the prime aim of any free enterprise firm within a capitalist economy.

The profit objective has had considerable re-examination in recent years as to whether it is the real prime goal of an enterprise. Much of the discussion seems to confuse means and ends. Our view is simply that a capitalist society relies upon its industry to create wealth which can then be distributed, by way of pay to staff, dividends to shareholders, taxation to government and thus to support social services which in themselves are not wealth-creating. It is therefore both the purpose and duty of a capitalist firm to create profit; if it fails to do so not only do the firm and its members suffer but also society as a whole. The profit objective must always have been prime. What has changed is our concepts of the best ways to achieve the objective and, having achieved it, the fairest means of distributing the profits.

Difficulties of implementation

Few managers would disagree with the logic of the above analogies and yet the marketing concept is still not fully implemented in the vast majority of companies. Marketing is far more difficult to practise than to preach because there are inherent conflicts within this concept of organising the firm's resources and functions to satisfy consumer needs at a profit. The two major sources of these conflicts are the relationship of the functions within the firm and the relationship of the firm with its customers. They will be exposed by an examination of the marketing system.

The marketing system is made up of five elements, the market, the company, the marketing mix (which is what the company offers the market), the distribution system and the environment within which the system operates. (See Figure 1.1.)

The market and its segments

The market consists of a number of actual and potential buyers with needs to be satisfied. However, the term itself can be misleading when used in the sense of "the market for cars" or "the market for machine tools." There is an underlying implication that "the market for cars" is similar in its homogeneity to the "production for cars," the latter being concerned with creating products, the former with consuming them. Even a brief examination reveals that although the product – that is, "cars" – remains physically the

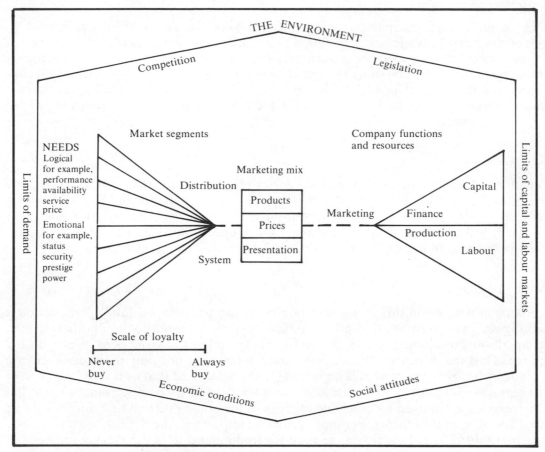

Fig. 1.1 The marketing system

same in both phrases, the acts of creation and consumption differ vastly. The striking feature of modern production techniques is the ability to produce vast quantities of exactly similar goods. It is easy to assume, therefore, that vast quantities of exactly similar people consume them. If a closer look is taken at any market it can be seen that this is not so.

Each individual customer is, in fact, different in terms of his or her needs. Some of these needs will be logical, others emotional. In some businesses these differences are so critical that each customer must have a product that is specifically made to fit that unique need pattern, for example, bespoke tailoring. Even where a standard product is acceptable, the particular need satisfactions it offers will vary from one customer to another. The same car may be bought by one person because of its performance and by another because of its boot space. Obviously it is impractical for most companies to offer tailor-made products as this would slow down the production process too much and thus increase the cost. Nevertheless it is unwise of any company to ignore these need differences. The problem of relating mass production to individual customer needs is being tackled in some industries by extension of the product range and particularly by offering a variety of alternative specifications for certain product groups. The motor industry demonstrates this trend, having moved from an attitude of "any colour you like as long as it is black" to today offering a very wide variety of engine and body trim configurations for each model. Thus while the basic theme of a car remains constant and can be mass produced, variations on the theme enable customers to match their individual need patterns.

Definition of segments

Most sophisticated companies regard their markets not as homogeneous masses of customers but as a series of segments. Each market segment represents a number of buyers or potential buyers who have similar enough need patterns to be tempted to buy the same products for the same reasons. The number of segments in a market will vary greatly but there will always be at least two. There is always a number of buyers who are more interested in performance than price and always a group of customers for whom cost is all-important.

Buyer loyalty

A further dimension on the market is the degree of buyer loyalty to a particular company which can range from total – that is, the buyer will buy a particular company's product repeatedly – to nil (he will never buy from that company). Loyalty to a particular company will vary from segment to segment, based upon how successful the company has been in the past in satisfying customers with that particular need pattern.

Nature of competition

Looking at markets in this way gives a new definition to "competition." Competition is usually seen as companies that offer products or services similar to one another. In fact, competition exists where goods or services compete for the same need or purchasing power. Thus the domestic steam iron manufacturer must not only monitor other iron producers but also watch what is happening to the basic need that he is satisfying, that of the removal of creases by the housewife. The laundry industry competes in the sense that the creases are removed by someone other than the housewife and therefore her direct need for an iron disappears. Perhaps even more important, the development of crease-resistant fabrics could eliminate the need for ironing and thus the market for irons.

In industrial terms, the need to purchase a particular piece of plant – for example, a forklift truck from a manufacturer – might be eliminated by hiring it from a leasing firm or by a change in the industrial process concerned, such as installing a conveyor.

Competition for purchasing power is equally important. For a farmer to buy new grain storage equipment, he might have to forgo purchasing a new tractor. On the broader scale of government expenditure, hospital and school building programmes may have to be financed by cutting back on defence spending. Thus, the manufacturer of guided missiles is competing in a very real sense with the producer of educational equipment.

The market must be thoroughly analysed from all these facets if a company is to organise itself to supply customer needs at a profit. This is the process of marketing research which is beyond the scope of this book. However, it is apparent that the sales manager must be familiar with the nature of the market in order successfully to gain orders from it. Already it is clear that the sales management function within a marketing strategy is very different from simply distributing what production makes. Moreover, in many companies the marketing research process itself will require an input from the field force, as this is the major point of customer contact. Once the nature of the company is examined and, in particular, the relationship between the company and its markets, it will be easier to identify the detailed role of sales management within the marketing function.

The company: its resources and functions

The typical company today consists of two major resources, money and people, and is organised in three functional streams: finance, production and marketing. If it is well run it will have identified corporate objectives such as desired profitability, needs to be satisfied, etc. However, despite these overall goals, it is common to find conflict existing between the three functions which prevents the full implementation of the marketing concept. This is because, regardless of the nature of the corporate targets, the individual functional goals seem to be of necessity at variance. A brief and highly generalised look at the goals and concepts of each function will demonstrate this paradox.

Finance

Finance is the function concerned with the money resources of the enterprise. Its basic objective is to view the revenues and expenditures of the organisation and see how the resultant profits can be utilised to satisfy the three requirements of the capital invested. First, to ensure there is enough money to continue in business, the requirement of security; second, to provide for future expansion, the requirement of growth; and third, to reward the owners of the capital, the requirement of yield. The finance function is concerned largely with giving an account of the past history of the company – thus the term "accountancy."

The way in which the expenditure of money is regarded is peculiar to the function. Marketing costs, for example, are seen as money that is spent and thus lost to the company. This is consistent with the general concept of the finance function and no criticism of the process is intended. Accounting duties are as essential to the health of the company as are the more glamorous aspects of the marketing department, and most accountants perform other vital tasks, such as providing management information, investment analyses, cash flow forecasts etc.

Production

Like the finance function, production is concerned largely with events within the company. In concept the objective of production management is to optimise output and cost. It is concerned, therefore, with such considerations as the effect on unit cost of expanding output. As overheads will be spread further, will the unit cost decrease or will it be increased by the need for new machinery and labour? In terms of the time scale on which finance was placed in the past, production is concerned more than any other function with the present, particularly if round-the-clock working is being used. Production lost in a three-shift system can never be made up as all time is already utilised. This concern with the present is demonstrated in many production managers' offices by the charts on the wall which record output on the previous shift and even hourly production targets and achievements.

Marketing

The marketing managers' graphs are never in such detail. Sales are not recorded by hour in most companies. [One work study officer once remarked when he first examined a sales department that he felt a calendar would be more use than a stop watch!] There are even more significant differences between the functions. Marketing is concerned with selling the maximum output to the ultimate user at a profit to the company by arranging production to suit the needs of the market. As there is inevitably a time-lag between finding out needs, producing the goods and selling them to the customer, marketing must be concerned with the future. What is happening in the market-place today (particularly in overseas markets) is usually beyond the reach of the marketing man. It is clear, therefore, that marketing management must be forward-looking and outward-looking. It is worth noting that only the marketing staff of all company personnel spend the majority of their time looking and working outside the company.

The way in which marketing management regards money is different, too. Marketing is concerned with causal relationships where effects – that is, revenues and profits – result from the arrangement of a number of causes (all of which involve expenditure). Therefore, marketing costs by definition are investments, albeit often with indefinable returns.

Interfunctional conflicts

Having considered finance, production and marketing as separate functions with differences of objectives, orientation, time scales and attitudes to money, it is now possible to analyse their relationships with each other. Two cases will demonstrate the problems of conflict which were stated earlier.

First, in the case of a sales decline, finance management will normally argue that as revenue is decreasing, expenditure must be cut in order to maintain profits. This is logical within the concept of finance. But marketing management equally rationally will suggest that to cut back on the causes (for example the advertising budget) can only be detrimental to the effects (the revenue). In theory, at least, every £1 spent on marketing is designed to produce over £1 to the company. Thus, not spending the £1 can only leave the company worse off, assuming the money was going to be well spent.

Second, in the case of an argument about what products should be made, production management will normally argue in favour of those products which show the best output/cost relationship. Marketing management will strive to get products which are most easily saleable. The two are seldom identical. Production management will usually favour a reduction of the product range to gain longer runs, marketing management an increase in the number of products to attract a wider variety of customers. Again, both functions are being logical in attempting to achieve their functional objectives. It is the interrelationship that causes the problem.

The resolution of these interfunctional conflicts is one of the prime tasks of the chief executive and the decisions that he will take will vary according to the circumstances of the company. In general terms, however, the marketing view must be given prominence when the company is in a highly competitive situation. This is because it is the only function that is deeply concerned with consumer need satisfactions, which will be the ultimate determinant of the company's success. Obviously if the company has a heavy investment in one type of production, it is unrealistic for marketing to demand overnight changes. Likewise, if the money is not available it is unreasonable to plan vast marketing expenditure. There are times in even marketing-oriented companies when the marketing operation is concerned with selling what is made within arbitrary cost limits. Even so, the long-term strategy must be to make what is saleable and to spend according to the volumes desired.

The marketing mix

Company/customer conflicts

Marketing is concerned with arranging the relationship between the company and its markets to the satisfaction of its customers and to the profit of the firm. Here again, however, there is an inevitable conflict which can be demonstrated by examining a simple case from the buyers' and sellers' viewpoints. In buying a suit, most men try to achieve three basic objectives. First, that the suit is tailor-made to the individual's measurements. Second, that the price of the suit relative to the quality chosen is as low as possible. Third, that the intrinsic value or the cost of the suit is as high as possible and ideally above the price paid. This is what is known as a bargain.

From the manufacturer's point of view, these three objectives are diametrically opposed to his own. If he can avoid it he will not want to make products to suit individual needs, thus losing the major economies of mass production. Certainly he will want to obtain the highest possible price for his product while minimising its cost. This is what is known euphemistically as "improving margins!" The danger of a monopolistic situation is that the producer is likely to achieve his objectives at the expense of the customer who has no other choice. Conversely, the problem of monopsonistic situations – that is, buyer-dominated – is that the producers' future is likely to be jeopardised by being forced to satisfy consumer demands unprofitably.

Most companies, most of the time, exist somewhere between these extremes; in fact, in most capitalist countries there are countervailing forces to ensure that this happens. One of the great paradoxes of the capitalist concept is that while deriving its strength from competitive forces, each competitor attempts to eliminate competition by trading, merger or acquisition. Thus left unchecked a capitalist economy moves from a situation of competition towards one of monopoly. The natural tendency of capitalism towards monopolistic situations is opposed by increasing government legislation covering restrictive practices and cartelisation.

The arrangement of the compromise between producer and consumer objectives is the prime task of marketing management. It is their job to fulfil customer needs but to ensure that it is done at a profit.

This compromise is effected through the arrangement of three basic variables, the product range, the price structure and the presentation of the product/price package to the market.

Product range

The product range can be varied either to suit consumer needs better or to satisfy the requirements of production. In most successful companies these processes of product development, value analysis and variety reduction run concurrently, adding on more satisfied customers at one end and removing dead products at the other.

Price structure

The price relationship can also be varied to suit either company or customer (or indeed intermediary agents such as wholesalers, retailers, distributors, etc). When the company has a "quality" product – that is, one that suits customers' needs particularly well – a premium price is charged. When a competitor is in this happy position, prices may have to be reduced.

Development of product/price parity

In theory, therefore, the firm has a wide latitude of decision on products and prices. In practice, this is seldom so. One of the inevitable results of the process of capitalism referred to above is that the larger firms in an industry tend to get larger by growth, acquisition or merger. The remaining smaller firms are forced to specialise or to go out of business. Thus an increasing percentage of industry is in fewer and fewer hands; many markets have already reached the permissible ultimate. In Britain, for example, many markets are dominated by a handful of corporations. For example there are only two major soap powder companies, only four major banks. Three oil companies control over 80 per cent of all outlets. This is a process which has already transcended national frontiers in many industries – for example, oil, cars, computers – and has resulted in a handful of giant corporations dominating world markets.

Any of these vast companies is quite capable of matching its competitors in terms of resources and, therefore, if one company achieves a major product advantage, it is not long before the competitors copy it (even assuming that they were not developing something similar themselves, which is so often the case). The consumer goods industries provide many examples of this process from the constant product leapfrogging of Unilever and Proctor and Gamble in the detergent and toothpaste markets to the rapid spreading of new concepts such as hatchbacks across competing motor manufacturers. Likewise, because the giant companies are achieving the same economies of scale, product costs and thus prices tend to be similar for similar products.

Thus, in product/price terms the offerings of competing companies are getting increasingly alike as the big companies increasingly dominate industry. This is not to say that good products and prices are any less important than they ever were; simply that the chances of making a significant difference in product/price terms and maintaining it are getting less. It is perhaps encouraging to note that it is still possible for smaller firms to challenge the giants with new products as long as they follow through with strong marketing activity. For example, McCain, basically a catering company, launched oven chips, a new concept in that they can be cooked without oil, into the retail market in February 1979 and although the leader, Birds Eye, responded in August 1980, McCain still managed to maintain its dominance by heavy advertising and below-the-line promotion. Thus some differences still occur, particularly in the nature of the product technology, but in terms of need satisfactions to the consumer products are becoming increasingly similar. For example, the digital wristwatch is technologically different from the normal spring watch. However, they both satisfy the basic consumer need to know the time. Moreover, there is an occasional product breakthrough where one company maintains a major product advantage over another for a time, as occurred in the fields of float glass, electrostatic photocopying and stainless steel razor blades. In general terms, however, the position is that most companies for most of the time must face the fact that the best they can hope for is product/price parity with competition.

Presentation

Thus increasing emphasis is thrown on the third variable of the marketing mix, presentation, by which is meant the communication of the offering of the company to the market. This involves using all the available tools of communication, public relations, advertising, sales promotion, merchandising and the sales force. It is in these areas that the differences between competitors are increasingly made, as is apparent from an examination of the basic concepts of purchasing.

How buyers buy

Buyers buy to satisfy needs. These need patterns consist of logical and rational desires, such as the need to wash clothes clean in the detergent market, or the need to produce electricity at a certain price in the generator market. Buyers have subjective and emotional needs, too, such as prestige and security, which need to be satisfied. Obviously the mix of subjective and objective needs will vary vastly from market to market. In the case of consumer products, like cigarettes, the buyer is concerned almost exclusively with emotional satisfactions, although having objective considerations such as price and quality of manufacture in mind. The industrial buyer purchasing, for instance, glass bottles, will be concerned with cost, delivery and quality of manufacture, but he, too, has subjective feelings. He wants to feel confident that he is making the right decision, that he is dealing with a good company and that he can trust the salesman. (See Figure 1.2.)

In situations where products and prices are similar emotional needs become relatively more important. The buyer, either housewife or engineer, faced with this parity between offerings is forced to choose on other than purely rational grounds. This choice will be much influenced by the information given by the company and particularly the manner in which it is presented.

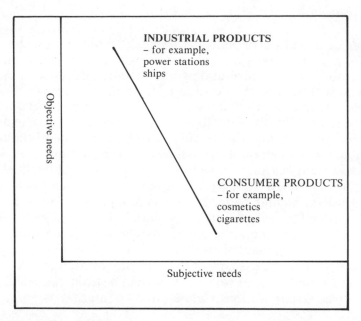

Fig. 1.2   Consumer need mix

This diagram is illustrative of the relationships; it is not intended as a quantitative guide. Note that the graph touches neither axis, indicating that there is no need pattern that is wholly objective or subjective

Role of the sales force within marketing

The strategy of marketing is concerned with arranging the resources of the company so that the needs of customers can be satisfied by presenting to them a product/price offering. This strategy is implemented through a number of tactical tools, some concerned with finding out what the needs are (marketing research), some with ensuring the product/price offering is correct (product development and testing), and some with presenting the offering to the customer. The sales function is a major tactic in this last area, while having a role to play in the first two.

Contributions of the sales force

The importance of the sales function cannot be over-emphasised in those companies where the bulk of the presentational effort is carried by the sales force. This covers most industrial and speciality markets and many consumer goods industries. In fact it is not going too far to say that in some markets, for example, office equipment and life insurance, the major difference between competing companies is the relative quality of their sales forces. In such fields the buyer's decision is virtually wholly influenced by who calls on him, what is discussed and how the discussion is organised.

Moreover, the sales force can make valuable contributions in the definition of market segments and customer needs, and product development and rationalisation. This is particularly true in industrial markets, where formal market research is less used. Obviously as salesmen tend not to be trained researchers, the information they collect has to be treated with care. Nevertheless, as they are usually the only regular and continuous contact with customers, they can gather considerable and valuable data.

The distribution system

For many companies the only economic way of reaching the end-users or consumers is through some form of distributive network (i.e. wholesalers, retailers, distributors, dealers etc). Traditionally, the distribution system was regarded as an inert "channel" through which goods flowed at the decision of the manufacturer to the marketplace. Today it is only too apparent in most industries that the distribution network has changed dramatically in its nature and structure. In most major markets the system has polarised into a handful of large powerful distributors controlling the bulk of the business and a relatively large number of small outlets handling a minority of the sales. In the chemist trade for example 30 multiples now account for over 50 per cent of retail sales, leaving the other 50 per cent to be covered by about 90,000 independent chemists supplied through around 100 wholesalers. Similar patterns are commonplace in other consumer goods industries (e.g. food) and growing in many industrial markets (e.g. bearings).

Understanding the nature and structure of the distribution network and how it is evolving is vital to the development of an effective sales activity. For many companies it will be the key determinant of the shape of the sales organisation, the kind of sales staff needed, the knowledge and skills in which they should be trained, even the level of their sales targets. All of these implications will be explored later.

The environment

The marketing system does not operate in a vacuum. It is bounded on all sides by restrictions such as limitations of demand and shortage of money (or more accurately shortage of profit opportunities greater than the cost of investments). Major constraints include competitive activity on both national and increasingly international levels, legislation affecting both marketing strategy (e.g. limiting promotional activity in industries such as pharmaceuticals and cigarettes) and the operation of the firm (e.g. employee protection), social attitudes (e.g. consumerism, unionism) and, perhaps most important of all, the general economic environment which has been typified since the beginning of the oil crisis in 1973 by recurrent recession, inflation, currency fluctuation etc.

The marketing man must function cognisant of all these pressures. The sales manager, as a member of the marketing team, must likewise recognise the nature of the system within which he has to live, its conflicts, opportunities and limitations.

The development of marketing has caused deep changes in the nature of the sales manager's task. In a sense his job is more limited within this concept of marketing but it has become more vital to the health of the company. It is this function which will now be explored.

ACTION PLANNING CHECKLIST

Questions	Answers and action	Timing of action and evaluation
1 What is the company's definition of marketing? If there is no definition, write one in here		
2 Are all management and staff aware of what marketing is and why it is necessary? If not identify action to be taken		
3 What markets is the company in, in terms of need satisfactions?		
4 What segments have been identified in these markets? If unknown, what action should be taken to define them?		
5 Can we identify for each segment? *(a)* Number of customers actual and potential *(b)* Size of customers *(c)* What they buy *(d)* For what purpose *(e)* In what quantities *(f)* At what frequency *(g)* Competition		
6 Does friction exist within the company between various functions? If so, what should be done about it? *(a)* Improved communications *(b)* Education *(c)* Organisation		
7 What product/price advantages and disadvantages do we have compared with our competitors? Which should we concentrate on in our promotional effort?		
8 What function does or should the sales force perform in our total communications to and from the market? For example: *(a)* Market research *(b)* Prospecting *(c)* Order-taking		
9 Does the sales force understand its responsibilities for these functions? If not, what action should be taken?		
10 How far does our environment limit our growth? If it does, what action should be taken?		

CHAPTER 2

The Job of the Sales Manager

The sales manager must first and foremost be a manager. Like other managers in the company he is responsible for getting things done through other people towards economic objectives. This simple definition has many implications.

"Getting things done" implies that the sales manager must be action-orientated and must be concerned with results rather than means. He will be judged by what is ultimately achieved rather than by the processes he manages. "Through other people" suggests that the results will be, in fact, achieved by others. He is not there to do their job for them although this is what far too many sales managers do. It is often easier to handle personally a difficult customer than to develop a salesman to cope with him. "Towards economic objectives" means that the sales manager must constantly consider the financial implications of his actions.

Financial responsibilities

Traditionally, the major financial responsibility of the sales manager has always been sales revenue; increasingly, however, sales management is being held responsible for some form of "bottom line". This makes for a significant change in the sales management job. The type of customers sought by a sales manager aiming for revenue or unit volume goals can be very different from the sort of buyers who will be most profitable to the company. For example, the large customer, buying on maximum discount, taking a long time to pay and demanding constant attention from the sales force, may be less profitable to the company than the prompt paying, medium-sized buyer who requires little servicing. As companies are in business to make profits it is obviously desirable that sales managers should be orientated to this objective. In some firms revenue and profit have such a close relationship that increasing the former will automatically increase the latter. As markets become more competitive, however, and the laws of diminishing returns begin to operate, it is too often the case that increased volume can only be gained at a relatively higher increase in cost, thus leading to a decline in profitability and, in extreme cases, to a fall in total profits. On the other hand, the sales manager cannot be totally profit responsible because he does not control all the elements that affect profits. Items such as production costs, overheads and advertising expenditure are normally beyond his authority. The prime area of influence must be revenue but he must be guided in the gaining of that revenue by the relative profitability of different sources of revenue. It is essential that he understands the basic financial mechanisms of the company and how he can utilise them to the betterment of the company's profits.

In essence, assuming that the company is concerned with return on capital employed, he must be aware of the equation:

$$\frac{\text{Profit}}{\text{Capital employed}} = \frac{\text{Profit}}{\text{Sales revenue}} \times \frac{\text{Sales revenue}}{\text{Capital employed}}$$

– and lead his sales force not only to increased profitable revenue but also to higher utilisation of capital employed. This view broadens the approach of the sales manager so that he considers far more alternatives in planning his activities. (See Figure 2.1.)

---

1 Improve profit on sales

　(a) Improve sales volume at current prices and costs

　(b) Hold sales volume at increased prices retaining current costs

　(c) Hold sales volume and prices and reduce current costs

　(d) Hold sales volume but change product mix to sell more of more profitable items

2 Improve sales on capital employed – that is, turnover on capital employed

　(a) Increase sales volume at current capital employed – that is, no increase in stocks, length of credit, sales force, etc

　(b) Hold sales volume but reduce capital employed – that is, cut stocks in range or amounts, reduce length of credit, cut fixed costs of sales force, regional offices, etc

---

Fig. 2.1 **Managing for profit checklist**

The six basic functions of the sales manager

In order to fulfil his basic duty as a manager of the company, the sales manager must carry out six specific functions:

1 *Plan* objectives and strategies for his team.
2 *Develop* an organisation structure capable of achieving the objectives.
3 *Recruit and select* staff who can perform the jobs laid down in the organisation structure.
4 *Train* them in the further knowledge and skills required to perform the jobs.
5 *Motivate* them to perform their jobs to the best of their abilities.
6 *Evaluate and control* them to ensure the objectives are achieved.

Particular problems of sales management

In performing the six functions the peculiar difficulties of sales management must be recognised. Unlike any other body of staff in the company, the sales force is normally geographically well spread. Thus they cannot be supervised as closely as in other departments. This causes particular problems of motivation, communication and control for the sales manager and feelings of isolation for the salesman.

Again, unlike other sections of the firm the sales force spends the vast majority of its time with people other than company employees, usually, of course, with customers and prospects whose viewpoints are very different from those of the salesman. This can cause attrition whereby the salesman's attitudes and skills are worn down by the constant contact with opposing views. For example, it is difficult for a salesman to maintain that his product has a particular advantage when buyer after buyer for month after month (whether correctly or not) says that it is no better than competition.

Furthermore, the kind of people who choose this isolated and wearing life are often, paradoxically, those least capable of coping with it. Men who choose selling as a career are normally gregarious individuals, yet the structure of the job ensures that they spend a minimal amount of time with their colleagues.

Need for leadership and training

Because of the particular difficulties of the sales job, sales management must provide strong leadership and training to overcome them. The training programme must be powerful enough to inculcate methods of working which will be followed despite the lack of close supervision. Training must also be continuous to counter the attrition of dealing with customers. The leadership shown by the sales manager must be clear and strong enough to support men who are widely spread and whose nature requires a high level of social contact. Some of these problems can be eased by skilful organisation, careful selection and attractive commission systems. However, the basic conditions of the sales job make it imperative that the sales manager places great emphasis on leading and training his team.

The sales manager as a decision maker

In carrying out his six specific functions, the sales manager is faced with a variety of decisions at every stage, based on the answers to the following questions:

1 What sort of objectives should be set?
2 How many salesmen are needed?
3 What kind of men should be selected?
4 How should they be trained?
5 What standards should be used to control them?

In fact it may be argued that the fundamental task of any manager is that of choosing between alternatives, that the basic difference between good and bad management can be traced back to the subsequent accuracy of decisions made. Yet, even when the importance of decision making is recognised, the state of knowledge about it is remarkably low.

Decision making by analogy

Traditionally sales managers have been the most qualitative in their judgements. When question as to how things are going, the answer tends to be expressed in vague generalisations. The difficulty of quantifying sales activity is extreme, as with most other sociological situations. If managerial performance is to improve, efforts must be made to evaluate results in measurable terms. Because of this lack of measurement, many decisions seem to be made on the basis of experience whereby analogies are drawn, often subconsciously, between today's problems and past difficulties. The choice of action is then made by repeating previously successful solutions. This can be verified by looking at the requirements in job advertisements. Time and again the only significant qualification needed for a sales management position is a number of years of appropriate experience.

Limitations of experience

With some managers, however, the decision by analogy approach not only stifles the search for new solutions but also inculcates a false sense of security. After lengthy experience in a particular industry, it is dangerously easy for the manager to believe that he has seen all possible eventualities. Thus, when a new problem arises, he adopts the most appropriate solution from his past experience, although the current situation may differ in significant respects from anything he has come across previously. As the business environment appears to be becoming increasingly volatile, the chances of the past being repeated diminish.

Method of the working hypothesis

It would be equally wrong, of course, to deny the values of experience. But its limitations must be recognised and new approaches sought to decision making. One technique that forces a broader view is the method of the working hypothesis or the "scientific method." It is neither unique nor infallible, but to follow such a procedure ensures that decision making is approached logically, systematically and with a consideration of the alternatives available. If, in addition, the steps are formalised in writing, major decisions taken in this way can be recorded and evaluated at a later date.

Step 1: Setting objectives. Before any action can be considered the objectives of the exercise must be set. Unless you know where you are going you cannot plan how to get there or how to measure your progress. For the objective to be valuable it must be as specific and as quantitative as possible. Goals such as "increasing sales," "improving customer service" and "reducing costs" are useless, as they provide no basis for measurement. If the aim is to increase sales it should be specified by how much and within what time period.

Step 2: Evaluating the objective against other company objectives. When a clear, precise goal has been established it should be compared with other company aims to ensure compatibility. Failure to do this is common, particularly in large companies. This results in different sections of the firm working towards objectives which in themselves are reasonable but which when put together become mutually exclusive. For example, the sales manager plans to increase sales at a time when production is being rationalised and no extra output is available. In one television company marketing two brands of receiver, the marketing division decided to concentrate on promoting the two product lines as entirely different. At the same time the engineering department was following a policy of making as many parts as possible common to the two brands. Thus the dealers were faced with the sales force stating that they should stock both brands as they were different, and letters from the engineering staff advising reductions in parts stock because of the commonality. Not surprisingly, the dealers were somewhat confused. When faced with a customer who wanted a brand A set when they had only a brand B stock they simply sold the brand B on the basis that it was really the same as brand A. Thus dealers found they needed less stock to satisfy demand, the products in effect competed with each other rather than with the brands of other companies and sales and profits began to fall.

Each objective in itself might have been reasonable; together, they caused chaos.

Step 3: Collecting Information. Information can now be collected from which plans can be developed. It is unwise to commence this data collection stage until clear, compatible objectives have been defined, otherwise vast quantities of useless figures will be assembled "for information" or "in case we need them." The hunger for information has been stimulated by the development of research techniques and the introduction of the computer. It is a great temptation to the sales manager to call for information simply because he knows it is available. Mountains of figures may give a sense of security but information is costly to process and is only useful (and economic) when it contains answers to precise questions which have direct bearing on the decisions it is possible to take.

Step 4: Analysing the information. It is the objective which will guide the manager towards the questions to be answered and thus the information needed. Likewise the lines of analysis to be followed will be indicated by such questions. For example, if the sales manager of an engineering firm is faced with declining sales in one area of the country which he suspects are due to the larger customers buying from competition, he should not ask for "everything we know about the market." What he really needs is sales in that region broken down by customer type, possibly compared with similar figures for another area. From this analysis he will begin to see if there is a pattern of steady or improving sales to medium and small customers, and static or declining sales to large accounts. This, in turn, will suggest further lines of analysis to him. Is the product more suited to the needs of smaller customers? Is the price, discount and credit structure competitive enough on the big accounts? Is the sales force allocating its time in correct proportion to the volume of business done? All these specific questions can lead to particular analyses of competitive position and sales force organisation which will be far more valuable than dozens of different breakdowns purporting to tell all about everything.

Step 5: Developing alternatives. The whole basis of this method of approach is to encourage the manager to think more broadly and creatively about possible solutions to his problem. It is too facile to fire the salesman any time that sales decline. There could be a dozen different reasons for a falling sales graph. By the processes of analysis, hypotheses will begin to emerge as to how the objective of, say, increasing sales in area X by 10 per cent within the next six months can be achieved. In a few cases, of course, the solution will become obvious from systematic processing of the data; in the majority of instances, however, no clear cut answer will be found. It could be in the engineering example used that three basic approaches seem possible. First, the sales force could be reorganised to concentrate more heavily on major accounts. Second, the price structure could be changed to give lower prices to large customers. Third, the product could be modified (at a cost of course) to suit the bigger people.

Step 6: Choosing the "best" alternative. This is the heart of the decision making process. It is unlikely that all three solutions can be implemented; one must be chosen. To help in this choice, four criteria should be considered: cost, time, risk, resources.

The costs of each alternative can be calculated and compared against the objective. Assuming that all three approaches appear to be capable of achieving the objective, this might provide the basis for choice. However, the other yardsticks should also be used. Time taken might be a critical factor, particularly in this case, where a 10 per cent improvement in sales is sought within six months. The third solution of modifying the product is likely to take much longer than changing the prices and perhaps will be ruled out on that score. However, the risk of a price change for one group of customers is high not only because other customers may demand the same treatment but also because it is a strategy easily and quickly matched by competition. This would seem to leave sales force reorganisation as the best hypothesis; but when the availability of resources is considered it might be found that there were both insufficient salesmen to arrange such a concentration and insufficient management time to plan it. The choice of the "best" alternative therefore is based on a consideration of all the advantages and disadvantages of all the possible alternatives. It is at this stage that experience can be particularly valuable. The criticism of experience made earlier that it can be limiting will already have been overcome by the systematic search for alternatives.

Having made the choice, at least the manager will be well aware of what he has done in terms of the possible drawbacks of his decision and the discarded alternatives. It will thus be easier at some time in the future to look back and assess why such a decision was, in fact, made.

Step 7: Communicating the decision. This is a step too often omitted. And yet unless all concerned know what is being done impact will be lost. It is commonplace to find salesmen whose first knowledge of an advertising campaign is gained from customers. The communication must be systematically planned. The information may well have to be passed by different methods and in different forms to different people. Assuming the decision has been made to implement the third alternative, that of sales force redeployment, many different groups of people will have to be informed. The sales force itself, for example, will have to be told in detail about the new scheme. This is perhaps best done at a series of meetings. The accounts department may need to know so that the sales force costing information can be reorganised; a memo may suffice for this. The managing director may wish to be kept informed and here a telephone call from the sales manager briefly outlining the action will probably be all that is needed. By communicating only necessary information by the most appropriate methods, far better results will be gained than by a blanket memorandum with copies to everybody.

Step 8: Setting up the control system. It will be noted that this stage occurs before implementation. This is because in many cases the process of implementing a plan destroys the ability to evaluate it. For example, in a situation where it is believed that the sales force lack product knowledge, the decision might be taken to run a training programme. At the end of the course a test is given in which the average score is 90 per cent. It might be concluded, therefore, that the programme was successful. But as there has been no measurement of what the test score would have been at the beginning of the programme, in fact it can never be known whether it was successful or not. Moreover, it is of course impossible to turn the clock back after the course to take such a measurement. It is imperative therefore that the control system is decided before any action is taken.

Step 9: Implementing the decision. Putting the decision into action should now be easy. It will have been clearly stated what is to be done towards what objective, why that particular action has been chosen, all concerned will have been informed and the system of evaluation will have been set. Research has shown that if change is to be implemented then specific tasks should be allocated to particular people and deadlines defined by which the tasks will be completed. Vague requests for action sometime will inevitably result in failure.

Step 10: Evaluating the decision. Again assuming quantitative objectives, clear decisions and predefined control systems, evaluation is simple. The problems of control and evaluation in sales management are caused by the lack of clear yardsticks against which to compare. If the sales manager simply sets broad qualitative goals of increasing sales and improving customer service, he will have the utmost difficulty in evaluating the results. There will usually be no common definition of what constitutes an increase or an improvement.

Figure 2.2 shows in summary form the decision making steps, the major points to check at each step and a typical example of a decision taken by this method.

The sales manager as a marketing man

It has already been emphasised that sales management is a function, often the most important, within the marketing strategy. Because of this, it is essential that the sales manager is at least aware of the other tactics of marketing so that he can contribute to and benefit from them.

Marketing research, for example, is an area in which the sales manager is often involved. If he is to be able to collect meaningful data and to use the figures provided by the marketing researchers, he must know something of the techniques used. Other parts of marketing where some knowledge and skill are required include:

1 New product development.
2 Distribution strategy.
3 Pricing
4 Advertising and sales promotion.
5 Public relations.
6 Marketing planning and control, particularly the financial aspects of these.

In some companies the sales manager will directly control some of these areas; in others, they will be looked after by marketing staff. In every firm, the sales manager must integrate his activities with the rest of the marketing effort if the maximum value is to be gained from marketing expenditure.

Conclusion

The sales manager is the key man in developing a successful sales operation. He must do this by managing his team not by doing their jobs for them. As a manager he is responsible for getting things done through others towards economic objectives. As a sales manager the implementation of this process is hindered by the particular difficulties of dealing with geographically spread subordinates who spend the majority of their time with people other than their colleagues. Constantly he faces the choice between alternative actions and he must develop a systematic approach to his basic task of decision making. Finally he must integrate his effort with the rest of the marketing strategy.

To do his job successfully, the sales manager must possess knowledge and skill in four major areas; selling, management, sales management and marketing. Only then can he claim to be a fully productive member of the executive team. (See Figure 2.3).

Steps	Check	Example
1 Setting objectives	Are they specific and quantitative?	To increase sales revenue in west region by 10 per cent in next six months compared with same period last year. To increase customers to 1000. To hold sales costs at same percentage as last year
2 Evaluating the objectives	Do they conflict with other goals?	Production is available also promotional help
3 Collecting the information	Have the questions to be answered been clearly defined?	Need last year's sales broken down by customer, product and salesman. Also market research data on potential available and competitive activity
4 Analysing the information	Is it known what is being searched for?	Specific questions to be answered include: Can current customers buy more? How many prospects are there? What is current sales force call rate? What is order: call ratio?
5 Developing alternatives	Have all possibilities been listed?	(Assuming above work done) *(a)* Increase call frequency on customers *(b)* Increase prospecting rate *(c)* Improve selling skills by training
6 Choosing the "best" alternative	Have all alternatives been evaluated in terms of cost, time, risk and resources?	*(a)* Cost increase because need more men. Delay in recruiting. Risk in taking on more new men. Personnel dept resources involved *(b)* No cost – can do with existing force. Some time to reorganise. Low risk. Low resource use *(c)* Cost of training. Time for training. Experience elsewhere shows training effective therefore risk low. No resources, can use consultants. Choose *(c)* as likely to be most effective though not cheapest
7 Communicating the decision	Have the right people been told the appropriate information by the appropriate methods?	Advise marketing director by memo. Brief sales force at meeting. Give terms of reference to consultants at meeting
8 Setting up the control system	What will be measured, how and when?	Best yardsticks of increased effectiveness are order: call ratio and average order size. Monitor now before action starts
9 Implementing the decision	Have specific tasks been allocated with specific timings?	Run training programme. Revise sales targets. Concentrate on lists of customers with further potential
10 Evaluating the decision	Has the decision been evaluated against the objectives?	Appraisal of training programme. Actuals *v* targets on monthly basis

Fig. 2.2   Ten-step decision making

ARE YOU A FULLY COMPETENT SALES MANAGER?

Rate your knowledge and skill in each area

1   Highly knowledgeable and skilled – no further training needed at the moment

2   Above average – could benefit from further development but not urgent

3   Below average – need deep training which should be arranged soon

4   Low – need training immediately. Dangerous to take decisions in these areas without consultation

Better still, ask your superior to rate you

	1	2	3	4	Action
1 Sales knowledge and skill					
(a) Product knowledge					
(b) Company knowledge					
(c) Sales techniques					
(d) Negotiation techniques					
(e) Personal organisation					
2 Management knowledge and skill					
(a) Principles of management					
(b) Financial techniques					
(c) Objective setting					
(d) Decision making					
(e) Communication					
3 Sales management knowledge and skill					
(a) Planning the sales operation					
(b) Developing sales organisation structure					
(c) Recruitment and selection of staff					
(d) Initial and continuous training					
(e) Motivation of staff					
(f) Controlling the sales operation					
4 Marketing knowledge and skill					
(a) Marketing research					
(b) Product development					
(c) Pricing					
(d) Distribution					
(e) Public relations					
(f) Advertising and sales promotion					
(g) Marketing planning					

Fig. 2.3   Knowledge and skill checklist

ACTION PLANNING CHECKLIST

Questions	Answers and action	Timing of action and evaluation
1 What is the company's definition of management? If there is none, write one in here		
2 What are or should be the financial objectives of sales management?		
3 Using Figure 2.1 what are the major profit opportunity areas for the company?		
4 What are the particular difficulties of sales management in the company and how can they be overcome?		
5 How are major decisions taken? Does the Scientific Method offer improvements? (Use Figure 2.2 to work out an actual example). If so, how can it be used in the company?		
6 What areas of marketing knowledge and skill should the sales manager be familiar with?		
7 What further training does sales management need to become fully competent? (Use Figure 2.3)		

PART TWO

HOW TO MANAGE A SALES FORCE

CHAPTER 3

How to Plan the Sales Operation

To achieve maximum efficiency the sales manager must plan the utilisation of the resources at his command. This involves deciding in advance what actions he will initiate. Planning as a concept is often heavily criticised by sales management on the grounds that it provides too many restrictions and that an experienced sales team must be capable of reacting quickly to changes in the market-place. These are criticisms, in fact, of bad planning not of planning as a whole. The aim of the plan is not to create a strait-jacket. It is to ensure that the men, money, facilities and time involved are used to the best advantage. Moreover, without a plan it is difficult to ensure that correct priorities are allocated or that minor but still important facets of the company's business are not overlooked. Perhaps most important of all, the sales effort cannot be fully integrated with the rest of the company unless there is foreknowledge as to its nature and scale.

The objectives–planning–control continuum

The planning process is only one part of the basic and repetitive management activity necessary in any company seeking to grow. The firm must continuously answer three fundamental questions:

1 Where are we going? – this is the objective-setting process.
2 How will we get there? – this is the planning process.
3 How will we know if we are getting there? – this is the control process.

These questions first appear at top management level and the answers constitute the corporate objectives, corporate plans and policies and corporate control mechanisms. Typically they will result in a statement of the profit objectives of the company usually expressed in terms of return on capital employed, a description of the business the company is in and its desired position in that industry, its plans and policies for each function of the company and specific goals and targets to be met within specific time periods.

The whole process will then be repeated for each function of the company. Thus marketing, production, R & D, finance, and so on, will each set its objectives, plans and controls. Within the marketing framework, the sales manager must formulate his answers to the three questions in order to produce a format for his staff to work to. Each salesman may well be required to repeat the process with individual customers.

This continuum is essential if the company is to move forward purposefully. Without it, the company will have to try to react to pressures both internally generated and externally imposed. The individual sections of the company will be likely to get out of phase and clash with each other; competitive and market pressures tend to be unpredicted and cause confusion. The lack of a basic planning concept such as this prevents the growth of many companies which may have been successful as small enterprises.

The sales manager's role in the continuum is obviously critical. If he fails to set clear objectives that are compatible within the hierarchy and does not initiate the appropriate action, the whole firm must suffer.

Setting sales objectives

The sales manager will commence by considering the overall marketing objectives, policies and strategies and control criteria. He will probably have a forecast of sales by revenue and volume, a forecast of gross and nett profit required, perhaps an expense budget ceiling, a description of the product range available with additions and deletions, price structure, promotional support, etc.

Forecasting sales

In many firms the sales manager will be involved as a member of the marketing team in the definition of these items. The process will normally start with forecasting sales for the next period. This is the most critical prediction in the company as it will determine the production schedule, raw material and finished stocks, promotional expenditure, etc. It is best to approach the forecast in two stages. First, what will sales be, assuming all variables in the situation are the same in the future as they have been in the past? Second, which variables will change and what will the impact be? Some of the variables will be internal factors which management decides to change, others will be external factors which are uncontrollable by the company but whose effect must be predicted.

There is a wide variety of methods of sales forecasting and many of the more sophisticated techniques are beyond the scope of this book. They can be followed up in the references given in the Bibliography.

Statistical methods

The first phase of the forecast, that of extrapolating the past experience into the future is basically a statistical one. Simple graphical methods can be used where the continuation of the sales line is estimated by eye. More precisely, time series analysis can be employed which enables the sales figures to be analysed into components of trend and seasonality before it is projected into the future. In particular circumstances where the available data is limited and where recent events are likely to be particularly relevant, a technique known as exponential smoothing can be used to attribute weights to the most important figures so that they figure larger in the calculation of the expected sales.

In many companies such sophistications of method are not practicable, either because the statistics are too few or too small or because the product line is so long that such processing would be an extremely costly business. Simple graphical estimation or calculation of percentage change during the past few years may be all that is justified. (See Figure 3.1).

In many sales situations, particularly industrial ones, often the best way to predict what will happen in the future is to ask the salesmen for forecasts by customer or customer group. If the sales force is to be involved in this way (and it is preferable from a motivational viewpoint that they are), great care must be taken to ensure that they base their judgements on as many facts as possible. They must be encouraged to study the past sales history of their customers and made to justify large increases and decreases in their predictions.

Estimating economic changes

The second stage of the forecasting process is to estimate the impact on the basic prediction of changes in the external world – for example, government legislation, market trend, competitive activity, etc, and the actions planned within the firm – for example, production capability, product policy, promotional campaigns, etc. Again, sophisticated techniques of economic analysis exist but are beyond the scope of this book and the resources of most sales managers. Thus the estimation of the change of variables will largely be a judgement process but one which is eased by separating the forecast into its two phases.

Moreover by this two-stage approach, all concerned are forced to think creatively about the business. One of the great problems of any sales manager is to implement change. This method in effect encourages innovation, particularly at salesman level. Each man can be asked, first, what will happen if the company continues as before; second, what actions can be initiated to improve sales beyond that figure.

Relationship between forecasting and targeting

The sales forecast forms the hub of the sales manager's objectives. It will of course influence the plans he formulates and in turn will be influenced by them. It also represents the heart of each individual salesman's objective in that the overall forecast should equal the summation of the individual sales targets.

In many companies, however, forecasting and targeting are seen as two different processes. Often the sales forecast is increased by an arbitrary figure to form sales targets which will give the salesmen "something to go at." This approach usually leads to problems, as the sales force quickly realises that it has been asked to achieve more than the sales manager really believes is possible and he thus loses credibility. Moreover, the sales manager is faced with a dilemma when informing his production colleagues. Should he give them the sales forecast or the sales target? If he gives production the former and the salesmen achieve their targets, he will have a demand he cannot satisfy. If he gives production the same figure as the sales target and the sales forecast turns out to be accurate, there will be an unwelcome overstocking. Those companies who try to work on more than one set of figures inevitably must cause themselves problems; whatever figure is achieved will be wrong for some purpose.

The simple solution is to make the best forecast possible and use that for all purposes of targeting, production scheduling, stocking, etc. Then at least the company is working towards a common objective.

This common sales forecast or target will be expressed usually in terms of revenue and unit volume by product, by time period and in some cases by customer. A further refinement which is particularly useful in static markets where additional business can only be gained from competition is to split the forecast and particularly the targets into repeat sales and new sales – that is, from new customers, new lines introduced to old customers, increased usage by old customers, etc.

		Cumulative sales and percentage			
		First quarter	Second quarter	Third quarter	Total
Three years ago	Sales	10 000	40 000	80 000	100 000
	%	10	40	80	100
Two years ago	Sales	12 000	42 000	82 000	100 000
	%	12	42	82	100
Last year	Sales	8 000	38 000	78 000	100 000
	%	8	38	78	100
Average		10	40	80	100
This year	Sales	12 000	44 000		

Fig. 3.1   Sales forecasting by percentage analysis

Analysis of the past three years shows that on average 40% of average sales had been achieved by the end of the second quarter. Therefore, by calculating of what figure 44 000 is 40% a 1970 total of 110 000 is forecast

Developing the sales plan

Having set the sales forecasts and targets, the manager must now consider how they will be achieved. Obviously some thought will already have been given to the plan in formulating the objectives. After the plan is written it might well be necessary to reconsider the goals that have been previously identified.

Basically, the sales manager has to ponder five questions:

1   What is to be sold?
2   To whom?
3   At what price?
4   By what methods?
5   At what cost – effectiveness?

In some of these areas, notably the product range and pricing structure, he may well have limited influence; they are often controlled by the marketing planning department, through a brand or product management structure. In respect of all five facets he will certainly have to consider the inputs of other parts of the business. What stocks will be available from production, what money is available from finance, what advertising and sales promotion support is planned, etc?

What is to be sold

This is the product range definition and here the sales manager can at least advise his marketing planning colleagues on the saleability of the various items in the range as well as new product requirements. From a sales management viewpoint he will have to decide whether the full range should be sold to everybody. In some capital equipment markets where the distributor has to make a heavy investment in stock it may not be in the interests of the company to supply dealers whose financial resources may be overreached if they purchased the more costly products. Likewise, companies who have to make after-sales service arrangements may well decide not to sell products to customers who are geographically isolated.

To whom

Next, the sales manager must consider the customers and prospects for his products.

First, he will study the existing markets and decide whether business with them is likely to increase, decrease or remain static. This judgement will be based on a study of previous buying records. By analysing customers in terms of their potential and actual purchasing of the various products he has to offer, he can identify the areas to be attacked. Prospective customers can be analysed in the same way. Such customer analysis can be most systematically done by construction of matrices which have the advantage of clearly identifying the market segment/product relationships.

Market/product matrices

In the simple example given (Figure 3.2), a construction equipment company has broken down its situation in terms of its three product lines and its three major markets. Each

Products	Markets				
	Government	Local authority	Industry	Trend	Total
Bulldozers	Potential				
	Actual				
Scrapers			800 p.a.	Sales up 20%	
			500 p.a.	Market up 30%	
Loaders		1000 p.a.			
		800 p.a.			
Trend		Market declining			
Total					

Fig. 3.2 **Planning matrix for a construction equipment company**

market segment/product cell shown potential and actual sales, thus identifying which are the significant portions of the market to be aimed at and what penetration is being achieved. At the end of each column is entered the trend of that particular product line or market segment so that management is aware of future possibilities. For example, it might be that a high penetration has been achieved in the loader/local authority market but the market as a whole is declining and therefore future growth must be sought elsewhere. Alternatively, a 20 per cent increase in sales may be registered in, say, the scraper/industry market but the trend comment might be that this area in total has grown by 30 per cent and therefore performance has slipped relatively.

The degree of detail that the sales manager will identify on the market/product matrix will obviously vary from industry to industry. The example shows broad divisions: in some companies the products can be listed individually. The markets also might be split in different ways. Thus a frozen vegetable processor might evolve a matrix as shown in Figure 3.3. Each cell in the matrix could then be developed in more detail to show past, present and future positions (Figure 3.4).

The categorisation of products and markets and the degree of analysis of product/ market relationships will obviously vary from company to company, and may also be varied within a firm to identify different facets of the business. The paucity of information may prove a limitation to many sales managers. Nevertheless, categorisation is worth undertaking if only in the broadest terms because it focuses managerial attention on both problem areas and growth opportunities. Generalisations such as "this market is expanding by x per cent a year" or "that product is declining" are pointless. In the vast majority of markets and products the overall picture is an amalgam of increasing, decreasing and static situations. For example, total UK passenger car production declined dramatically during the 1970s from a peak of 2 million vehicles in 1972 to only about 1 million by 1980. However, the performance of the various segments of the industry varied considerably throughout the period; for example in the mid 1970s when the total market was fairly static this stability resulted from declines in the sectors from

Products	Markets					
	Multiples	Voluntary groups	Co-operatives	Independent	Trend	Total
Peas						
Beans						
Cauliflower						
Broccoli						
Brussel sprouts						
Trend						
Total						

Fig. 3.3 Planning matrix for a frozen vegetable processor
"Markets" in this example are defined by distributive type. This is a particularly important categorisation where networks are evolving at different rates.

1000cc to 2800cc being offset perhaps surprisingly by a steep rise in the sales of larger cars (i.e. over 2800cc). (See Fig. 3.5.)

It is one of the prime tasks of sales management to guide the company into growth areas; such basic strategies can only be identified by analysis of this nature.

By what methods?

Having identified from the product/market analysis the segments to be attacked, the sales manager can now consider the methods that will be most likely to achieve the objectives set.

His basic promotional tool is the sales force. The particular areas of interest are the determining factor in the type of sales effort required. The first question to be answered is – what sort of service should the sales force provide in order to influence the buyer? If, for example, the manager of a food firm has identified an area of great potential with supermarkets this will lead him to consider what he can do to persuade supermarkets to buy more of his products. The best way to approach any problem of selling to a distributive network is to consider what help the dealers need in order to sell the product. Therefore, in this case, he will recognise that supermarkets will only buy more if they can sell more. One way of selling more is to merchandise the product in-store, so the sales manager may well organise his field force towards that objective. Obviously such a conclusion will have important implications for the selection, training, organisation and control of the field force. These aspects will be covered in ensuing chapters. The same thinking applies to companies in other industries. For example, a crop protection firm pondering how to increase sales to agricultural merchants will have to consider how the merchant will market the product to farmers. Perhaps the job of the sales force in this case will be to help the merchant develop his own marketing skills.

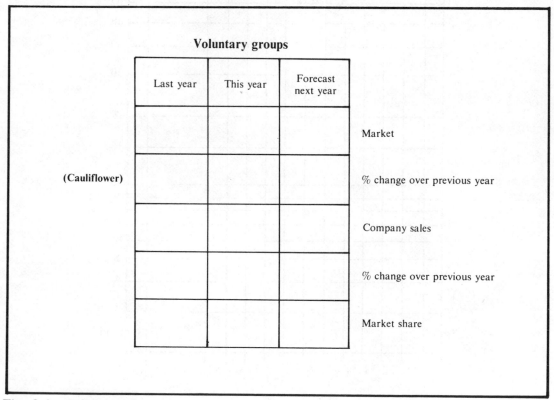

Fig. 3.4   Cell analysis
An example of a single cell developed from the planning matrix in Figure 3.3

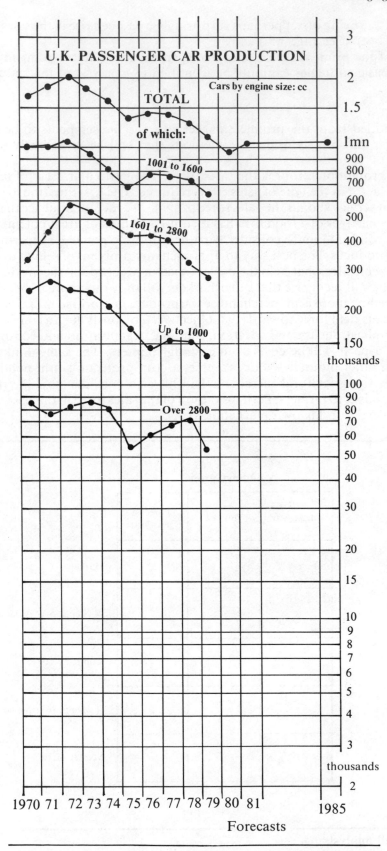

Fig. 3.5   U.K. car production in total and by segment

Even where distribution networks are not involved, the sales manager must still give thought to what service to provide to the buyer. For example, a packaging company must consider whether the buyer needs salesmen who are technical experts in the packaging itself, the packaging process and the machinery required, or the particular packaging problems of individual industries. On the other hand, perhaps the salesman should be more of a design consultant or maybe have a high degree of financial knowledge so that he can discuss the cost-effectiveness of his products. Most important of all in selling packaging, the salesman will need an appreciation of his customers' own marketing problems. Thus the successful industrial salesman selling packaging to, say, a food company will certainly have an awareness of the problems of the food company selling to the retail trade; and, moreover, the retail trade's problems selling to the housewife.

Such an analysis of what kind of sales effort is needed will lead to identification of the sales methods that are appropriate. The complexity of seller/buyer relationships becomes rapidly obvious. It is only by such definition that the sales manager can develop the presentational approach that will enable him to succeed in the face of product/price parity.

Having identified the nature of the sales method he can then consider the scale of effort required. He must calculate how many customers and prospects should be called on how often. The customers are relatively easy to specify because they are known by name to the company. However, it may be uneconomic to have very small customers visited personally, except very seldom. The level of prospecting is more difficult to calculate as in many companies potential customers cannot be identified by name. At least, however, the sales manager can indicate the characteristics of likely prospects. Such a profile can then be used by the sales force to select prospects to be called upon. Alternatively, the sales manager can plan simply to allow a certain percentage of time or calls for the process of looking for new business, giving the salesman the responsibility of using the time or calls wisely.

How often calls should be made is always difficult to assess. Obviously different categories of accounts will require or demand different call frequencies. In some trades where there is an established buying frequency, usually little is gained by calling at a different frequency. For most companies, however, the call frequencies have to be decided by management and the best rule of thumb to follow is to call as infrequently as possible without jeopardising the business. Many companies over-call because they fear that if they are not on the customer's doorstep as often as possible they will lose business. It is worth while to experiment with call frequencies to see if slowing down the frequency does actually affect sales. Even marginal changes can have a dramatic impact on cost. If, for instance, a sales force is calling on average every four weeks and this could be altered to every five weeks, the company could possibly save up to 25 per cent of its sales costs.

The support of the field force will also be covered by the sales manager's study of the methods required to achieve his objectives. It is often the case that various parts of the supplier/buyer relationship can be more economically handled by techniques other than personal visiting by representatives. Telephone selling is one method that is successfully used to handle routine ordering, thus freeing the salesmen's costly time for more creative work. In the consumer goods trades, where point of sale display work is common, many firms have split their field forces into salesmen and merchandisers. In industrial selling, the sales force has often to be supported by technical staff who can advise more expertly on the product and its applications. In the computer market the salesman is usually backed by a team of experts who can advise the customer on systems design, programming and installation.

Furthermore, parts of the sales task may be better handled by other non-personal promotional techniques. For example, it may be more economic to generate prospects for a life assurance company by advertising and direct mail than by cold canvassing by the salesmen. Customer education in using the product may be better handled by producing films than by individual tuition from the salesman.

In other words, the sales manager's task in deciding the nature and scale of the methods necessary to achieve his objectives should not be limited to a simple consideration of how to deploy salesmen. His criteria for selecting techniques must not only be effectiveness and use of his sales force but also cost and use of total company resources. Obviously the majority of the effort will be through the sales force in most companies; this should not lead, however, to ignoring other possibilities.

At what cost – effectiveness?

The planning focus of most companies has been traditionally on growth, particularly profit growth coming naturally from sales volume or at least revenue increases. However the situation facing many industries is one of stagnant, even declining markets, prices under pressure and most costs rising rapidly. In such circumstances the planning focus has to change from one of simple growth to a search for increased productivity.

Productivity is the measurement of the interrelationship between inputs and outputs, well acknowledged if not totally understood in production processes, but far less well explored in sales because of historic assumptions about year on year sales increases. Improving productivity is not simply a question of cost reduction, the dreaded "head count" exercises for example. Paradoxically such efforts often actually reduce productivity as senior, highly paid sales management have to do the work left behind when junior, lower paid jobs are eliminated.

To analyse and subsequently to increase productivity there must be a clear understanding of what outputs are desired, what inputs are necessary and the nature of the relationship between the two in terms of causation (i.e. what effects result from what causes) and correlation (i.e. how much a change in input will affect the output). Typical desired sales outputs include volume, revenue, product range, mix, market share, gross margin, and net margin. The relative importance and achievability of these will of course vary from company to company and situation to situation. Thus a firm which has traditionally sought volume increases may now have to concentrate on margin protection.

Sales inputs are characterised by the kind of sales activity used (e.g. field force, telesales, van sales), the number of sales personnel (both in the field and in the sales office) and the type of person employed (management: staff ratios, calibre, pay etc).

There are so many different measures of sales productivity that a sequential approach is needed to focus management attention on the key figures and, what is more important, their underlying causes.

A good starting point is to measure the ratio of sales to sales cost. Sales will normally be taken as revenue, but should be analysed by volume, price and mix relative to target. Sales cost will usually include not only field force costs, but also the costs of the sales office, sales management, training etc. This overall measurement can be further analysed as shown in Figure 3.6.

Comparisons within the sales force are often illuminating too. An analysis should be made of the differences in performance between the most successful salesmen and the average and the reasons for the differences. All of these productivity measures become much more valuable if trends from year to year can be identified and comparisons made with other similar companies. Organisations such as the Institute of Marketing publish surveys from time to time which provide useful yardsticks.[1]

---

1   For example, *Sales Force Practice Today* published by the Institute of Marketing in 1979 analysed the performance of 35000 salesmen in almost 2000 companies.

Ratios	Comments
1. Sales:sales costs	What is the trend?
2. Sales per salesman	Are there big differences?
explained by	
3. Number of customers/contacts per salesman	Are there big differences?
4. Number of calls per day	Relationship to sales?
5. Face-to-face time:total time	Enough time with customers?
6. Orders:calls	Trends in "strike rate"?
7. Average order value	Differences between salesmen?
8. Field sales costs:total sales costs	Too much "indirect" cost?
9. Percentage of labour turnover	Is the sales force stable?
10. Most successful salesman:average salesman	Difference gives some indication of improvement potential

Fig. 3.6   Assessing sales productivity: ten key ratios

Such quantitative assessments of current productivity will usually highlight key areas for improvement and at the same time indicate the underlying causes that have to be modified if results are to be improved. Furthermore, evaluating sales performance in this way forms a sound basis for the whole planning process.

Major customer planning

Most companies' sales exhibit strong 80:20 tendencies, i.e. a small percentage of large customers taking the bulk of the sales and vice versa. These major customers are so important that they require special planning attention from sales management and, usually special handling which will be explored later.

In planning this key aspect of the business, the sales manager must consider first what is the maximum proportion of sales revenue that top customers should account for. One service company for example will not allow its top 5 accounts to represent more than 40 per cent of the sales revenue because above that level it considers itself too vulnerable. An industrial components company decided that no single market should account for more than 15 per cent of its output and that each market segment ideally should consist of

CUSTOMER		
	£ TOTAL	% GSV
1 Gross sales value		
2 Less: Invoiced discounts		
3 Net sales		
4 Less: Manufacturing cost		
5 : Distribution		
6 Customer gross profit		
7 Less: Sales allowances		
8 : Marketing allowances		
9 : Consumer deals		
10 : Other marketing*		
11 Customer contribution		
12 Less: Direct sales force		
13 : Sales overheads*		
14 : Marketing overheads*		
15 : General and administration*		
16 Trading profit		
17 Less: Payment discount		
18 : Debtor interest		
19 : Stock interest		
20 Profit after interest		

*Allocations

Fig. 3.7   Customer profit and loss account – consumer goods example

no more than 5 firms controlling 80 per cent of purchases. Of course, it is not always easy or even possible to control the customer/sales mix in this way, but at least having a sales policy on this key issue is a good start so that if and when major customers are predicted to become too dominant, appropriate action can be taken for example to broaden the customer or market base of the firm.

Second, the profitability of major customer business should be analysed as it is too facile to assume that because they produce most of the sales they must inevitably produce most of the profit. In fact because large customers demand large discounts, tend to take longer credit, need more stock back-up, expect considerable promotional support etc., the costs of servicing them are usually disproportionately high. In order to analyse and control major customer profitability an increasing number of firms produce profit and loss accounts for each top customer. Figures 3.7 and 3.8 show example formats for

---

Customer ....

Period ....

		£
1	Gross sales volume	
2	Less: Invoiced discounts	
3	: Credits	
4	: Delivery charges	
5	Net sales	_____
6	Less: Cost of goods sold	
7	: Product royalty	
8	Customer gross margin	_____
9	Less: Negotiated discount	
10	: Direct sales costs	
11	: Product trial costs	
12	: Installation costs	
13	: Invoicing costs	
14	: Customer operation training costs	
15	Customer gross contribution	_____
16	Add: Invoiced service and spares	
17	Less: Direct service costs	
18	: Spares costs	
19	Customer contribution	_____
20	Less: Debtor interest	
21	: Stock interest	
22	Operating profit	_____
23	Less: Sales overheads	
24	: Service overheads	
25	: Warehousing	
26	: General and administration	
27	Net profit	══════════════

Fig. 3.8 Customer profit and loss account – industrial goods example

consumer goods and industrial companies. When this process is first installed, it usually shows to the horror of management that their key customers produce much less profit than they had believed and in many cases actually show a net loss. However, only by analysing performance in this detail can a realistic basis be laid for future planning and negotiation.

Involving the sales force in planning

So far, the construction of the plan has been examined as a sales management task. The quality of the plan and the likelihood of its achievement will be enhanced if the salesmen themselves are involved. This is because they possess detailed local knowledge which the sales manager may not have and also because by being involved they will feel more committed to achieving the objectives.

It is always worth while consulting the sales force on the forecasts and targets that should be set. Curiously enough, it is usually discovered that when the sales force is asked for its views on the future they are more optimistic than the manager. To avoid excesses of optimism the manager must stress to each man that his forecast must be based on facts concerning what has happened in the past and what action is proposed for the future.

Developing customer strategies

Having set the targets jointly, the manager should then ask for details of the actions that will achieve the targets. This process will cover not only what the salesman himself intends to do but also what support he needs from elsewhere in the company. As the basic unit of a salesman's work is the customer, a systematic way of planning this level is to develop customer strategies. (See Figure 3.9.) These focus particular attention on the large customers and ensure that the relationship with such important buyers proceeds purposefully. The development of a customer strategy commences with a matrix analysis similar to the more global tabulations drawn up by the sales manager to identify areas of potential business. Targets are then set sector by sector. The salesman identifies who is to be called upon within the customer company and how frequently, what is to be done during the visits, and what support he needs. Further refinement can be added by producing actual and forecast profit and loss accounts (see Figures 3.7 and 3.8). Such strategies provide a means of dealing with at least the big customers and a method for controlling the salesman's performance on a continuous basis. The two examples (Figures 3.10 and 3.11) show how the technique can be used in both consumer and industrial markets. Obviously the sales manager will amend where necessary if he feels the targets are unrealistic or the actions not feasible. He can then agree and consolidate the strategies to form the basis of his total plan. Also items will be added, amended or deleted to suit particular company requirements. For example, market shares can be readily calculated, the product/use definitions can be changed to suit particular needs and the detailing of support required from other departments may be curtailed if this is outside the salesman's jurisdiction.

CUSTOMER STRATEGY FORM

Salesman _____ Date_____

Name and address_____

Current contacts _____
(names and positions)

_____

Product/Market matrix
– this year

		MARKETS				
		(a)	(b)	(c)	Trend	Total
P R O D U C T S	A	Potential Actual				
	B	P A				
	C	P A				
	D	P A				
Trend						
Total		P A				

Competitive activity _____

_____

Targets

		MARKET			
		(a)	(b)	(c)	Total
P R O D U C T S	A				
	B				
	C				
	D				
Total					

Action

Contacts to be made _____

Call frequency_____

Objectives of calls _____

Support required _____

Fig. 3.9   Customer strategy form

CUSTOMER STRATEGY FORM

Salesman _____R. Kelly._____ Date ____11th October____

Name and address of customer _____Head Office,_____T.V. Chain Stores Ltd.,____

_____High Street,_____

Branches throughout Great Britain_____London_____Tel. 01-935-3330.____

Current Contacts _____L. Brown – Purchasing Director._____

_____S. Black – Merchandising Manager._____

_____Q. Jones – Regional Controller – South._____

Product/Market matrix
– this year

PRODUCTS		MARKETS			Trend	Total
		South	Midlands	North		
	Small	P 2000	1500	1200	Declining	4700
		A 1000	500	300		1800
	Large	P 1500	2000	1500	Static	5000
		A 800	800	400		2000
	Video recorders	P 1000	500	400	Rapidly	1900
		A 300	100	100	expanding	500
	Trend	Increasing	Static	Increasing		
	Total	P 4500	4000	3100		
		A 2100	1400	800		

number of sets

P = Potential
A = Actual

Competitive activity

Competition relatively strong in Midlands and North regions because of traditional ties with local factories.

Product competition particularly on small colour sets.

Fig. 3.10   Customer strategy form
Consumer goods example – television sets

Targets		MARKETS			
		South	Midlands	North	Total
P R O D U C T S	Small	1200	500	400	2100
	Large	1000	800	500	2300
	VCR	500	200	200	900
	Total	2700	1500	1100	5300

Action

Contacts to be made. Each region is virtually autonomous for buying purposes under general policy guidance of purchasing director. Must make contact therefore with Regional Controllers for Midlands and North.

Call frequency. Recommend maintenance of four-weekly cycle to purchasing departments and eight-weekly contact with merchandising to arrange special display, etc.

Objectives of call

1.   To ensure Midlands and North Controllers fully aware of our product range, pricing structure and after sales service.

2.   To arrange at least four special promotions of our range during the year, especially VCR.

3.   To arrange contract purchasing of large sets.

Support required

1.   Our Northern and Midlands representatives to concentrate on Regional Controllers.

2.   Sales Promotion to provide merchandising ideas for 4 in-store promotions during year.

3.   Finance to advise on better contract arrangements for large sets.

4.   Distribution to advise on best possible stockholding (delivery position for Midlands and North) so that we can fight local competition.

Fig. 3.10   *(continued)*

CUSTOMER STRATEGY FORM

Salesman _____ R. McCarthy. _____ . Date ___ 11 October

Name of customer _____ XYZ Bottlers Company Limited _____

_____ Main Street _____

_____ Newtown _____

_____ Telephone Newtown 123 _____

Current contacts _____ F. Smith, assistant buyer _____

_____ J. Jenkins, works manager _____

_____

Product/Market matrix
– this year

number of units in grosses

			MARKETS			
		Gin	Whisky	Vodka	Trend	Total
P R O D U C T S	Miniature	1 000 600	5 000 3 000	? 500	Increasing because of airline business	6 000 + ? 4 100
	½ litre	10 000 5 000	20 000 12 000	? 500	Static	30 000 + ? 17 500
	1 litre	25 000 5 000	50 000 18 000	? 500	Decreasing because of price increases	75 000 + ? 23 500
	Trend	Static	Slightly increasing	New line seems to be increasing		
	Total	36 000 10 600	75 000 33 000	? 1 500		

Competitive activity

Competition very strong in 1 litre bottles because of price. Also trying to attack our miniature bottle sales

_____

_____

_____

Fig. 3.11   Customer strategy form
Industrial goods example – glass containers

Targets

		MARKETS			
		Gin	Whisky	Vodka	Total
P R O D U C T S	Miniature	700	4 000	500	5 200
	½ litre	6 000	15 000	500	21 500
	1 litre	10 000	20 000	500	30 500
	Total	16 700	39 000	1 500	57 300

Action

Contacts to be made:

1. Must establish contact with Chief Buyer as he handles vodka line where we have little information. Must also contact Marketing Department to try and establish brand plans.

   Suspect Company will put strong effort behind vodka, and ease off gin

Call frequency. Need to increase to every four weeks except in pre-Xmas period when every two weeks.

Objectives of call:

1. To identify size of vodka business and future intentions.

2. To stress our technical expertise to combat price competition.

3. To increase gin business by indicating better bulk discounts on slightly larger order.

4. To increase whisky business by offering stock back-up.

Support required.

1. Agreement to increase whisky stock back-up. Technical staff to visit customer to advise on running bottle line.

2. Member of senior management to help contact Chief Buyer.

3. Market Research department to supply any information available on vodka market

Fig. 3.11 *(continued)*

ACTION PLANNING CHECKLIST

Questions	Answers and action	Timing of action and evaluation
1 Is the objectives-planning-control continuum understood and accepted in the company? If not what action is needed?		
2 What are the current marketing objectives, strategies and control criteria?		
3 What are the current sales objectives?		
4 What forecasting procedures are used? Should they be improved? If so, by adopting what methods?		
5 What is the relationship between the company's forecasts and targets? Should it be changed?		
6 In what terms and categories are the targets expressed? Are they sufficiently detailed?		
7 Is there a clear picture of market segment/product relationships? If not use Figure 3.2 (Planning Matrix) to identify these		
8 What services should the sales force provide to customers?		
9 Are all the sales methods used efficient? What areas should be studied for cost-effectiveness and how?		
10 Are major customers identified, analysed and planned separately and in sufficient depth?		
11 Should the sales force be involved in planning? If so should they develop Customer Strategies (Figure 3.9)?		

CHAPTER 4

How to Organise the Sales Force

Many sales organisations have developed without regular objective analysis of their purpose or structure. Today they are out of date and unable to fulfil the purposes for which they were originally designed. This is because the traditional hierarchical structure (see Figure 4.1) is based upon conditions which no longer hold true in a great number of firms. Such organisations assume that there is a large number of relatively small, geographically separate and independent buying points all with similar requirements, and that these can be serviced by a large number of geographically separated salesmen who can perform similar tasks and who represent the major promotional activity of the company.

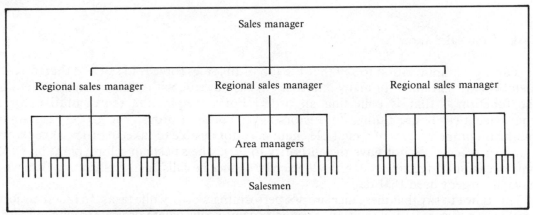

Fig. 4.1   Traditional sales organisation structure

Changes in buyer/seller relationships

These suppositions have been made obsolete by a number of fundamental changes in the buyer/seller relationship.

First, as has been discussed, the buying power in many industries is no longer evenly distributed. In a large number of markets a few big firms (either distributors or end-users)

47

control the majority of the purchasing. Because of their buying power and importance it is not usually feasible to delegate sufficient responsibility and authority to the salesmen in whose territories they happen to be located. Furthermore, the large customers themselves are increasingly centralising their purchasing so that their branches or subsidiaries who at one time might have been direct customers for other territory salesmen no longer are allowed to buy.

Second, the development of new marketing techniques has meant that some tasks traditionally performed by the sales force can be more economically or efficiently handled by other methods. The growing use of techniques such as telephone selling, contract ordering, broking, auxiliary or commando sales forces and even franchising is having a significant impact on the nature and scale of the field sales effort required. Broking organisations, for example, seem to be expanding very rapidly and already cover the food, chemist and hardware trades in the UK. If the evolution of the US market is any guide to the future, it is significant to note that 65 per cent of all food sales are now handled by brokers.

Not surprisingly the reduction in number of buying points to be called on and the development of other methods of customer servicing have together caused major changes in the size and function of many companies' sales forces. The most dramatic examples are to be found in the consumer goods industries where typically sales forces have been reduced by up to 50 per cent in the last 5 years, e.g. the Brooke Bond Oxo sales force of 1000 in 1975 numbers around 300 today.

It is evident that the sales manager must consider these major influences in planning his organisation. In order to fit his sales team to the needs of his customers he must identify:

1　What the task of the sales force is.
2　How many salesmen are needed.
3　How they should be organised.
4　How they can be managed.
5　How the sales organisation can be integrated with the marketing organisation in particular and the rest of the company in general.

Task of the sales force

It is an oversimplification to say that the job of the sales force is to sell and therefore its members are salesmen. In many industries this is not true within the normal concept of the function – that is collecting an order. For example, the representative for a pharmaceutical house calling on doctors never takes an order. The grocery salesman calling on branch stores of a multiple chain may not be able to take an order, as the store manager often does not have the authority to buy. The salesman selling plant hire will only occasionally get an order himself when by chance he calls on a construction firm who have an urgent need that day.

This is not to say that these men are not performing worth-while tasks. In fact their jobs need even more careful definition. Even in organisations where orders are gained by the salesman, he usually has many other functions to perform which must be identified. The soft drinks salesman calling on licensed premises will probably spend a proportion of his day in debt collecting. Merchandising occupies much of the time of many consumer goods salesmen. The computer salesman's work will be largely occupied with investigating the information systems of his prospects before he can even think about what they might buy.

The prime objective of all salesmen is to gain business directly or indirectly. From an organisational point of view, however, *how* they are to achieve their goals must be defined in order to identify what kind and quality of skills are required.

Deficiencies of organisation theory

Classical organisation theory always suggests that the salesmen do the selling while the managers do the managing. Such a simple division is no longer practicable. One result of the process of concentration of power is that the big buyer often wishes to deal with his supplier at a higher level than the territory salesman. This may be because he wishes to negotiate prices to levels beyond the salesman's authority or simply that the spread of his business is far broader than the salesman's geographical area. Regional sales management may be able to cope with the medium-sized buyer who is wholly within their territory. But inevitably the big national or international customer wants to deal at national or international level with his suppliers. Thus, despite efforts to thrust sales responsibility downwards (as is demanded, quite rightly, by classical organisation theory) management is forced to become increasingly involved in sales situations. In those companies where the organisation is built on the supposition that managers do not have to spend time selling, the manager's workload becomes intolerably high as he tries to fit an increasing amount of selling time into an already fully committed day. A typical example of what might happen as a result is that of the marketing director of a frozen food firm who found that he was working very long hours and was personally selling some 50 per cent of the total company turnover despite having a staff of forty-two. Moreover, further analysis showed that there was little he could do to delegate this large sales responsibility. The 50 per cent of turnover that he handled consisted of major national accounts which demanded his personal attention.

Matching the sales effort to customer requirements

Organising the sales effort so that it matches the reality of the market-place can alleviate such problems. First, the level and quantity of customer service must be defined and the personnel concerned identified. Then job descriptions can be developed, which will be discussed in the next chapter. Such an analysis will also begin to identify the workloads of each level and suggest ways of grouping the various elements so that they can be better managed. (See Figures 4.2 and 4.3.)

For example, in the consumer goods analysis (Figure 4.2) senior management are noted several times to handle national accounts. A common way of regrouping these activities so that line management is freed from much of the work is to appoint a national accounts manager. Likewise, in the industrial goods analysis (Figure 4.3) perhaps national and local government bodies should be grouped under one manager.

An increasing number of companies are using field research to help them identify more accurately the buying motivations and influences of the various types of customers and thus to specify the sales services to be offered. Perception surveys are a powerful technique to establish what services the customers rate as important and how they view the competitive suppliers of them. They are conducted by providing a checklist of factors to a sample of customers, asking them to rate their relative importance and then rank order the competing suppliers in terms of their performance. The deeper understanding of customer motivation and perceived supplier competence gained from such surveys can be of significant value in organising the nature and scale of the sales effort. For example, an industrial component firm had believed that the key buying need was for their high product quality until a perception survey revealed that their customers felt that all major suppliers offered sufficiently good quality products and that therefore they made most of their purchasing decisions based on quite different criteria notably rapid availability. This led them to reconsider the type of salesmen required, the basis of their training (traditionally highly technical) and the overall sales policy on stockholding and supply.

Type of account	Number of accounts	Services to be provided	Personnel responsible
1 National multiples		Contract purchasing	Marketing director and sales manager
		Price negotiation	Marketing director and sales manager
(a) Head offices	20	Own brand deals	Managing director and marketing director
		National promotions	Merchandising manager and sales manager
(b) Branches	1000	Local ordering	Territory representative
		Merchandising	Territory merchandiser
2 Co-operative societies		Contract purchasing	Marketing director and sales manager
		Price negotiation	Marketing director and sales manager
(a) Head offices	10	Own brand deals	Managing director and marketing director
		Promotions	Merchandising manager and sales manager
(b) Branches	500	Merchandising	Territory merchandisers
3 Voluntary groups		Contract purchasing	Marketing director and sales manager
(a) Head offices	6	Price negotiation	Marketing director and sales manager
		Own brand deals	Managing director and sales manager
		Promotions	Merchandising manager and sales manager
(b) Branches	5000	Nil	N/a
4 Regional multiples			
(a) Head office	50	Purchasing	Regional manager
		Regional promotions	Regional merchandising manager
(b) Branches	200	Local merchandising	Territory merchandiser
5 Independent stores	5000	Purchasing	Territory representative
		Account collection	Territory representative

Fig. 4.2   Customer service requirement analysis
Consumer goods example – food

Type of account	Number of accounts	Services to be provided	Personnel responsible
National building companies	20	Purchasing	Marketing director and sales manager
		Price negotiation	Marketing director and sales manager
		Technical advice	Technical service manager
		Samples and trials	Development manager
Regional building companies	100	Purchasing	Regional manager
		Technical support	Technical representative
Local building companies	500	Purchasing	Area representative
		Technical support	Area representative
Architects	500	Technical advice	Architectural representative
		Assistance in specifying	Architectural representative
Local authorities	300	Technical advice	Area representative
		Assistance in specifying	Area representative
Government departments	20	Purchasing	Sales manager
		Technical advice	Technical service manager

Fig. 4.3   Customer service requirement analysis
Industrial goods example – building products

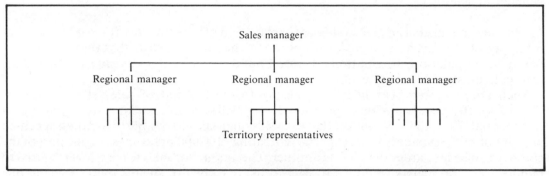

Fig. 4.4   Traditional geographical structure of a glass container company

The sales force structure should also be scrutinised. A geographical split may be most economical in that travel time is minimised. It may not, however, be the most effective. In one glass container company it was seen that the prime service to be provided to the buyer was a technical knowledge of bottling as applied to the customer's particular industry. Thus the sales force was regrouped on an industry basis changing the organisation structure from that shown in Figure 4.4 to that shown in Figure 4.5. Obviously there was some increase in travel costs because each industry group worked nationally but this was more than offset by the increase in sales.

At sales force level common groupings other than geographical are by industry, by customer size category – for example, big and small accounts – by customer function – for example, purchasers and specifiers – or by service to be provided – for example, order-taking and merchandising. By conducting a customer service requirements analysis the sales manager can identify which organisational approach is appropriate.

An increasing number of companies are recognising that different structural decisions may be appropriate for various sectors of their markets. For example, a company making drinking glasses identified the different customer service requirements of its two major market sectors, the licensed trade (i.e. bars, hotels, restaurants) and the retail market. An employed sales force is used to service the former, either direct to major accounts or via specialist wholesalers for the smaller outlets. The retail market has traditionally been serviced direct to large accounts (e.g. departmental stores, mail order) and again through wholesalers to smaller stores (china and glass shops). However, increasingly glassware is being sold through supermarkets where neither the company nor its wholesalers had any strong connections. It has responded to this market development by providing a field sales activity through a broking firm as the most likely cost-effective solution. Furthermore, a contract merchandising field force is used to boost in-store display in ailing trade sectors.

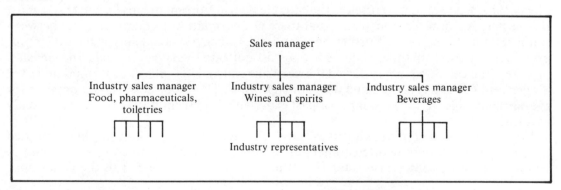

Fig. 4.5   Current industry-based structure of a glass container company

Number of salesmen needed

Many sales managers can give no logical explanation of why the sales force is the size that it happens to be. Even when explanations are forthcoming, such as that the sales force is based on population distribution, county boundaries or sales revenue per man, the rationale must still be in question.

Such criteria often bear little relationship to the amount of sales effort required. Counties differ greatly in size; population density will seldom correlate directly with sales or potential. Even the assumption that each salesman should be able to handle a specified amount of sales revenue is very suspect. Generating £100 000 of business in one part of the country can be far harder than it is in another. The amount of sales force effort required to handle 100 customers spending £10 each is likely to be far greater than servicing one account of £1000.

Sales force workload analysis

The aim of building an organisation from the bottom up is to give the appropriate level of service to each customer and the appropriate amount of work to each man. The only common factor between salesmen is the number of working hours and this should be the starting point for a workload analysis, which is the only really logical way of constructing a sales force. The amount of work per salesman can then be calculated by assessing the elements of the sales job. If a sophisticated approach is needed, work study and method analysis can be used to establish these elements and the time taken on each. Typically, they include: *prospecting, travelling, waiting, selling* and *report-writing*. If the number of actual and potential accounts to be visited and the frequency of visiting can be assessed, it is possible to calculate the number of salesmen needed.

Practical short-cuts can be taken and an answer arrived at quickly and simply if four basic factors are known.

First, the number of accounts to be visited by the sales force should be listed. It is usually easy to identify existing customers by name, location, type and number; potential customers may be more difficult to specify and in some cases impossible to define in detail. For example, in some door-to-door sales activities, every house can be a prospect. Where these cannot be specified, but a level of prospecting is decided, then allowance can be made later.

Second, the call frequency per type of customer must be assessed. As a general rule, the larger the customer the more frequent the call; but this may not always be so. For example, a customer buying £90 000 worth of goods per annum and having further potential of £10 000 may warrant less frequent calling than a customer spending £70 000 with the company who has a further potential of £50 000.

Third, the average call rate per salesman is calculated. Some managers seem to believe that the number of calls is irrelevant as long as orders are gained. Although the goal must always be one of sales, nevertheless the call rate is an important means to that end in most businesses. It can be demonstrated that there is a correlation in many markets between number of calls and sales. Furthermore, call rates when averaged across the sales force and over a period of time, such as a year, do not often vary very much. In one case, although the call rate per day varied between one call and ten calls, it was found that over 80 per cent of the days contained seven or eight calls. Therefore, it is usually possible for the sales manager to take a sample of past experience and from it to fix the average daily call rate.

Finally, the number of working days per year is calculated, a working day being defined as a day spent dealing with customers as opposed to attending in-company meetings, training sessions, conferences, etc. Then the four factors can be put in the equation:

$$\frac{\text{Number of actual and potential customers} \times \text{Call frequency}}{\text{Average daily call rate} \times \text{Number of working days per year}}$$

– and a total sales force size can be calculated. (See Figure 4.6.)

The formula can also be used to check the workload per man. If figures are inserted for any salesman's work, the answer should be 1.00 if he is fully loaded. In sales forces constructed on bases other than workload, such a check normally reveals a range between 0.75 and 1.25. In other words, some men are underloaded, others overworked. This does not normally mean a vast difference in the time put in by different salesmen. The men simply adjust the work to fit the time available by altering the call frequencies. Thus, the underloaded man typically overservices his accounts, calling more frequently than is justified; the overloaded salesman calls more seldom or cuts out accounts altogether. Unfortunately the omitted calls are often those on prospects which are vital to any company's future growth. Time for prospecting can be built in as described above by nominating potential customers in the same way as actual accounts are listed. Where this is not possible but where a percentage of prospecting time should be allocated, the annual call total (which is the product of the top line of the equation) can be increased by the appropriate percentage. In the example described in Figure 4.6, the annual call total was 68 000. If this represents only existing customers and the sales manager wants his men to spend one day per week looking for new business, then this total should be increased by 20 per cent to 81 600 calls a year. Dividing this by the calls per man a year of 1720, gives a total sales force of about forty-seven.

Territory organisation

The organisation of each salesman's workload can now be considered to ensure the territory is covered as effectively as possible. Customers to be called upon have been identified, call frequencies have been set and call rates calculated. Using these three factors the territories can be built up to form appropriate workloads per man. How the workload is handled will have an impact on achievement and cost, and many salesmen if left to their own devices will work in almost random fashion round the territory, "territory" in this case implying a group of customers, not necessarily a discrete geographical area, so the comments are applicable to industry-based territories as well as geographical areas. Some will tend to call more frequently than is necessary on customers near to home and will ignore accounts in distant parts of their areas. Others, particularly industrial salesmen, may give too much attention to customers whom they find technically interesting or from whom they get a pleasant reception rather than allocating their time in accordance with sales potential. The prime aim of territory organisation analysis is to maximise selling time by minimising travel time in particular.

Pie system

Two of the major causes of increased travel time are the retracing of routes to pick up previously abortive calls due to buyers' absence and so on, and to detouring to deal with urgent inquiries and complaints. Both these situations can be alleviated by organising the week on the so-called pie system.

The territory is divided into five segments, each segment representing a day of the week. A map of the territory drawn thus is shown in Figure 4.7. It is assumed in this case that the salesman lives near the centre of his territory and travels to and from home every day. Each segment is then divided into a number of portions equivalent to the number of weeks in the journey cycle and containing one day's work. If the journey cycle – that is, the call frequency – is every four weeks for all customers, each segment is divided into four

NUMBER OF ACTUAL AND POTENTIAL CUSTOMERS × CALL FREQUENCY
AVERAGE DAILY CALL RATE × NUMBER OF WORKING DAYS PER YEAR

Customer categories and call frequencies

Category *A* (over £50 000 a year)	500 × 12 visits p.a. =	6 000
Category *B* (£25 000–£50 000 a year)	2000 × 9 visits p.a. =	18 000
Category *C* (£10 000–£25 000 a year)	5000 × 6 visits p.a. =	30 000
Category *D* (under £10 000 a year)	7000 × 2 visits p.a. =	14 000
	Annual call total	68 000

Average daily call rate = 8

Number of working days

Total days in year		365
Weekends	104	
Holidays	15	
Sickness	5	
Training	10	
Conferences	5	
Meetings	11	150

Number of working days 215

Call total per salesman 215 × 8 = 1720

Number of salesmen required $= \dfrac{68\ 000}{1720} = 40$ salesmen

Fig. 4.6   Calculating sales force size

portions. Where varying lengths of journey cycle are used, a common denominator is found. If calls are to be made at four-weekly, eight-weekly and twelve-weekly intervals, each segment will still be divided by four as this is the module which fits all frequencies. The map will then appear as shown in Figure 4.8.

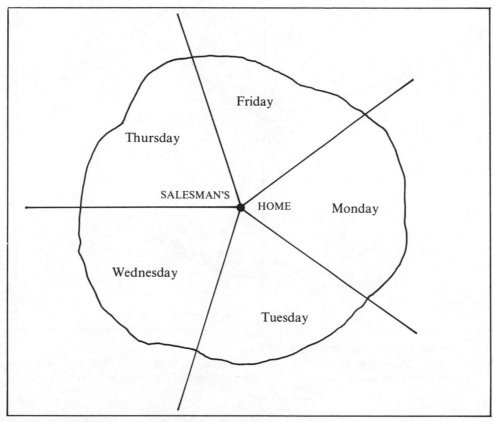

Fig. 4.7   Organising a sales territory – Phase 1
The territory divided into five segments, each segment representing a day of the week. The sequence of the days is adjustable and can be altered to fit in with factors such as half-day closing, etc

By working to this system the salesman will visit each segment of his territory each week. Thus, if a call is missed on Wednesday of week 4 it can be picked up by a short detour only seven days later on Thursday of week 1 without making a special journey or waiting four weeks until the next journey cycle visit. Likewise, if an inquiry comes in from any part of the territory, it can be handled within a week of its arrival, as each segment is visited each week. There are always urgent calls that have to be made which necessitate a special journey, but it is surprising how few calls cannot wait for a few days until the salesman is next in that segment.

Petal system

Further time can be saved by logical organisation of the work each day. Mileage can be minimised by adopting the "petal" system, whereby the midpoint of the calls is the mid-point of the journey. If a typical day's portion is examined it can be seen that the petal-shaped route is the shortest distance between the points of call. (See Figure 4.9.)

It is certainly more economic than two policies commonly adopted by sales manage-ment. Some managers believe it is better for the salesman to drive to the furthest point of his territory and work his way back; others think he should work his way out and drive back at the end of the day from the furthest point of call. Assuming the number of

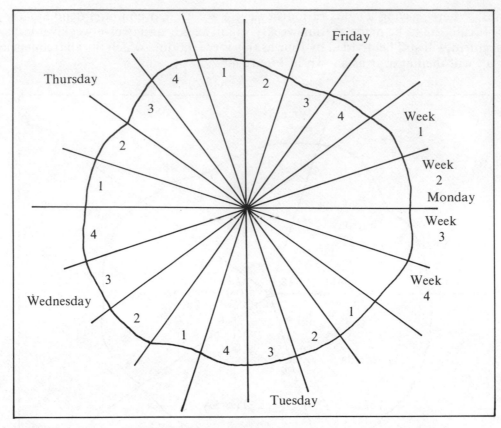

Fig. 4.8   Organising a sales territory – Phase 2
The five segments of Phase 1 divided into four portions equivalent to the number of weeks in the journey cycle. In this example the journey cycle represented can be one of four, eight or twelve weeks

working hours to be equal whichever method is adopted, both these views will lead to longer travel time than the "petal" system.

Organising the sales force by these techniques will certainly improve its efficiency in many companies. Obviously, however, any system must be tempered by the practicalities of particular situations. It is often not possible to implement these methods fully because the salesman has many urgent calls that must be handled, or he has to stay away from home, or the road system does not match the ideal requirements or a host of other factors. Nevertheless, in most companies some of the elements can be applied and will provide benefits. At least the manager will be able to evaluate his judgements against an ideal and thus be aware of the risks he is taking when diverting from the most economic ways of running his sales force.

All of these systems will have to be assessed in the light of the financial position of the company. Although the workload analysis may indicate that fifteen men are required to make the necessary number of visits on the appropriate number of customers to achieve the targets set, in the short term the company may only be able to afford twelve. The system at least allows the manager to calculate what must be eliminated if twelve is the number he has to have.

In cases where there is doubt over the economics of a particular territory, this should be calculated in terms of the likely revenue from the territory and the total costs of the salesman. Specifically, if the direst costs of the salesman are equal to or greater than the gross margin on the revenue generated, obviously the firm will make a net loss on that territory. Even that might be acceptable if there is potential for development.

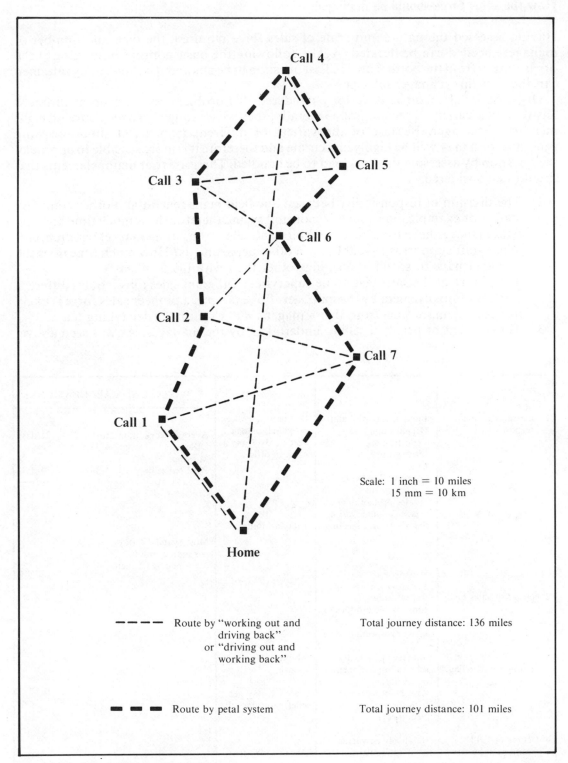

Call 4

Call 5

Call 3

Call 6

Call 2

Call 7

Call 1

Home

Scale: 1 inch = 10 miles
       15 mm = 10 km

– – – – Route by "working out and   Total journey distance: 136 miles
         driving back"
         or "driving out and
         working back"

▬ ▬ ▬   Route by petal system   Total journey distance: 101 miles

Fig. 4.9   Minimising travel time

How the sales force should be managed

Having assessed the nature and scale of sales force required, the type and number of managers needed can be decided. Again, following the basic concept of looking at the organisation from the bottom up, the first question to be answered is: how many salesmen can the first-line manager manage?

Organisational theorists have long pondered this problem and arrived at different answers by a variety of techniques. Generally, their views range between four and eight men to a manager. Because of the variety of different managerial situations, any generalisation may well be highly inaccurate and therefore it is more sensible to approach the question by assessing the workload to be handled. There are four major elements that should be considered:

1   The division of responsibility between line field management and other company staff. For example, how much responsibility and therefore how much time does the field manager have to spend on recruitment, sales promotion, market research, etc? What staff support is available from other departments? How much time does the manager have to spend in meetings other than with his own staff?
2   The nature of the sales task to be supervised. Different sales jobs require different degrees of involvement by the manager. For example, a pioneer sales force is likely to need far more time from the manager than a routine order-taking team.
3   The amount of personal selling undertaken by the manager. As was seen above,

			WORKLOAD CALCULATION	
1 Sales management responsibilities	Final selection of staff Organisation Field training Motivation Control Other staff provide: recruitment sales promotion sales administration Sales manager meeting	Because of services provided, manager needs only 1 day a week in office 1 day a month	Average working month Office 4 days Meetings 1 day Personal selling 4 days Must spend 1½ days per man a month ∴ can manage 8 men	21 days 9 days 12 days
2 Nature of sales task	Repeat selling of consumable product to industrial buyer Little prospecting			
3 Amount of personal selling by manager	Manager personally sells to big customers on territory Also helps salesmen with their larger customers	About 4 days a month About ½ day per salesman a month		
4 Degree of field training necessary	Relatively new team needing regular field training	About 1 day per salesman a month		

Fig. 4.10   Sales management workload assessment

some industries demand a large amount of personal sales time from the manager, either operating on his own or as a part of a sales team. It is common practice, for instance, in capital equipment selling for the manager to lead a team of men on important sales projects.

4 The degree to which field training is necessary. This will depend on the type of salesmen and the sales activity as well as on the seniority of the men concerned. A recently recruited speciality salesman – say, in office equipment – is likely to need far more field training than a senior van salesman who has long experience of his job. However, because of the attrition process that all salesmen undergo, some field training is necessary in virtually every situation.

Analysing these four elements on the sales management workload assessment form (Figure 4.10) will provide a logical approach to deciding the span of control. This workload approach can be used for any job assessment and provides the most logical basis not only for deciding spans of control but also for identifying job standards and recruitment criteria.

Process of delegation

It also ensures that the process of delegation is properly implemented. Delegation consists of three elements, responsibility, authority and accountability.

The delegation of responsibility seems very common in most companies but far too many managers overlook the basic point that no man can really accept a responsibility unless he has the authority to discharge it. Therefore what passes for delegation is not delegation at all in many cases because the power given does not enable the task to be performed. This is particularly true of the so-called delegation of profit responsibility. Many firms try to make lower levels of management responsible for profit generation when, in fact, they have no control over many of the elements that directly affect profitability. If the factory goes on strike because of poor industrial relations management, can the sales manager be held responsible for the subsequent loss of profit?

The third facet of delegation, the maintenance of accountability, is the difference between delegation and abrogation. Giving a subordinate a responsibility and the required amount of authority to discharge it does not mean that the manager himself is no longer involved. The delegative process implies that he still holds the subordinate accountable for his actions and thus requires regular reporting from him regarding the performance of the task in question.

Workload analysis facilitates the process of true delegation because the identification of the tasks quickly identifies the necessary responsibility, the authority and the accountability. For example, if a manager identifies the task of complaints settlement as one to be performed by the sales force, he can specify within what time and financial limits complaints should be finalised. Thus the responsibility for the task can be clearly identified, the power of the salesmen to negotiate can be defined and the type and time period of reporting back specified.

How the sales force can be integrated within the company

For the sales force to function efficiently it must be viewed as an integral part of the total company effort. Much has already been said about the need for this linking together in Chapter 1.

In order to achieve this, there must be a clear concept of the role of the sales force in the total communication process with the market-place. In far too many companies the various promotional tactics are seen as separate units. Thus it happens that the first time the sales force hears about a product modification (which they should be using to sell with) is when a customer comments on it. Even more important is the relationship between the sales force, who are basically an implementational weapon, and the marketing planners. Unless great care is exercised, particularly in firms with product management structures, the sales organisation is continuously torn between different brand objectives and plans.

The best way to overcome these difficulties is to involve sales management in the marketing planning process and for the marketing plan to be the basic operating document for everybody in marketing.

Because the sales force is usually the most frequent if not the sole contact with the customer, it is often used for all dealings with customers regardless of whether they are strictly sales tasks or not. For example, many firms use the sales force to collect overdue debts, although the salesmen may not be involved in the credit rating of customers and thus in a sense it is not their fault if over-long credit is taken. Some companies operate product testing using the sales organisation, although it might be basically a research and development function.

There are good reasons for such tasks being given to salesmen, the prime one of which is that they are the only members of the company who are skilled in dealing with customers. On the other hand, such jobs eat into scarce and valuable selling time. They must be very strictly controlled, otherwise the sales force will be so busy with market research, literature distribution, accounts collection, product testing, and so on, that they have no time left to get orders!

ACTION PLANNING CHECKLIST

Questions	Answers and action	Timing of action and evaluation
1 Has the sales organisation been evaluated recently against the changing scale and nature of the marketplace?		
2 What services should be provided to customers by whom? (See Figures 4.2 and 4.3)		
3 Is the sales force structure cost-effective, not simply the cheapest?		
4 How many salesmen are required to perform these services? (See Figure 4.6)		
5 Do the salesmen cover their territories efficiently and systematically? (See Figures 4.7, 4.8 and 4.9)		
6 Has the workload of sales management been assessed? (See Figure 4.10)		
7 Is the process of delegation carried out properly?		
8 Is the sales force fully integrated with the other elements of the marketing function?		
9 Is too much sales force time being used for functions other than order-getting?		

Chapter 5

How to Staff the Sales Organisation I: Defining the Jobs to be Done and the Men to Do Them

It has been calculated that it costs between £18 000–£20 000 per annum on average to employ a salesman. This level of investment in equipment would require considerable justification and great care would be taken to ensure the right machine was chosen. It is surprising, therefore, that so much of salesmen selection is so carelessly conducted. In many firms, the recruitment process is too often a question of "stick another ad in just like last time," although the previous advertisement did not produce the right calibre of candidate. Selection technique is frequently highly subjective, being based on unproven criteria, such as: "a limp handshake indicates weakness" or "if he can't look you straight in the eye, he is deceitful."

While appreciating the shortage of time in modern business, the sales manager must realise that unless he staffs his organisation carefully and systematically, the rest of his work will be abortive. No amount of organisation and training can change men whose personalities are entirely unsuited for selling, into dynamic, persuasive order-creators.

Salesmen performance factors

The performance of a salesman will depend upon three basic factors. His innate character traits, his training and his motivation. The objective of the staffing process is to choose men whose inborn characteristics are suited to the sales job and who can then be developed and motivated. Obviously there are some individuals whose intrinsic personalities are such that little or no training or incentives are required. These are the "born salesmen." However, they tend to be few and far between and gravitate towards those industries where their outstanding sales skills are directly rewarded by high commission rates, such as life assurance, office equipment and other forms of speciality selling.

Most sales managers must plan not only to pick staff with the appropriate characteristics but also to train and motivate them. In order to choose good salesmen, it is necessary to understand some basic concepts of the staffing process and to have a system for handling recruitment and selection.

Basic concepts of staffing

When a sales manager needs to find a new man, he is faced with a predictive problem. How will a man that the manager knows little about perform in a job that the man knows little about? By some means, the manager must match the one with the other, and it is failure to achieve congruence that causes many of the staff problems in industry. The manager must therefore appreciate that he is not looking for just a good man but a man who is appropriate for a particular job. He is trying to pick horses for courses.

The first stage in the process will be to define carefully the job to be performed. From the organisation study that has already been conducted, the general framework of the position will have been delineated. Now it can be specified in the form of a written job description.

From this document the manager can identify the characteristics that a successful incumbent would possess and thus construct a man profile.

These two statements contain the criteria against which candidates will be assessed and present incumbents appraised. If new men are required, applications can now be generated by recruitment techniques using one or more of such sources as internal staff, newspaper advertising, consultants, etc. In order to begin to assess applicants, the manager must first gather information about them and, second, have some methods for evaluating and checking this data.

Whenever a prediction has to be made of how a man will perform in the future, it is wise to examine in depth what he has done in the past. Psychological research indicates that in terms of basic behavioural patterns, people do not change very much, particularly after the age of maturity. (In fact some psychologists argue that fundamental personality patterns are settled by the age of seven. As most salesmen are well over this age, the precise date does not really matter.) The selection process, therefore, is concerned with collecting detailed information about the man from as far back as possible, verifying that the facts are as stated and then analysing to identify repetitive behavioural traits.

The techniques that can be used for this collection, verification and analysis process are the application form, psychological tests, reference checking, the structured interview and the placement analysis.

Altogether, there are eight steps in a systematic staffing procedure:

1 Writing the job description.
2 Constructing the man profile.
3 Recruiting candidates.
4 Assessing application forms.
5 Checking references.
6 Psychological testing.
7 Structured interviewing.
8 Evaluating and placing successful candidates.

Writing the job description

Job descriptions are one of the basic tools of any sales manager. Not only are they essential for selection but they are also of great value for staff appraisal and checking that all duties in the organisation are covered. They act as a motivational influence for the men concerned, who tend to feel more secure when they know more precisely the limits and opportunities of their jobs.

The job to be described should first be analysed in terms of its organisational position and the responsibilities and authorities that are necessary. The customer service requirement analyses (described in Chapter 4, Figures 4.2 and 4.3) will help. The job description can then be written up using the format in Figure 5.1. Two examples of typical job descriptions are shown in Figure 5.2.

Obviously the examples shown in Figure 5.2 are generalised and somewhat fore-shortened. Care must be exercised, however, to keep job descriptions terse, otherwise they will not serve one of their primary purposes, that of guiding the man in his everyday duties. Some companies have job descriptions which run into thousands of words, many of them meaningless – for example, the job description for a large international chemical firm says: "Attain through personal development individual community stature appropriate to his position as representative of XYZ Company in his territory."

The *job title* should ensure that the job is described in an accurate manner, otherwise the wrong candidates may well be attracted, nor should the motivational influence of the job title be underestimated. (See Chapter 11 for fuller discussion of the motivational effects.) Some firms seem to neglect job titling completely and names are given that are certainly baffling today even if they had a meaning at some earlier date. One brewery company, for example, called its field supervisors "abroad clerks." It is doubtful whether such a nomenclature would attract dynamic candidates!

The *prime job objective* is a concise statement of the major reason for the existence of the position. As far as possible it should be specific and quantitative so that it can be used as a yardstick for evaluation. Many job descriptions contain so many objectives that it is obvious that they can serve as no more than a very general guide to the job function. Such goals should be listed in the next section, *subsidiary objectives*, thus indicating the priorities of the job.

The *person to whom the holder of this position is responsible* should next be specified. It is a cliché that a man can only have one manager and yet it is surprising how often, in practice, a salesman's loyalties are divided by faulty organisational structure. This is particularly true in companies where there are several product ranges, each with a manager and salesman, but only one field management structure. In such cases it may be unclear whether the salesman for product *A* in Devon and Cornwall reports to the western regional manager or the divisional manager for product *A*.

The position *duties* can be now indicated. This section contains the tasks that the man must perform in order to achieve his objectives. His degree of responsibility and authority should also be listed. Obviously it will be impractical to specify every detail that he should control. Attention should be focused on those tasks that are likely to have a major impact on the prime job objective.

If quantitative objectives have been set, the definition of *performance evaluation* procedures is simple. Wherever possible, performance should be measured in specific terms, such as achievement against sales target, prospecting rate, call rate, expense budget, etc. Some items, however, may have to be qualitatively evaluated. At least the timing of such appraisals can be indicated so that, for instance, the salesman knows that his field performance will be considered on a monthly basis.

The *remuneration* of the job will have to be evaluated in relation to the objectives to be achieved and responsibilities carried. In addition to obvious factors such as salary and commission, all tangible rewards of the job should be specified so that both the manager and the man can clearly see the worth of the whole "package." (See Figure 5.2.)

```
┌─────────────────────────────────────────────────────────────┐
│                     JOB DESCRIPTION                          │
├─────────────────────────────────────────────────────────────┤
│                                                             │
│   1   Job title:                                            │
│                                                             │
│                                                             │
│                                                             │
│   2   Prime job objective:                                  │
│                                                             │
│                                                             │
│                                                             │
│   3   Subsidiary objectives:                                │
│                                                             │
│                                                             │
│                                                             │
│   4   Responsible to:                                       │
│                                                             │
│                                                             │
│                                                             │
│   5   Duties:                                               │
│                                                             │
│                                                             │
│                                                             │
│   6   Performance evaluation:                               │
│                                                             │
│                                                             │
│                                                             │
│   7   Remuneration:                                         │
│       (salary grade, commission system, bonus payments,     │
│        car, fringe benefits)                                │
│                                                             │
└─────────────────────────────────────────────────────────────┘
```

Fig. 5.1   Job description form

	CONSUMER EXAMPLE small hardware company expanding its distribution	INDUSTRIAL EXAMPLE well established pharmaceutical company
1 **Job title**	Territory salesman	Senior medical representative
2 **Prime job objective**	To achieve sales targets for all products each month	To call on GPs on your territory at least quarterly and detail the products laid down
3 **Subsidiary objectives**	To open at least ten new accounts a month. To erect at least four displays a month. To demonstrate to at least one women's association meeting a month	To call on all hospitals at least twice a year. To visit all wholesalers at least monthly. To visit all retailers at least annually
4 **Responsible to**	Sales manager	Regional manager
5 **Duties**	Operate the laid-down journey plan. Make at least ten effective calls a day. Always carry full range of product samples and literature. Report weekly on activities to Sales Manager. Report monthly on state of trade and competitive activity to sales manager. Collect overdue accounts as advised by credit department. Follow all laid-down administrative procedures on cars, expenses, etc	Operate the detail schedule. Make at least six GP calls a day. Arrange trials of products. Always carry full range of samples and supporting evidence. Report on each call and send in daily. Attend medical conferences in your area and others as designated. Keep up-to-date with medical literature
6 **Performance evaluation**	Actual sales *v* target per product per month. Actual *v* target call rates, new account display. Field appraisal by SM at least quarterly to assess sales presentation	Actual *v* target – call rates, call frequencies on GPs, hospitals, wholesalers and retailers. Field appraisal fortnightly to assess adherence to detailing schedule, medical knowledge and doctor relationships
7 **Remuneration**	Salary Grade 5 Commission 5% of all revenue from territory. Car allowance. Contributory pension. Expense allowance.	Salary Grade 7 Annual bonus based on estimated territory performance and company progress. Ford changed every 2 years. Non-contributory pension. All business expenses reclaimable against vouchers

Fig. 5.2   Outline job description examples

Elements of the man profile

The definition of the sort of man required to fulfil the job description can now be completed. The type of person needed is analysed under four main headings, under each of which are listed seven different facets. (See Figure 5.3.)

---

1   Quantitative factors
(a)   Age
(b)   Education (including professional qualifications)
(c)   Experience
(d)   Special qualifications (languages, marital position, car owner, achievements in other fields)
(e)   Intelligence (as measured by test)
(f)   Availability
(g)   Health

---

2   Character traits
(a)   Stability – maintaining same jobs and interests
(b)   Industry – willingness to work
(c)   Perseverance – finishing what he starts
(d)   Ability to get along with others
(e)   Loyalty – to the employer
(f)   Self-reliance – self-starting, decisive
(g)   Leadership – ability to manage others

---

3   Job motivations (not already satisfied off the job)
(a)   Money
(b)   Security
(c)   Status
(d)   Power
(e)   Perfection
(f)   Competitiveness
(g)   Service

---

4   Degree of emotional immaturity
(a)   Dependence
(b)   Disregard of consequences
(c)   Incapacity for self-discipline
(d)   Selfishness
(e)   Exhibitionism
(f)   Pleasure-mindedness
(g)   Unwillingness to accept responsibility

Fig. 5.3   Man profile form

Quantitative factors

First, and easiest, is the identification of the quantitative factors of the man. These are sometimes referred to as the "can-do" qualities. In other words, if a man is of the right age and has the right experience and qualifications, and so on, the sales manager can be reasonably sure that the applicant is appropriately equipped for the job. All too often, however, despite possessing such relevant attributes, salesmen fail because of weaknesses of character, of motivation or of emotional maturity. Because these items are far more difficult to identify and measure, they tend to be overlooked and attention is paid only to the quantitative factors, although these are extremely important in themselves.

The great advantage of this first section over the other three is that, as its name implies, each factor can be quantified. The sales manager can and should specify the standards necessary for the job so that he can measure candidates against them.

The first two items listed, *age* and *education*, will vary so widely from company to company that it is hard to generalise about them. The type of *experience* required should be thoroughly reviewed. Simply to say *x* years' experience in allied trades is not enough. It might be that the company who needs the new salesman is small and breaking into the field. Experience with large, well-established competitors may therefore not be of too much relevance. It is better if the nature of the desired sales experience can be specified in terms of prospecting, handling complaints, building in-store displays, etc. This will be far more meaningful than simply "grocery trade experience" or "selling to farmers."

The *special qualifications* category needs careful thought. Ideally, should the candidate be married or single? If there is a lot of entertaining of customers and their wives, it is easier if the salesman is married. In some industries to have salesmen with sporting achievements has proved to be of help in opening recalcitrant buyers' doors. Some companies do not provide cars for their salesmen, a fact which should be indicated if it is essential that the man be a car owner. Almost certainly he will need a driving licence and it is worth specifying the maximum number of endorsements the company is willing to tolerate.

The *intelligence* of the man will affect his trainability, although little correlation has ever been shown between intelligence and sales results. His *availability* might be a critical factor particularly if he must be in the field by a certain date because of other marketing schemes. Although it is always the best general policy to wait for good staff rather than to be panicked into employing men who happen to be available, this is not always practical.

Good *health* is needed for most sales tasks and is essential for some. Each job can be evaluated individually regarding health hazards. For example, it would be unwise to appoint as an agricultural seeds salesman a man who suffered from hay fever. Overweight is a serious handicap to the salesman who has to deliver goods and merchandise displays in stores, particularly on low shelves. Virtually every sales job demands a considerable amount of car driving and it does seem that the design of car seats exacerbates back trouble. The sales manager should therefore be wary of candidates with recurrent histories of slipped discs, etc. Obviously it is not for the layman to evaluate health characteristics but medical inspections can often be made more informative by careful identification of the major health requirements of the job, including any particular physical attribute the man should possess.

Character traits

The second section is far more difficult to complete. Nevertheless, if the manager has thoroughly analysed the job requirements, valuable comments can be made.

The degree of *stability* desired will depend upon whether the job is to be a career appointment, a precursor to management or a short-term project. The location of the job may influence the degree of stability required. It is often helpful when selling in well-established communities to have men who have roots in the locality. More cosmopolitan customers might be handled more easily by salesmen with broader backgrounds.

The amount of *industry* required varies from job to job. Some routine sales positions are not very demanding on the man; whereas speciality selling almost always requires men who are willing to work hard and long to achieve results. Some jobs need considerable *perseverance*, particularly where the sales process is lengthy. For example, in the computer industry the average time between first contact and order placement is about two years. The salesman must therefore persevere in his communication with the customer if he is to be successful.

Ability to get along with others is a basic requirement of any job concerned with interpersonal relationships. It can be overemphasised, however, and it is not uncommon to find salesmen who have plenty of friends but too few customers. Also, the type of people with whom the salesman is compatible is important. Has he to be able to sell to people like himself, or to those higher or lower in the social scale? There are many salesmen who are competent in dealing with buyers but who cannot handle senior executives or technically qualified personnel.

Loyalty to the company is particularly important when the firm is undergoing problems of, say, delivery or product quality. As soon as the buyer suspects the salesman has little confidence in his product and company, he will be less inclined to buy.

The degree of *self-reliance* needed will vary according to the closeness of supervision. In the very simple sales position of the shop assistant, very little self-reliance is required. Help is always near. On the other hand, the export salesman negotiating large contracts may have to make quick decisions without reference to his head office in order to get business. The danger that should be avoided is that of putting a self-reliant man in a totally structured situation; the converse could be even more serious. In the first case, he will be bored and will eventually leave. In the second, the individual, unable to make a decision when it is imperative that he should, will be a complete disaster.

Finally, *leadership* qualities are needed in some jobs, particularly where the salesman has supervisory responsibilities over, for example, junior representatives or merchandisers. Also, in companies selling through an enfranchised dealer network where the salesman is operating as a kind of consultant to his distributors, he often has to demonstrate real leadership ability. In most sales situations, however, little leadership ability is needed and its existence can be threatening to the structure of the organisation. The need for future management might well dictate having latent leaders in the sales force.

Job motivations

Here the sales manager is concerned with specifying what is the likely motivational pattern of successful candidates.

The first item deals with *money*. If the job to be filled is a routine order-taking task paid by straight salary, there is little point searching for the dynamic go-getter who expects to be rewarded by results. However, high-flying speciality sales positions remunerated by straight commission do not constitute *security* for most people. That is why they tend to be highly paid. Risk and reward correlate throughout the whole of competitive business.

Some jobs, such as selling high quality motor cars, confer social *status* on their incumbents. Others, such as door-to-door sales activities, rank low in the social scale and thus a man to whom position is extremely important is unlikely to be attracted by them.

As has been indicated, some men enjoy wielding *power* and find a highly structured sales situation frustrating; others, when faced with a situation in which they have to be powerful, feel very insecure. Generally speaking, the sales job does not offer much power to command and men with such motivations usually gravitate towards more authoritarian positions – for example, those in the police force or services.

Perfectionists often find sales jobs unsatisfying because in marketing, as in the rest of business, it is not economic to have sufficient resources to do everything perfectly. This is not meant as a cynical comment but simply as a reflection of reality. Consider, for example, spare parts service: no company could afford to offer 100 per cent ex-stock availability on all lines. However, there are some sales tasks where one attribute of *perfection*, attention to detail, is absolutely vital – for example, recommending drugs to doctors or dealing with architectural specifications – and a degree of this motivation is of help.

How much a spirit of *competitiveness* is needed will depend upon the management style of the company. If contests are used as a basic motivational tool – that is, salesman of the year awards and so on – then it is obviously important that the salesmen are competitive. Where the salesman is treated as an individual who stands or falls by his own efforts, it is less crucial.

The *desire to serve* must be present in all salesmen as serving is basically what they are doing. Every salesman must want to help his customers but only as long as such service contributes towards the objectives of the firm. One industrial salesman selling adhesives spent several weeks mixing up various compounds to glue back into position a fireplace of a stately home without spoiling its appearance. The squire's eternal gratitude did not compensate for the loss of a large but routine contract in another part of the man's territory. As the salesman himself said afterwards, he just did not have time to call on the large contractor!

Some of the man's motivations may well be satisfied off the job. The sales manager must be concerned with those that have to be satisfied within his working life. The point must be recognised, however, that the applicant is one whole man not two separate people, of whom one exists from 0900 to 1700, and the other from 1700 to 0900, as is believed in some companies. It is possible sometimes for a socially conscious man to be happy in a low scale position because he is a senior member of the village council in his social environment. In one speciality selling firm, the sales manager correctly identified that the man required for a sales job should have a high need for income, and appointed such a candidate. He found out too late that although the man did need a great deal of money to maintain his standard of living, he had a private income and by working only two days a week he could comfortably generate the additional amount required!

Emotional immaturity

The process of growing up or maturation is a process of losing childhood characteristics. If the list of factors is examined it is easy to identify most or all of them in children. Children tend to be highly dependent upon their parents. They disregard the consequences of their own actions. Hence they run out on the road after a ball, although they know it is dangerous. They have little self-discipline and find it hard, for example, to save sweets for another day. They are often selfish in their play and will not share toys with their friends. They delight in showing-off, usually to the horror of their parents. They dislike unpleasant things like getting dressed or washing their faces, preferring to use such time for enjoyable games. They find it hard to accept responsibility and so when an ornament gets broken it is really Teddy who did it.

Most people lose these characteristics in some degree as they grow up; few people, if any, however, lose all of them entirely. Therefore the manager must consider what degree of immaturity he can afford in his candidates.

If the job has been identified as highly structured, it is of little consequence if the salesmen are *dependent*. It is dangerous, however, to have men who have a *disregard of consequences* in the way they act, and, for instance, promise delivery dates to customers that they know cannot be achieved. Likewise, the amount of self-discipline required will be high in those jobs where there is little or no check on when the salesman starts and finishes work or what he does during the day. This of course covers most sales positions and therefore an *incapacity for self-discipline* is a feature of immaturity that cannot normally be tolerated.

Some aspects of immaturity can be of positive benefit. If the sales force is remunerated by individual commission, a degree of *selfishness* is advantageous. Where the salesmen have to make public speeches or demonstrate the product to audiences, *exhibitionism* is valuable. If the sales manager wants to run sales contests where the prizes consist of holidays abroad, *pleasure-mindedness* will prove a strong motivation. On the other hand, the manager must be careful that such hedonistic tendencies do not lead to every afternoon being spent on the golf course.

The need for responsible people will be related to the amount of responsibility that has to be accepted. Where the salesman is in a position to make major commitments on his company's behalf, he must act responsibly. In a van sales force, where the amount of responsibility is strictly limited, more immature attitudes can be tolerated, and *unwillingness to accept responsibility* is not of paramount importance.

Writing the man profile

To complete the man profile the sales manager has to make judgements based on twenty-eight different facets of the type of candidate required, assuming he has not added further items, particularly to the quantitative factors.

Analysis of past experience

The best way to approach these decisions is to analyse current and past employees of the company to identify what correlations, if any, there are between particular types of individual and sales results. Do younger or older men tend to be most successful? Are the better educated better salesmen? Is the sales force unstable or perhaps too stable?

Far too often judgements on the kind of men required are made in contradiction to all the facts. This is a particularly frequent happening in industrial sales forces, where beliefs that technical training is essential continue to be held despite the obvious success of unqualified salesmen.

Compatibility of factors

Another check on the quality of the judgements that have been made is to examine their compatibility with each other. If a high degree of stability has been specified, a strong security motivation and a great deal of dependence are also likely to be present. Obviously it would be illogical to specify a need for self-reliance alongside an unwillingness to accept responsibility.

Conclusion

Having completed the man profile (and the examples given in Figure 5.4 should help with this), the sales manager can be confident that he has summarised the major facets of the type of person required to do the job. There are many other points of character, motivation and maturity that could be explored but professional psychological help will generally be needed to establish these. It might be argued that even to identify the

		TERRITORY SALESMAN – HARDWARE	SENIOR MEDICAL REPRESENTATIVE – PHARMACEUTICAL
1	QUANTITATIVE FACTORS		
(a)	Age	22–25	28–35
(b)	Education	5 "O" level including maths	At least 2/3 "A" levels inc. a science. Preferably some pharmaceutical or medical training
(c)	Experience	Cold canvassing, opening new accounts and merchandising in consumer durable field	At least 3 years selling on repeat basis to professional people preferably GPs. At least 2 years in pharmaceuticals
(d)	Special qualifications	Must be car-owner. Preferable creative bent for display work	Preferably experienced in antibiotics. As some company material from Holland preferable if speaks Dutch
(e)	Intelligence	No more than average (IQ around 100)	Above average (IQ around 110)
(f)	Availability	Immediate	Within 3 months – territory currently covered
(g)	Health	Must be fit enough to: Drive 30 000 miles p.a. Lift product crates weighing 25kg Merchandise at high and low levels	Must be fit enough to withstand proximity to patients in doctors' surgeries
2	CHARACTER TRAITS		
(a)	Stability	Expect 2–3 year staff turnover therefore fairly low	Career opportunity – needs to be highly stable Well established business
(b)	Industry	Must be willing to work very hard to build up territory	Average industry required
(c)	Perseverance	Must have high perseverance to continue opening new accounts	Medical profession readily accept company representatives – average perseverance required
(d)	Ability to get along with others	Average ability required as low call frequencies and short calls	Very important to establish close contact with profession at business and social level
(e)	Loyalty	Average	Very important as industry and company under public criticism
(f)	Self-reliance	High degree required. Little field supervision. Must be self-starter	Average – highly structured job with close management
(g)	Leadership	No requirement	Small requirement. Occasionally will have to supervise new men during field orientation

Fig. 5.4   Outline man profile examples

		TERRITORY SALESMAN – HARDWARE	SENIOR MEDICAL REPRESENTATIVE – PHARMACEUTICAL
3	JOB MOTIVATION		
(a)	Money	High – commission major factor	Low – straight salary only. Little opportunity to make higher income
(b)	Security	Low – if territory sales not increased, must replace	High – career position running well-established territory
(c)	Status	Low – junior member of small company in non-prestigious trade	Above average – large company, quasi-professional job, not order taker, some technical training required
(d)	Power	Low – fixed price list, no decision making latitude	Low – operating laid-down detail schedule
(e)	Perfection	Low – must sell and move on, product selling on price rather than high quality	High – must describe product accurately and in detail Meticulous in claims and sample testing
(f)	Competitiveness	Low – will work and be paid as an individual	Average – regular interpersonal and interregional contests
(g)	Service	Average – but must avoid doing retailer's job for him, e.g. delivery, shelf-filling	High – must wish to serve profession and community
4	DEGREE OF EMOTIONAL IMMATURITY		
(a)	Dependence	Low – must be on his own most of the time	Can be above average – well supported by management
(b)	Disregard of consequences	Average – not too relevant	Must be low. Because of nature of work must be well aware of implications of what he is doing
(c)	Incapacity for self-discipline	Must be low – must be self-starter	Average – discipline largely imposed
(d)	Selfishness	Must be high to be motivated by individual achievement	Must be low – must act as member of team
(e)	Exhibitionism	Above average – must be capable of speaking in public at women's associations, etc	Low – to be acceptable within profession
(f)	Pleasure-mindedness	Low – must wish to work hard and long	Low – must fulfil routine calling continuously
(g)	Unwillingness to accept responsibility	Average – little responsibility to accept	Above average – need to be responsible in all dealings in this type of selling

Fig. 5.4   *(continued)*

characteristics listed in Figure 5.3, sections 2, 3 and 4, the manager has to be at least an amateur psychologist.

This is indeed true. Psychology, according to the *Shorter Oxford English Dictionary*, is "the science of the nature, functions and phenomena of human soul or mind." So, to a large degree, is management.

By using these basic concepts and techniques of staffing, the sales manager can take stock of his sales force. He can now ensure:

1   All necessary functions in the organisation are defined and covered.
2   The desired knowledge, skills and characteristics of the men are defined.
3   The current sales force is appraised and weaknesses identified.

ACTION PLANNING CHECKLIST

Questions	Answers and action	Timing of action and evaluation
1 Is there a systematic staffing procedure? If not, detail elements needed here		
2 Is there a salesman's Job Description? If so, check against Figure 5.1. If not, develop using Figure 5.1		
3 Is there a Man Profile? If so, check against Figure 5.3. If not, develop using Figure 5.3		
4 Appraise current sales force against job descriptions and man profiles		
5 Identify gaps between desired and actual performance		
6 Are all functions necessary to achieve objectives covered within jobs?		
7 Are all jobs covered by existing staff?		

CHAPTER 6

How to Staff the Sales Organisation II: Recruitment and Selection

When modern concepts of staffing and detailed techniques of job description and man profile construction are first introduced, the sales manager will often notice a gap between what is necessary to achieve the objectives and what exists in his organisation.

This discrepancy will frequently have to be overcome by the appointment of additional or replacement staff. Having completed steps 1 and 2 (described in the previous chapter) of the staffing procedure, it is possible to recruit and select using these basic documents. This chapter is concerned with the six steps to be taken in attracting and choosing good salesmen from outside the current sales force.

How to recruit candidates

There are three major sources:

1 The company's own staff.
2 Employment agency lists.
3 Advertisements.

The present staff should always be checked first for possible candidates. Not only is there less risk with current personnel because of the manager's broader experience of them but also there is a significant motivation in promoting from within. Even where suitable men are not available inside the company, often the existing staff can introduce friends or relations who are worth considering. If small rewards are paid for successful introductions, this can be a fruitful source of new candidates.

There are some employment agencies who specialise in sales staff and who for a fee will submit candidates from their records. This can be valuable, particularly when a detailed job description and man profile is available for the agency to use to evaluate its list. Unfortunately, however, there is a demand situation for good salesmen, seemingly all over the world. As the good man has little difficulty in finding his own jobs, the agency lists tend to be filled with many poor candidates.

Thus the recruitment process is usually one of attracting the otherwise happily employed man from another company. The most likely way of doing this is by newspaper advertising.

Constructing the advertisement

As space is very expensive it must be used carefully and properly. Like any other sales presentation, a job advertisement must attract attention, create interest, arouse desire and result in buying action. The manager should therefore transfer his persuasive skills to writing. The advertisement should contain five basic points:

An impact headline.   To attract the candidates' attention, the advertisement must make an immediate impression. A good technique is to use a question to arouse curiosity, particularly where the question contains a dramatic point from the job or its rewards. Thus:

> "Are you worth £10 000 a year?"

or

> "Can you sell to Managing Directors?"

or

> "Do you want to be a manager within two years?"

Failing all else, the job title should be used.

A brief description of the job and its rewards.   This should concentrate on the salient points of the position – location, type of business, product range and the like – and the salary and fringe benefits. If details of remuneration are omitted, the quality and quantity of replies will be reduced. Where, for internal reasons, it is impossible to publish the salary, at least some guidance should be given, such as:

> "The successful candidate is likely to be currently earning more than £x."

or

> "This position is graded up to £y."

A brief description of the man and his qualifications.   This should cover only the quantitative aspects contained in the first part of the man profile, that is, such items as age, education, experience, etc. It is a waste of time and space to say "must be industrious, persevering and able to get along with others," etc. Everybody thinks he has such qualities and therefore the advertisement will not act selectively. It is wise to separate the essential qualities from the desirable in order to avoid deterring basically qualified candidates.

A statement of the action the applicant should take.   If the company calls for lengthy descriptions of careers at this stage, it will deter some of the best applicants who are relatively satisfied with their current jobs. To attract such people the initial effort demanded of them should be minimal. An invitation to write, ring or call for an application form is often the best solution. Thus, by simply picking up the telephone the

JOB APPLIED FOR ....

1   May I have your name? ....

2   Your address where you can be contacted? ....

....

....

3   Telephone numbers where you can be contacted
     Working hours ....

     Other times ....

4   What kind of a job are you looking for? ....

                                                     Must be sales

5   What do you expect to earn? ....

                                           Must be in line with what is being offered

6   What are you earning now? ....

                                               Compared with 5 is he being realistic?

7   What are you doing now? ....

     Who for? ....

     How long for? ....

                                     Is it good experience for this job? Good company?
                                                        Stable?

8   And before that? ....

     Who for? ....

     How long for? ....

                                 Is it good experience? Has he shown progression?
                                              Good company? How long for?

9   How much time per month can you spend away from home? ....

                                                     Is it sufficient?

10   Are you willing to move home? (at our expense?) ....

                                                       Flexible?

11   When can you be available? ....

                                                   Is that soon enough?

12   Are you married? ....

     Children? ....

                                                        Stable?

                                     Completed by ....

Fig. 6.1   Typical telephone screening form for a sales job

man can start the process. One technique that seems to appeal to applicants is to ask them to request an application form with which is sent a copy of the job description. Having read the job description and decided whether they can fulfil it, they are then invited to apply. This approach, perhaps because of its challenge and frankness, appears to attract good candidates. There is the objection, of course, that it is easy for competitors to obtain the company's job description but that can be a small risk and worth taking.

A statement of who to contact.   Many advertisements are a nonsense in that they ask the applicant to write "in full detail and in strictest confidence" to a box number or to a company. One can only write in confidence to an individual. A person should be identified as the receiver of all communications. In any case, box numbers do seem to inhibit the quality and quantity of replies. Perhaps salesmen are afraid that they might be applying to their own company.

A specialised form of the newspaper advertisement is the "telephone-in ad." This is normally placed on Sundays and candidates are invited to telephone on that Sunday to discuss the job with the company. It has a two-fold appeal in that it is easy for the man to apply and that he can call from home. It has been shown that such a technique draws from two to five times as many replies as a normal advertisement. More important than quantity is the fact that often calls are received from people who had not thought of applying for another job until that moment. In order to handle the telephone calls systematically, a telephone screening form is needed (Figure 6.1), which will at least eliminate the totally unqualified. The form can be adapted to meet the requirements of each new recruitment but should not contain more than ten to twelve questions, being intended only for quick screening. When the applicant has successfully answered the questions he can then be handled like any other candidate by being sent an application form, etc.

Alternatively, the applicant can be brought in and interviewed that day. Where time is critical the "telephone-in ad" is a powerful approach; in one extreme case, a job was advertised on Sunday morning, a man rang up about it during the afternoon, he was interviewed and appointed on Monday and started on Tuesday. This compares with an eight- to twelve-week lapse, which is the normal period between advertising and starting the job. Telephone-in advertisements have further advantages:

1   A national response can be gained quickly by inviting reverse-charge calls.
2   Candidates looking for jobs other than that of sales often apply, and can be quickly screened.
3   The normal working week is not disturbed because the bulk of the replies is handled on Sunday.

Samples of normal and telephone-in advertisements are shown in Figure 6.2.

Placing the advertisement

Britain is fortunate in having excellent national newspaper coverage which, although expensive, can achieve a widespread immediate impact. Furthermore, there are many good regional and local papers which can be used for jobs in particular geographical areas. These media can be supplemented by trade and technical press advertising where appropriate. However, it is the experience of many companies that the power of the national press is such that often little or nothing is gained by using more limited circulation media as well, particularly when attempting to fill positions for which there is a shortage of good candidates.

Are you worth £10 000+?
Then phone us today

Glitter Paints, already established as a brand leader in the industrial market, is now marketing a comprehensive range of protective coatings to industry

Big opportunities!

Expectations for this new range are high and we now need two more people based on Sheffield and Leeds to join our existing team. They will analyse the needs of potential clients, and specify the company's products to meet them

Big jobs!

The men or women we are looking for will be experienced in selling in the industrial sector, preferably in the chemical industry in particular. They will be accustomed to negotiating up to board level and a formal qualification in chemistry will be an advantage. Age is less important than ability to analyse a complex situation and find a logical solution

Big pay!

Starting salary for these positions will be at least £10 000 p.a. A company car is provided and there are generous fringe benefits

Ring now!

To find out more about this opportunity, and to tell us about yourself, telephone today (Sunday) between 0900 and 1600 and speak to Mr Brown or Mr Robinson, reversing the charges if you wish

Glitter Paints Limited
061-543 1234

Are YOU good enough
to be a Splshperson?

Splosh Limited markets a new range of soft drinks direct to the licensed trade and supermarkets. The company is part of the well known Splurge Group and turnover is now in excess of £50 million

The Jobs

We are now broadening the distribution of Splosh nationally, backed up by TV advertising campaigns, and consequently expanding our sales force. Three of our existing salesmen have just been promoted to management, and we are now in need of six new people to join our team – two based in London, the others centred on Bristol, Birmingham, Manchester and Leeds. The persons we are seeking will, after initial training, open new accounts in the areas covered, and will maintain and service these with the help of a central merchandising team

The People

Successful candidates (either men or women) will be aged 22–35 and educated at least to "O" level standard. They should have at least two years' experience in selling direct to retail outlets, preferably in grocery products. A clean driving licence is essential and applicants should already be living within easy travelling distance of one of the locations above

The Rewards

Starting salary will be approximately £7500 p.a. and in addition there is a monthly bonus scheme, based on realistic targets, which should bring average total earnings up to about £9000 p.a. A company car is provided and there is an excellent pension scheme.
Because of our continued expansion plans, prospects of promotion for the right people are excellent

Please telephone or write for application form to

John Smith Sales Recruitment and Training Officer
Splosh Limited, 100 North Road, London A1
Telephone: 01-487 5811

Fig. 6.2   Samples of recruitment advertisements

It is imperative that sufficient space be taken to attract applicants' attention away from the many competitive offers. It is not very convincing to advertise "a fantastic sales opportunity with fast-growing international corporation" in a tiny space at the bottom of the classified columns. As a very rough guide, in today's papers a $2\frac{1}{2}$ to 3 in double column space at least is needed to stand much chance of success. Obviously the attractiveness of the job and the company will influence the size of space taken but when the financial importance of having good salesmen is analysed, an investment of even several hundred pounds in advertising can be recognised as reasonable.

Other sources of candidates

Other sources of recruitment include executive search (or "head-hunting" as it is commonly known), university, college and school-leavers, ex-servicemen's associations and the professional registers at employment exchanges. Experiences vary so much with these methods that it is hard to make a firm recommendation. However, when top-level salesmen are needed in very specialised industries, for example, some types of high cost capital equipment, head-hunting can be successfully employed as it is likely that there will be a very limited number of possible candidates. Several reputable executive search organisations exist but they will not usually accept commissions on jobs under £12 000/ £15 000 a year. Some firms with sophisticated and lengthy training programmes prefer to take on staff direct from their place of education. Other companies, particularly with relatively high status sales jobs, can directly attract ex-servicemen and use them successfully to obtain sales interviews.

Planning recruitment

A recruitment plan should be drawn for each vacancy, covering the sources and media most likely to provide candidates. A study of the origins of the current sales force can be enlightening. For example, a company selling labelling machinery to shops discovered that a number of its most successful salesmen had at some time in their careers worked for trading stamp firms or life assurance organisations. (This is not very surprising as both these categories of selling require prospecting and cold canvassing ability, which are prerequisites to success in the speciality selling of the labelling machines.) The result was that the advertising was angled to attract men from these two fields.

The aim of the recruitment process is to attract a number of qualified candidates. The manager must be careful here not to stray to either extreme. It is easy to generate vast quantities of replies simply by setting out the requirements so broadly that virtually any healthy adult fits the qualifications. One example of such an advertisement in England called for four or five sales trainees for a large American company with opportunities to work in the States and Europe. High salaries were offered for few qualifications and little experience. Six hundred replies were received, creating a phenomenal screening task, made almost impossibly difficult by the absence of criteria against which to appraise the applications.

On the other hand, advertisements which specify suitability in too much detail will not attract enough candidates. The wise sales manager will list the essential standards which must be met and the desirable qualities which, ideally, candidates should possess. Thus, while attracting sufficient quantity, the advertisement will also act as the first screening process to avoid the time-wasting procedure of examining applicants who are patently unqualified.

It is difficult to quantify how many replies should be expected. Obviously one application from the perfect candidate is the ideal. Generally speaking, however, if less than 20 and more than 60 responses are received for a sales job, it is likely that something is wrong with the recruitment campaign. In the former case of too few replies, either the

APPLICATION FOR SALES POSITION
(All information treated confidentially

Date..

Name (Print)_____ Home telephone number_____

Present address_____ How long have you lived there?_____

Previous address_____ How long did you live there?_____

Business address_____ Business telephone number_____

Sex: ☐ Male ☐ Female. Birth____19__	☐ Married; Date_____19__	Number of Their children_____ ages_____
Height_____Weight_____	☐ Single ☐Engaged ☐Separated ☐Widowed	Number of other dependants____Ages____
Are you a British citizen? ☐Yes ☐No	☐Divorced. Date_____19____	

Position applied for_____ Earnings expected £_____

Why are you applying to this company?_____

Who referred you to this company?_____
Have you ever applied to, or been
employed by, this company?_____If so, when?_____Where?_____

Names of relatives employed by this company_____

EDUCATION

Type of school	Name of school	Special subjects (where applicable)	Achievements	Special achievements (grants, prizes, etc)	Dates of attendance
Elementary					19
Public					19
Grammar					19
Secondary Modern					19
University					19
Technical College					19
Other					19

EXTRACURRICULAR ACTIVITIES (athletics, clubs, etc)
(Do not include military, racial, religious, or nationality groups)

In school_____ | In college, university, etc._____

_____ | _____

Offices held_____ | Offices held_____

_____ | _____

Principal source of your spending money while at college or university_____

Part of expenses you earned: ☐ None ☐ 0–25% ☐ 25–50% ☐ 50–75% ☐ More than 75%_____

What languages other than English do you speak?_____

Fig. 6.3   Application form for sales position

Work history

Beginning with the most recent, list below the names and addresses of all your employers: *(a)* Company name *(b)* Address and telephone number	Kind of business	Time employed				How was job obtained	Nature of work at start
		From		To			
		Month	Year	Month	Year		
1 *(a)* *(b)*							
2 *(a)* *(b)*							
3 *(a)* *(b)*							
4 *(a)* *(b)*							
5 *(a)* *(b)*							
6 *(a)* *(b)*							
7 *(a)* *(b)*							
8 *(a)* *(b)*							

Indicate by number _____ any of the above employers whom you *do not* wish us to contact

Were you ever fidelity bonded? ☐ No ☐ Yes. On which jobs?_____

_____

References (not former employers or relatives)	Address	Phone number
1		
2		
3		

Special activities
(List all activities participated in since leaving school. Do not include military, racial, religious, or nationality groups)

Type of organisation	Name or description of organisation	When did you actively participate?		Offices held during last five years	Average time now given per week
		From	To		
Luncheon clubs, mens clubs, etc					
Lodges, social groups					
Civic organisations or community activities					
Business, scientific or professional activities					
Athletics or sports organisations					

What are your hobbies?

Fig. 6.3 Application form for sales position *(page 2)*

142099

Work history (continued)

Earnings a year at start	Earnings Nature of work at leaving (state territory in which you worked)	Earnings a year at leaving	Supervisory positions held	Number of people supervised	Reasons for leaving	Name of immediate supervisor
						Name Title
						Name Title
						Name Title
						Name Title
						Name Title
						Name Title
						Name Title
						Name Title

Personal

Are you physically handicapped in any way? _____

If so, list handicaps _____

Any recent illnesses or operations? _____

Are you willing to take a medical examination at our expense? ☐ Yes ☐ No

Name of person to be notified in case of emergency Name _____

Address _____

_____ Telephone _____

Please summarise specific experience below

Selling in retail stores   Years_____For what firms?_____

Lines sold _____

Selling direct to home or farm   Years_____For what firms?_____

Lines sold _____

Selling to retailers   Years_____For what firms?_____

Lines sold _____

Selling to institutions or industrial firms   Years_____For what firms?_____

Lines sold _____

Other selling   Years_____For what firms?_____

Lines sold _____

Point-of-sale display work   Years_____For what firms?_____

Lines covered _____

Fig. 6.3 Application form for sales position *(page 3)*

Territory preferences, travel, car ownership

If your application is considered favourably,
on what date will you be available for work? _____ 19 _____ How much notice will you require? _____ days

Territory preferred _____ Why? _____

Is there any reason why you would not be willing to transfer? _____

How much time per month can you spend travelling away from home? _____

Do you have full use of a car for your work? ☐ Yes ☐ No. Make, model, and year of car _____

What type of licence do you have? _____ Any endorsements? _____

Does your insurance cover you for business purposes? ☐ Yes ☐ No

Other statements
Are there any other experiences, skills or qualifications which you feel would especially fit you for work with this company?

Signature _____

Applicant should not write below this line

Date application sent out _____ 19 ___ Date received _____ 19 ___ Reviewed by _____ Date ___ 19 ___

1 2 3 4: Disposition recommended _____

Action taken _____ Date _____ 19 _____ Action _____ Signature _____

_____ Date ____ 19 _____ Action _____ Signature _____

Fig. 6.3   Application form for sales position *(page 4)*

job limits have been specified too tightly for the salary offered or the advertisement has lacked impact. In the latter case, almost certainly the specification is insufficiently detailed and, when evaluated, the number of really qualified candidates will seem disappointingly low relative to the total number of replies.

Application form

All initial information about each candidate should be collected on an application form, otherwise the sales manager will have to judge between applicants on the basis of their letters, which will differ vastly in style, completeness and veracity. Any man writing for a job is obviously going to emphasise what he considers to be his strong points and skim over or ignore completely the less successful parts of his life. For the manager to make considered judgements he must be able to review as many facts as possible and compare one man against another.

The application form shown in Figure 6.3 ensures that a complete record is received detailing the candidate's activities from his school-days through his early career up to his present job. In addition, information is requested on how he spends his time outside working hours, availability, territory preference and car ownership. Finally, a space is left for him to give any reasons why he feels he should get the job.

The mere existence of such a form constitutes a screening device. Commonly, if there are, say, fifty requests for forms only about forty will be sent back completed. (Some of the unqualified but optimistic initial applicants when they receive the form to be completed realise they have little chance of bluffing their way through.) Also, there are usually some lazy applicants who cannot be bothered to fill in such detail, although they are making a major career decision, and possibly still one or two traditionalists who have a highly developed sense of personal privacy and who regard the form as too probing.

Reviewing applications

The manager can now review the completed forms he has received. The basic use of the application form should be as a rejection rather than a selection process. In other words, while he can eliminate many candidates totally on the basis of the application, it is unlikely that he will be able to decide that a man is worth employing without further checks.

The first review of the forms should be against section 1 of the man profile form (Figure 5.3). It is easy to evaluate rapidly each candidate against such quantitative yardsticks as age, experience, education, etc. Generally speaking, depending on the detail of the man profile this will eliminate at least 50 per cent of the applications. The remaining half can be reviewed again to attempt to identify the candidates' suitability against the other aspects of the man profile; character traits, job motivations and emotional maturity. In assessing these factors the manager must be careful not to place undue weight on single occurrences. He must search for patterns of behaviour. For example, in attempting to establish the degree of stability, he will assess how consistent the man was in his school life. Did he change from school to school or from subject to subject? Did he start off on one career then switch to another? How many jobs has he had and how long has he stayed in each job? Has he shown consistency and development in his career or has he swopped about for no good reason? Have his leisure interests been developed over a long period or is he a dilettante in his hobbies and sports? A fuller guide to the analysis of these factors is given in Figure 6.4.

The application form alone will seldom give sufficient evidence on these qualitative facets to form final judgements. However, when they are interpreted in this way, they will assist the manager to form an impression of the man that will guide him, at interview time, to probe areas of uncertainty.

Reference checking

One of the selection tasks that the sales manager must perform is to check the veracity of the information given. The data may be untrue in two senses. First, it may be an outright falsehood designed to hide something which the applicant fears may be damaging to his chances of employment. Second, it may be misleading because the applicant has given a conscious or unconscious bias to his answers. For example, it has been found that a candidate has described a previous job as that of assistant area manager, when the exact title should have been that of assistant to the area manager, or has neglected to state that the appointment was a temporary one. It is common to find that the earnings per annum figure is exaggerated. A man paid in part by commission is tempted to list the highest annual remuneration he has ever received rather than the average figure.

Written references

To verify that the information received is correct and to ensure that it is realistically interpreted, the manager has to seek data from other sources. This is traditionally done by asking for written references but in fact these are generally a waste of time. No man will give as a reference someone who will be critical of him, and few referees will comment adversely.

Telephone reference checking

The most powerful way of checking on the man is for the manager to speak in person or on the telephone to his previous immediate superiors. Hence the requests on the application form for the name, address and title of previous employers and for an indication which such people should not be contacted. Obviously, where an applicant forbids such contacts to be made, they should not be effected at this stage. He may well have good reason for fearing such contacts will lead to his present employers discovering that he wishes to move before he is ready to tell them. In such cases reference checking has to be deferred until the candidate's permission is obtained, normally after a favourable interview. Generally, however, most applicants allow contact to be made with all but their present superiors.

The past employer should then be telephoned or visited to verify and expand the facts already known about the man. This should be done in a structured way to ensure all relevant details are checked. (See Figure 6.5.) It will be seen from this form that the early questions are concerned with establishing that the facts as given are true. These initial queries, being factual, also confirm that the previous boss really does have a good knowledge of the man and gets him used to answering questions. Then follow some queries about how the man did his job, leading to Question 15 "would you re-employ him?" This is the most critical of all; often after earlier quite favourable answers, the respondent admits that he would not take the man back and, when pressed for an explanation, modifies his previous comments. The final questions give some background on the man's personal behaviour and whether it has affected his performance before concluding with a request for opinions as to his capabilities. The whole process takes some ten to fifteen minutes, depending on the further questions that occur during the course of conversation and the length and detail of the answers given.

Some managers object to this technique on the grounds that it probes too far into a man's background or that it could be misleading as a previous employer's judgement might be faulty. The first criticism is not valid as the applicant's permission has already been granted. The second is normally prevented by always making more than one reference check on each individual whenever possible, by pressing the previous superior to substantiate his comments, and in any case, by evaluating the information gained

SECTION 2 – CHARACTER TRAITS

Source of evidence	Stability	Industry	Perseverance
Family background: including parental and early childhood	Stable childhood? Parents together? Stable location?	Encouraged to work at home? Did he keep himself busy during leisure time?	Encouraged to continue with studies, etc? Did he have hobbies that needed time and care?
Educational history: including school, college, university and private study	Same school? Same courses? Same interests?	Work hard at school? Success? Take easy options? Choose undemanding leisure interests? Any self-motivated study?	Follow through courses started? Further education? Continued interests?
Work experience: jobs – reasons for leaving	Changed jobs? Changed type of work? Changed location? Good reasons for leaving?	Chosen hard or soft jobs? Attitude to hours of work, travelling?	Has work demanded perseverance? Continued trying in difficult circumstances, e.g. cold canvass?
Outside interests: sports, hobbies, social interests, part-time work	Continued same interests? Played sports with same people?	Do interests need work, e.g. council, committees? Need effort, e.g. vigorous sport?	Has he worked his way up in social activity, e.g. committee head after ten years?
Domestic situation	Marital status? Family? Time away from home?	Does he work at home? Developed personal financial situation?	Built up strong family and financial position?
Expressed desires and interview observations: Why this job? Territory preferences Travelling Other statements	Wants to stay in same location? Same type of work? Dislikes travelling? Sees career opportunity?	Sees challenge of job? Prepared for long hours and arduous work? Willing to take further training?	Determined to succeed? Building up long-term prospects?

Fig. 6.4   Applicant information analysis based on Sections 2 to 4 of Figure 5.3
(*NOTE:* Section 1 of the Man Profile form ("quantitative factors") has been omitted from this analysis as few managers find difficulty in rating these factors)

SECTION 2 – CHARACTER TRAITS

Ability to get along with others	*Loyalty*	*Self-reliance*	*Leadership*
Big or small family? Group or solitary pursuits?	Identifies with parents and background?	Encouraged to stand on own feet? When did he leave home?	Any positions of leadership while boy, e.g. Boy Scouts?
Take part in group activities? Enjoy group activities?	Attitude to school and/or college? Particular teachers?	Did he succeed on his own? Earn own expenses?	Positions of responsibility – in school? – sports? – social? – college or university?
Attitudes to customers? To colleagues? To others?	Loyal to previous employers? Team worker? Willingness to accept management?	Found his own jobs? Chosen jobs where on own? Enjoyed making own decisions?	Any positions of leadership? Ambitions?
Groups or solitary activities, e.g. team games, societies or fishing, stamp collecting?	Stayed with same groups and teams? Attitude to societies and associations of which he is a member?	Interests require self-reliance, e.g. climbing sailing, acting?	Leadership positions in outside interests?
Marital relations? Attitude to relatives and friends	Loyalty to wife? To relatives and friends?	Makes decision at home? Self-financing? Working wife?	Who wears the trousers?
Sees teamwork needed? Territory preferred because of other people? Dislikes loneliness of travel? Did he get along with you?	Wants job because all previous companies misunderstood him?	Wants job for own reasons or wife's reasons? Will go anywhere any time? Confident of ability to do job?	Looking for management job? Prepared to train for management?

SECTION 3 – MOTIVATIONS

Source of evidence	Money	Security	Status
Family background	Strong or weak finances at home? Attitude of parents to money. Any of own money earned?	Stable family background? Parentally? Location?	Socially conscious parents? Made to feel socially different?
Educational history	Interested in financial subjects? Earned own money whilst studying? Got qualifications in order to get more money?	Kept to same subjects because felt secure? Chose only things he knew and could do well?	Schools and colleges selected for status rather than educational achievement? Chose status courses?
Work experience	Sought high-paying jobs? Paid by results? Left jobs because of money?	Sought safe salaried jobs? Chose large companies? Enjoyed structure?	Picked status job with prestige companies? Enjoys status titles? Exaggerates level of job?
Outside interests	Increases earnings with part-time work? Makes money out of leisure interests?	Enjoys home-based leisure interests? Avoids dangerous sports, etc?	Chooses prestigious interests? Enjoys being council member, church warden, etc?
Domestic situation	Good standard of living within income? Expensive tastes?	Stable home environment? Low ambition?	He and/or wife need social status? Climbers? Children must go to right schools?
Expressed desires	Wants this job simply for pay? Willing to sacrifice to make more money? Ambition to be rich?	Wants this job because of career possibilities? Does not want to move or travel?	Wants job because of prestige? Wants to achieve social position in business?

Fig. 6.4   *(continued)*

SECTION 3 – MOTIVATIONS

Power	*Perfection*	*Competitiveness*	*Service*
Was father powerful? Did he exercise power at home?	Encouraged to perfection in manners, dress behaviour	Large or small family? Compete with brothers and sisters?	Encouraged to serve others? Church/scout-type activities?
Enjoyed being biggest boy or most senior because of power? Wanted to learn because of power?	Enjoyed research and detail subjects?	Enjoyed competing to be top of class or best at sport? Chose competitive situations – scholarships, awards, prizes, etc?	Worked for school? Helped others whilst at school?
Likes to dominate colleagues, juniors, customers? Wants bigger job even though money similar?	Likes detail work? Wants job he can do well?	Enjoys competition from colleagues and other companies? Compares himself with others?	Chose socially rewarding work? Wants jobs that contribute to community? Enjoys helping customers?
Enjoys power in outside interests? Sought chairman positions, captain, president, etc?	Indicates desire for perfection, e.g. model-building rose-growing, etc?	Chooses interests where he can compete, e.g. individual sports, enters competitions and shows?	Charity work? Social or church work? Helping others, e.g. Scoutmaster, part-time teacher?
He enjoys being boss in his own home? Attempts to decide children's future?	Spends much time improving house and garden? Wants perfect wife? Over-disciplined children?	Enjoys discussion with family and friends? Wants his children to be best at everything?	Works for family rather than himself? Encourages family in social work?
Sees job as giving power? Enjoys power of decision over whether he takes job?	Wants to do good job in detail? Asks lots of questions about job? Detailed application form?	Wants to know who he will compete with in future? Interested in sales contests? Regards success in competitive terms?	Wants to know about customers and what they want? Sees success in terms of customer satisfaction?

SECTION 4 – DEGREE OF EMOTIONAL MATURITY

Source of evidence	Dependence	Disregard of consequences	Incapacity for self-discipline
Family background	Overdominant parents? Not allowed to make own decisions? Only child?	Lack of parental concern for education? Poor choice of school, etc?	Never had to concentrate on studies or leisure activities?
Educational history	Choice of subject made for him? Always guided by someone?	Left school too early? Dropped subjects and later regretted it?	Could not force himself to study? Took easy options?
Work experience	Advised into career? Sought structured jobs? Changed job because of pressure from friends or family? Happy to be career salesman?	Chose wrong career to start? Left jobs without having employment? Promised customers impossibilities? Talks at interviews without thinking of implications?	Despite warnings unable to meet previous job standards of punctuality, report-writing, etc?
Outside interests	Chooses highly structured situations – military and para-military groups?	Has allowed outside interests to interfere with main job?	Has allowed interest to lapse because can't be bothered to fit them in?
Domestic situation	Highly reliant on wife or family? Likes quiet structured home life?	He or wife spend more than can afford? Have too big a family, too big commitments? Live beyond income?	Allows family to decide what he should do?
Expressed desires	Wants job because big secure company? Does not want to move or travel? Interested in own supervision and training?	Does not know why he wants job? Has not thought through career? Resigned before he got job?	Does not handle himself well at interviews? Badly 'prepared? Shows feelings easily?

Fig. 6.4   *(continued)*

SECTION 4 – DEGREE OF EMOTIONAL IMMATURITY

Selfishness	*Exhibitionism*	*Pleasure-mindedness*	*Unwillingness to accept responsibility*
Did what he wanted to? Left home when he wanted?	Enjoyed showing off? Encouraged to do so by parents?	Never developed interests that he had to work at?	Never had to face responsibility?
Thought only of himself? No regard paid to parent's interests?	Enjoyed activities such as dramatics, debating?	Avoided studies or interests that took up leisure time?	Sees failure at school as someone else's fault? Never held positions of responsibility?
Took job decisions without considering or consulting family? Sees previous employers only from own point of view? Only interested in how new job affects him personally?	Enjoys public demonstrations, display work? Shows off in his dress, manner? Talks of all his achievements? Drives too fast? Talks too much and too loud?	Dislikes hard work? Dislikes interference with leisure time? Enjoys trips, drink, food, golf too much?	Previous job failure always someone else's fault? Avoids positions of responsibility?
Follows personal interests contrary to family interests?	Chosen interests where he can show off?	Interests limited to pure pleasure – drinking, gambling, eating?	No interests where he has any responsibility?
Has he considered his family when choosing jobs? Time away from home? Relocation?	Is he the "life and soul" of the party? Enjoys showing off with friends	Are home activities all leisure-oriented? Spends a lot of time at the pub, parties, etc?	Allows wife to dominate him? Who decides family holidays, children's schooling, etc?
All questions asked relate to himself? Not interested in company and its future, or his colleagues?	Shows off at interview in dress, manner, speech? Claims vast achievements? Wants job because he can show off in company car?	Asks mainly about holiday and working hours? Enjoys talking about leisure pursuits? Sees his major achievements in that area?	Wants help and advice on career? Finds it difficult to decide on job? Wants to consult family and friends on all points?

REFERENCE CHECK ON SALES APPLICANT_____
                                                    Name of applicant

_____
            Person contacted   Position

_____
        Company   Address   Telephone number

1 I wish to *verify* some of the information
   given to us by Mr _____ who has
   applied for a position with our firm.
   Do you remember him? What were the dates
   of his employment with your company?   From_____19_____To _____19_____
                                                                Do dates agree?

2 What was he doing when he started?   _____
                                                                Did he exaggerate?

   When he left   _____
                                                                Did he progress?

3 He says he was earning £_____ ☐ Yes ☐ No £ _____
   per_____when he left. Is that right?   *Did he falsify?*

4 How much of this was salary?   £_____

   How much commission?   £_____

5 How was his attendance?   _____
                                                       Conscientious? Health problems?

6 What type of selling did he do?   _____
                                                      To whom? How did he get his contacts?

7 How did his sales results compare   _____
   with others?   *Industrious? Competitive?*

8 Did he supervise anyone else?   ☐ No ☐ Yes. How many? _____
                                                                Does this check?

   (If yes) How well did he handle it?   _____
                                                          Is he a leader or a driver?

9 How closely was he supervised?   _____
                                                          Was he hard to manage?

10 How hard did he work?   _____
                                                          Is he habitually industrious?

11 How well did he get along with other   _____
   people?   *Is he a troublemaker?*

12 What arguments did he have with   _____
   customers?   *Does he like selling? Can he control his temper?*

13 What did you think of him?   _____
                                                        Did he get along with his superiors?

14 Why did he leave?   _____
                                                          Good reasons? Do they check?

15 Would you re-employ him?   ☐ Yes ☐ No. Why not? _____
                                                              Does this affect his suitability with us?

16 Did he have any domestic or financial   ☐ No ☐ Yes. What? _____
   difficulties that interfered with work?   *Immaturity?*

17 How about drinking or gambling?   ☐ No ☐ Yes. What? _____
                                                                Immaturity?

18 What are his outstanding strong points? _____

19 What type of saleswork do you feel he   _____
   would do best?

20 What are his weak points?   _____

            Checked by_____Date _____

Fig. 6.5   **Reference check on sales applicant form**

against contributions from other sources.

When this system is used properly it is extremely helpful in evaluating candidates. It will eliminate some, identify areas to be probed further on others and reinforce the manager's already favourable opinion on good applicants. The questions printed directly below the answer lines will help the manager to interpret the information he is given; obviously these questions should not be addressed to the previous superior.

Psychological tests

So far in the procedure, no candidates have been seen by the manager. All the work has been concerned with rejecting applicants and picking those suitable to call for interview. One group of methods often used at this stage is the psychological testing of the candidates. In recent years, such testing has become very popular and there are several thousand tests on the market which purport to pick out the men who are likely to succeed in selling. Unfortunately, there are no tests which have been *proved* capable of identifying salesmen, despite the fact that research into such tests has continued for the last fifty years.

It might seem paradoxical, therefore, that there are so many tests sold. Their appeal for many managers is that they offer quasi-scientific quantitative solutions to difficult problems of judgement. The manager can abrogate his responsibility and always blame the test if an employee subsequently fails. Obviously it is worth while continuing experimentation with tests but the manager who uses them should be careful to define what he is testing and be rigorous in his assessment of the results.

First, he must identify what he is trying to measure; this might be intelligence, extroversion/introversion or personality as a whole. Tests can then be selected which aim to evaluate these factors. Second, and most important as this has never been satisfactorily achieved, the manager must correlate what is being measured with sales ability. Third, the results of the test must be related to actual success in the field and compared against the results achieved by other employees chosen by other selection techniques. Only when a test has been shown consistently to pick more successful salesmen than otherwise would be the case, can it be called truly validated.

At the current state of knowledge the only type of test that can be recommended is simple intelligence measurement. This is not because there is any direct relationship between intelligence and ability;[1] but there is a correlation between intelligence and learning ability and as almost all salesmen must assimilate at least a modicum of knowledge, it is worth while to know whether they are capable of learning. It can be fairly argued, however, that the factor of learnability can be assessed by other means, such as checking with past employers and interviewing.

Structured interview

The personal interview with a candidate is the most important stage of any selection procedure. As has been shown, it cannot be replaced by tests or any other form of non-personal evaluation. The interviewer, therefore, must know what he is trying to find out and how he intends to discover it. Otherwise, the interview degenerates into a conversation, at worst with the interviewer doing all the talking.

To ensure that interview time is used to the full, the interview should be carefully structured in advance. This implies the existence of an interview format which

---

[1] In fact studies conducted by Dr Robert McMurry the eminent psychologist in America indicate a slight negative correlation between intelligence and sales achievement. See *How to Build a Dynamic Sales Organisation*, McGraw-Hill, 1968, pages 105 *ff*.

identifies the areas to be probed, the questions to be asked and has space for the answers to be recorded. Such a form is shown in Figure 6.6. It also presupposes that the interviewer has carefully prepared himself by studying the application form and telephone checks against the job description and man profile and identified the specific lines of inquiry that have to be pursued with the particular candidate.

Candidate factors to be analysed

It is worth reiterating the concepts that are being employed here. The interviewer is attempting to predict how a man about whom he knows relatively little will perform in a job that the man knows little about. In order to make this forecast, and knowing that the best guide to how a man will behave in the future is to analyse how he has behaved in the past, the interviewer is attempting to verify and expand the facts he knows about the man in order to identify recurring behavioural patterns. The interviewer also will recognise that he must view the man as a whole individual as what he does outside working hours may well have a significant impact on his job performance. Some interviewers find it difficult to ask questions about the personal and home backgrounds of the candidates. When it is remembered that the whole man must be considered, for his own sake as much as that of the company's, such questions can be asked with confidence.

The nature of the sales job is such that the man is likely to have to work irregular hours, be away from home, do business at home, store display material in his house, etc. It is impossible for the job not to have an impact on his home environment and vice versa. If his wife (or mother-in-law) does not support him, feels that selling is socially unacceptable and reacts violently against intrusions into their leisure time, it is unlikely that the man will devote his full energies to his work. Moreover the sort of man he is will have been determined, as already mentioned, by his earlier life and to understand him as he is today implies knowing something of his background.

This is why these areas must be probed. In extreme cases, where the job fully involves the man's home life, such as living overseas, considerable entertaining involving the wife and so on it is wise to arrange discussions with the man and his wife. This is as much to ensure that both of them fully understand the nature of the job as to assess whether the man will be supported or undermined. There have been many cases of men taking jobs, often in other parts of the country or world, which mean considerable personal and social upheaval. Because their wives either did not fully understand the ramifications of the new job or cannot tolerate the conditions, considerable unhappiness is caused, with a consequent decline in performance. Such situations are far better prevented.

Conducting the interview

About one and a half to two hours should be allowed for each interview. This is not over-long when the seriousness of the decision and the amount of discussion required are considered. The whole of this time will not be used when candidates who seemed attractive turn out to be inadequate. The interview should be terminated as soon as the interviewer has sufficient information to decide, particularly if it is clear that the man is not suitable.

The atmosphere of the interview should be as relaxed as possible. The room should be private and pleasant, the chairs comfortable, the light not glaring in the candidate's eyes and the interviewer's attitude friendly and helpful. No interruptions whatsoever should be permitted. The aim of all these conditions is to relieve the tension of the situation and encourage the man to talk freely about himself.

To facilitate this, it is often best for the interviewer to commence by explaining the job to the applicant in more detail, possibly showing him a job description, brochures or

---

STRUCTURED INTERVIEW FORM – SALES POSITION

Summary

Rating ☐1 ☐2 ☐3 ☐4 Interviewer _____Date _____

Division_____Territory _____

Comments _____
In making final rating, be sure to consider not only the man's sales ability and experience but also his stability, industry, perseverance, ability

to get along with others, loyalty, self-reliance, competitiveness, and leadership. Is he mature and realistic? Is he well motivated for this work?

Are his living standards and his domestic situations favourable to this work? Does he have sufficient health and physical reserve?

Name_____Telephone number_____ Is it your phone? ☐No ☐Yes

Present address_____
Is this a desirable neighbourhood? Does it appear consistent with income?

Date of your birth_____Age _____Do you own a car? ☐No ☐Yes. Make _____Age _____
Will his car be satisfactory for this work?

What do you use your car for? _____
Will this interfere?

Have you served in H M Forces since 1940? ☐No ☐Yes. Which branch?_____

If rejected or exempted, what were reasons? _____

Why are you applying for this position? _____
Are his underlying reasons practical? Does he have a definite goal?

Are you employed now? ☐No ☐Yes. (If yes) How soon available? _____

Work experience. Cover all positions. This information is very important. Interviewer should record last position first. Every month since leaving school should be accounted for. Experience in armed forces should be covered as a job

Past or present position

Company _____Address_____From _____19___To _____19____
Do dates check with application?

How was position obtained? _____Superior _____Title_____
Was he trying to get into sales? Did he show self-reliance in getting this job? Have there been changes here?

Nature of work at start _____Earnings at start _____
Did this work require energy and industry?   *Salary or commission?*

Nature of work at leaving _____Earnings at leaving _____
Did this require steady industry? Was salesmanship used? Any indication of favourable motivation? Progress? Salary or commission?

How did you plan your work? _____How did you get your contacts? _____
Was he on top of his job?   *Was he on his own?*

Was there anything you especially liked about the position? _____
Has he been happy and content in his work?

Was there anything you especially disliked? _____
Did he get along well with people? Were his dislikes justified?

How much time have you lost from work?_____Reasons_____
Is he regular in attendance on the job?

Reasons for leaving_____Why right then?_____
Are his reasons for leaving reasonable and consistent?   *Do they check with records?*

Part-time jobs during this employment _____
Does this indicate industry? Ambition? Lack of loyalty? Will this interfere with the job under consideration?

Fig. 6.6   Structured interview form – sales position

Next to last position

Company _____Address_____From_____19___To_____19____
Do dates agree with application?

How was the position obtained?_____Superior _____Title_____
Was he trying to get into sales? Did he show self-reliance in getting this job? Have there been changes here?

Nature of work at start _____Earnings at start _____
Did this work require energy and industry? *Salary or commission?*

Nature of work at leaving _____Earnings at leaving _____
Did this require steady industry? Was salesmanship used? Any indication of favourable motivation? Progress? Salary or commission?

How did you plan your work? _____How did you get your contacts?_____
Was he on top of his job? *Was he on his own?*

Was there anything you especially liked about the position? _____
Has he been happy and content in his work?

Was there anything you especially disliked? _____
Did he get along well with people? Were his dislikes justified?

Reasons for leaving_____ _____Why right then?_____
Are his reasons for leaving reasonable and consistent? *Do they agree with records?*

Second from last position

Company _____Address_____From_____19___To_____19____
Do dates agree with application?

How was the position obtained?_____Superior _____Title_____
Was he trying to get into sales? Did he show self-reliance in getting this job? Have there been changes here?

Nature of work at start _____Earnings at start _____
Did this work require energy and industry? *Salary or commission?*

Nature of work at leaving _____Earnings at leaving _____
Did this require steady industry? Was salesmanship used? Any indication of favourable motivation? Progress? Salary or commission?

How did you plan your work? _____How did you get your contacts?_____
Was he on top of his job? *Was he on his own?*

Was there anything you especially liked about the position? _____
Has he been happy and content in his work?

Was there anything you especially disliked? _____
Did he get along well with people? Were his dislikes justified?

Reasons for leaving_____Why right then?_____
Are his reasons for leaving reasonable and consistent? *Do they agree with records?*

Other positions

Name of company	Nature of work	Salary at leaving	Date started	Date left	Reasons for leaving

1 _____
Has he got along well on his jobs? Has he shown energy on his jobs?

2 _____
Has he been consistent in being interested in sales work?

3 _____
Has he stayed in one line of work for the most part?

4 _____
Do his attitudes toward his employers indicate loyalty? Did he get along well with people?

5 _____
Has he shown self-reliance in obtaining work? Has he consistently improved himself and his position?

Of all the work which you have done, where have you been most successful? _____
Was he interested in contact work, merchandising work? In work requiring activity?

Which have you enjoyed most?_____Why?_____

To what kinds of customers do you like to sell?_____
Does he indicate lack of sales ability?

To what kinds of customers don't you like to sell? _____
Does he have biases or resentments which will stand in his way?

How do you like selling to retailers? _____Jobbers or wholesalers? _____
Is he excessively biased or prejudiced?

Industrial users?_____Consumers _____
Will his attitudes fit in?

What experiences have you had in starting new accounts? _____
Has he been successful in building up a clientele?

How much display work have you done? _____Why was it necessary? _____
Does he understand and appreciate displays?

What type of product demonstrations have you made?_____
Has he been well trained? Has he followed methods suggested by employer?

Fig. 6.6 *(continued)*

How many weeks have you been unemployed in the past five years? How did you spend the time?_____
Did conditions justify this time?   Did he use this time profitably?

_____How did you support yourself?_____
Does he depend upon himself?

What efforts did you make to obtain work?_____
Did he try to obtain sales work? Is he inclined to search for work or responsibility?

Have you ever drawn unemployment compensation ☐ Yes ☐ No (If yes) When and how long?_____
Has he been inclined to depend on others? Does he want to be employed steadily?

Have you ever been arrested? ☐ Yes ☐ No (If yes) What was the charge?____What fines have you paid?____
Will he be responsible and careful?

Is your driving licence clean?_____What accidents have you had?_____

Schooling

	Secondary school		College or university			
Name of school						
Dates of attendance	From	To	From		To	
Names of other schools						
Dates of attendance	From	To	From	To	From	To
Results	"O" level	"A" level	Degree		Thesis	
Scholastic standing; honours or prizes; scholarships or fellowships	*Did he show perseverance. If not completed why not?*					
School activities (exclude military, racial, religious, nationality groups)						
Offices in these?	*Does he get along with others? Were his activities purposeful?*					
Further studying or reading	*Has he shown leadership qualities?*					
Principal source of spending money	*Has he shown perseverance in his efforts to improve himself? Related to his work?*					
Part of expenses earned	*Did he learn to earn money early in life?*					

Does he show stability in his schooling?

Had he shown habits of industry and self-reliance while in school?

Family background

Are your father and mother living? Father: ☐ Yes ☐ No Mother: ☐ Yes ☐ No When deceased?____

Occupation of your father when you were in school?_____Average earnings of father_____
What was the family financial status?

Number of brothers and sisters____Number older____Number younger____Age differences_____
Was he the "baby" of the family?

Who brought you up?_____Who did the disciplining?_____
Overprotection? Wholesome background?   Any resentment of authority?

Was it necessary for you to help your family financially when you were growing up?_____
Did his early experience strengthen his character?

How did you spend your leisure time after school and on Saturday?_____
Did this help him form habits of industry and responsibility?

How did you spend your summer vacations while a boy?_____
Did he associate with others? Did he keep busy?

What part did you take in church activities? (Do *not* ask what Church)_____
Did he get along well with others?

To what groups such as Boy Scouts did you belong while a boy?_____
(Exclude racial, religious, and nationality groups) Did he get along well with others?

How far did you advance in these groups?_____Any positions of leadership?_____
Did he make progress? Were his reasons for dropping out justified? Did he show leadership as a boy?

How old were you when you became fully self-supporting?_____Age at leaving home_____
Has someone always carried him over the "rough spots"?

Fig. 6.6   *(continued)*

Domestic and social situation

☐ Married ☐ Single ☐ Widowed ☐ Divorced ☐ Separated. Date of marriage . Living with wife? ☐ Yes ☐ No
Are he and his wife compatible?
(If no) Specify_____ Dependants:Number ____Ages _____What plans do you have for your children? _____
Do dependants provide adequate motivation?
What difficulties or serious arguments have you had with your wife? _____
                                                                    Financial?   *Social?*   *Personal?*
Have you been married previously? ☐ No ☐ Yes. (If yes) How many times? _Dates_____What happened?

☐ Death ☐ Divorce ☐ Separation

(Unless death) What were the reasons? _____
                                       Do his domestic difficulties indicate immaturity?
What group meetings do you attend? (Exclude military, racial, religious, nationality groups)_Officer? _____
                                    Does this indicate that he likes to deal with people?   *Does he show leadership?*
What do you do for recreation? _____
                                Does his recreation show maturity? Will his hobbies help his work? Group or solitary activities
What hobbies? _____To what extent do you and your wife entertain? _____
                                                         Does he seem socially well adjusted?
What entertaining of customers have you done? _____How? _____

When did you last drink intoxicating liquor? _____To what extent? _____ ☐ Don't drink
                                            Is this sensible drinking?
What does your wife think about this job? _____
                                                       Will this affect his motivation?
How free are you to travel? _____To be transferred? _____

What do you think about working evenings, Saturdays and Sundays? _____

What types of people rub you the wrong way? _____
                                            Is he biased?

Present financial situation

Do you ☐ Own your own home? £ ____ ☐ Rent? £ _____ ☐ Live with relatives? £ _____ ☐ Board? £ _____
Is this a motive for working hard?
☐ Stay with friends? £ ____ Are you carrying a mortgage? ☐ Yes ☐ No £ ____ Own your furniture? ☐ Yes ☐ No
                                  Is this consistent with his past and future earnings? Does this condition indicate stability?
Number of rooms in home _____How much do you estimate it costs to live per month? £ _____
                                                                                Is he financially responsible?
Do you have any debts other than living expenses? ☐ Yes ☐ No. (If yes) Specify_____

When have you had to borrow money? _____
                                     Is he realistic in handling money?
In your last position, how much money were you able to save? £ ____What is your present net worth? £ _____
                                                          Is he frugal and provident?
Must you contribute to the support of your parents, relatives or others? ☐ Yes ☐ No. (If yes) How much? ___
                                                      Does he have other financial incentives for working?
Is your wife employed? ☐ Yes ☐ No. (If yes) What kind of work? ____ Is it steady? ☐ Yes ☐ No. Earnings £ _
                                                      Will this offset his motivations?
Do you have any other source of income? ☐ Yes ☐ No. (If yes) Specify_____
                                                      Will this other income affect his motivation?
Amount of insurance £_____Types of policy? _____
                        Does this indicate acceptance of responsibility?

Health

What serious illnesses, operations, or accidents did you have as a child? _____
                                                      Has he any infantile personality traits due to childhood illness?
What illnesses, operations, or accidents have you had in recent years or in the forces? _____
                                      Are his illnesses legitimate rather than indicating a desire to "enjoy ill health"?
When did you see a doctor last? _____For what reason? _____
                                Is he relatively healthy?
Does anyone in your home suffer ill health? _____
                                            Are his wife, children, or family relatively healthy?
Will you take a medical examination at our expense? ☐ Yes ☐ No

Fig. 6.6 *(continued)*

samples of the product. He then asks the candidate if he has any questions about the job or the company. This not only gets the interviewee talking but also begins to indicate how much thought he has given to the job, why he is interested in it, etc. Is he looking forward to the challenge or the pension? It is then an easy task to steer the conversation so that the applicant talks about himself, with the interviewer asking the questions.

The interviewer should follow the structured form without allowing it to act as a strait-jacket. The questions should be phrased in words appropriate to the occasion and if a topic comes up out of sequence it should be pursued not artificially delayed. Answers should be recorded during the interview in the spaces provided on the form. Otherwise, it is difficult to recall precisely which candidate said what.

The questions must be carefully constructed so that they do not bias the answers. They should begin with "why, how, when, what, who, where?" whenever possible. Two major dangers to be avoided are leading questions and moralising comments. It is only too easy particularly with impressive candidates, to assume the answers or to lead the candidate to the right answer. This is because, subconsciously, the interviewer does not want the man to disqualify himself and so he asks loaded questions such as:

"You must have enjoyed your cold-canvass work?"
"Am I right in thinking you were one of the top salesmen at that company?"

Sometimes an applicant will disclose attitudes that may be morally abhorrent to the interviewer. He might hold political or social views that are contrary to those of the manager. His personal life might be problematical. It is important when such situations occur that no moralising or critical comment is passed. This can only lead to embarrassment and/or argument and certainly will inhibit the candidate's conversation. If a difference in ethical standards is important then the interviewer should find out all he can about it; if it is not germane to the job, it is no concern of the interviewer.

All the way through, the interviewer will be listening and watching how things are said as well as what is said. Tone, manner, facial expression, posture and hands can all be revealing and it is usually easy to determine by such observations whether the whole truth is being expressed. Whenever doubts arise, particularly over dates and reasons for leaving, the interviewer should not be afraid to probe by persistent questioning. For example, inconsistency in timings are often found, particularly when the application form information is compared with interview statements. In many cases it is simply lapses of memory. In some it is an attempt deliberately to hide periods of time which might have been spent in socially unacceptable ways, such as, in an extreme case. in prison. This fact may not disqualify the candidate, but it is imperative that the interviewer knows about it. For example a pharmaceutical company appointed as a sales representative a man who had been sentenced for the serious offence of impersonating a doctor. To put such a man in a position where he could so easily repeat the crime is not fair to him, the company or the public at large. The interviewer had failed to verify the man's information by the techniques described; if he had he would have discovered discrepancies in the times the applicant was supposed to have spent with various companies. The candidate had simply covered his time in jail by stretching the jobs on either side of this unfortunate period.

To help quickly to identify this kind of falsification, it will be noted that the structured interview covers the same basic data as the application form, but in reverse order. Thus the liar has not only to lie consistently on two separate occasions; he has to lie consistently both forwards and backwards in time. Minor falsification is not rare and the problem is that it is impossibly to identify without such procedures when major forgery is taking place.

If the interview is conducted along the lines indicated a decision can usually be made on the basis of the single meeting. Some companies prefer, however, to recall candidates for final discussions about terms or to evaluate them for management potential. These are perfectly valid reasons. What is disturbing is the amount of both company and applicant time that is wasted by lengthy, repetitive interviews due simply to the interviewer's forgetting to ask all the right questions on previous occasions.

Who should conduct the interview

It is hard to generalise about who should do the interviewing. In some companies the personnel department will be involved along with general management, in others the area manager will recruit his own staff. It is very important that whatever the system the man's future superior must be involved and must have at least the right of veto. Otherwise, he could be landed with a man whom he did not choose and whose subsequent failure he can blame on the selectors rather than on his own managerial inadequacy. Furthermore, the number of interviewers should be strictly limited to prevent the situation becoming rather like an inquisition. Two or three interviewers at a time are generally the maximum.

Placement analysis

When all the information has been collected from and about the applicant by means of the application form, tests where used, telephone checks and structured interviews, it must be evaluated against the requirements of the job description and the man profile. The questions placed beneath the answer lines on both the reference check and the structured interview forms will guide the manager in forming judgements on individual items. The man as a whole should now be assessed, using the applicant information analysis (Figure 6.4) to help interpretation. Attention should be paid to the manner in which the applicant writes letters, fills in forms, approaches and handles the interview. Remembering that he is faced with a major career decision, it is reasonable to expect that these first tasks that he is performing for a potential employer should be carried out carefully. The way in which he performs them will indicate strongly any degree of immaturity, particularly aspects such as disregard for consequences and exhibitionism. In interpreting the information the manager should search for behavioural patterns and not place too much reliance on single facts. He should place more weight on the facts of what has happened rather than the applicant's opinions of what should have happened or what he intends to do. Otherwise it is easy to be misled by the glib.

For example, it is common to find men, say, in their early thirties, who profess to a desire to settle down and spend the rest of their career with the company. This is of course an expression of stability, security and dependence. When the facts are examined, it might be found that a particular individual came from a large family where he had to stand on his own feet early in life. He had to work to earn pocket money whilst at school. He left school and took a succession of jobs without being able to settle down to any particular trade. He lived away from home from the age of sixteen until he went into the services. He disliked army life because of its regimentation and did not progress very far. Since leaving the services he has had five different jobs, the first two in offices before going out as a salesman. His reasons for leaving are not logical in that he has shown little progression from job to job. He has moved around the country and spends a considerable amount of time travelling. He obviously is interested in the pay of this job and has not bothered to consult very deeply with his wife over this career change. His outside interests are very varied and he has not pursued any hobby or sport consistently. He is extremely self-confident at interview and quickly establishes rapport with the interviewer.

All this evidence would support an interpretation of an unstable, possibly hard-working, gregarious, self-reliant individual with little perseverance and probably little loyalty. He is motivated more by money than security, is independent, selfish and thinks little about the future. Certainly it is unlikely that he will do as he states and settle down with his new company. He may not even appreciate his own instability, rationalising his moves so far as gaining experience.

PLACEMENT SUMMARY					
Applicant's name					
Profile category	Rating				Comments
1 Quantitative factors	1	2	3	4	
Age					
Education					
Experience					
Special qualifications					
Intelligence					
Availability					
Health					
2 Character traits	1	2	3	4	
Stability					
Industry					
Perseverance					
Ability to get along with others					
Loyalty					
Self-reliance					
Leadership					

Fig. 6.7 Placement summary form

3 Motivations	1	2	3	4	Comments
Money					
Security					
Status					
Power					
Perfection					
Competitiveness					
Service					

4 Degree of emotional immaturity	1	2	3	4	Comments
Dependence					
Disregard of consequences					
Incapacity for self discipline					
Selfishness					
Exhibitionism					
Pleasure-mindedness					
Unwillingness to accept responsibility					

Overall comment

Recommendation

Rated by _____

Fig. 6.7   *(continued)*

The analysis of the example is neither critical nor praising. The man's suitability depends entirely on the job description and man profile criteria. It might well be that such an individual is perfect and the manager is willing to accept the fact that the chances are low of his staying more than two or three years.

In the judgement of people there are no certainties, only probabilities. There is a small chance that a man might change his whole career pattern; sometimes it is worth the risk. But most selection situations must be judged on the balance of evidence. The manager must also be careful to interpret major character change correctly if this seems to occur. Usually, what has happened is not that the man has been transformed but that his environment has been modified. Take for example the man who worked successfully for a large company for, say, ten years but who since leaving it has had a succession of jobs each lasting a very short term. Has such an individual suddenly become unstable? More likely than such a behavioural change is the interpretation that he is basically a dependent individual who was secure and happy within the structured environment of a large organisation. When he moved (whether for good or bad reasons) he put himself into a series of unstructured jobs and, as he lacked self-reliance and the ability to accept responsibility, became very unhappy and frustrated. Placed once again in a secure environment, it is likely that he will return to stability.

This approach to the analysis and interpretation of behaviour is as relevant to the assessment of present staff as to the selection of new employees. By understanding fully the character, motivations and maturity of his current sales force, the manager can weld them into a happy and productive team.

Making the employment decision

Having studied all the factors of the man, these should now be rated on the placement summary (Figure 6.7). The various facets of the individual should be compared with the requirements of the man profile and a score noted in the appropriate box. He should be rated 1 for a perfect match, 2 for an above average match, 3 for below average and 4 for totally unsatisfactory. Comments should be made in the appropriate column to explain apparent discrepancies. Overall comments can be made in the space provided.

The scores should not be totalled or averaged in arriving at the final recommendation, as the weighting of the various factors will vary. What the manager must do is to consider each candidate as a mixture of factors and by identifying strong and weak points come to a recommendation and score the man on the four-category scale. Category 1 men will normally be offered jobs immediately. Category 2 are not qualified in all respects but, failing the appearance of anyone better, are worth employing. Only in dire circumstances, when it is imperative that someone is employed, would category 3 men be taken on. Category 4 staff should never be employed however desperate the manager might feel, for they can only create worse problems than they solve.

Two further considerations that the manager must take into account in arriving at his decision are the compatibility of the man with his future colleagues and superiors and the future management needs of the company.

How well a man fits into a team can often determine his success. It is usually fatal to put a dynamic, aggressive, ambitious twenty-six-year-old into a sales force consisting of security minded senior citizens hanging on for their pensions. It is likewise dangerous to have a man who is over-compatible with his superior. This often comes about by "mirror-image" selection, a common fault of many inexperienced managers. Because a candidate happens to have a similar background to the manager – that is, comes from the same part of the country, went to the same school, shares an interest in water-polo, and the like – it is tempting to assume that he possesses similar business abilities. If a manager is prone to such temptations, it is better for him to ask a colleague to take over the interviewing.

Every company must look at its future management requirements as well as its need for career salesmen. Usually, these two demands will have to be met by different types of staff. Therefore, two different man profiles may be necessary when looking to fill similar sales positions. Those men with management potential should certainly score higher in the leadership, self-reliance and ability to accept responsibility categories than will career sales staff. Unless different standards are adopted, it can be that too many men of high potential will be employed who will quickly become frustrated and leave. If men who can be only career salesmen are taken on, there will be no potential management pool for the future. The relationship between the two categories will depend upon the spans of control, the number of management levels and the life-span of management in each job.

Conclusion

Defining the staffing needs and operating recruitment and selection procedures of a sales organisation is a complex and difficult process. It is imperative that it is done thoroughly, otherwise the whole sales operation will fail despite training and motivation.

Once, however, the systems are established, they do not take vast amounts of time to operate. The longest stage in the whole procedure is the structured interview which takes one and a half to two hours per candidate, little enough when considered against the size of the decision. All the other phases take only a few minutes each, and some of them can be delegated to other members of staff.

Two final points that every experienced manager must recognise. First, if in doubt, reject. Second, most candidates will turn out worse in practice than they did at the interviews, therefore it is usually a vain hope to believe that a border-line applicant "might just make it." It is this over-optimistic approach that leads to so many sales forces being full of "grey men," not quite bad enough to fire, hardly good enough to keep.

ACTION PLANNING CHECKLIST

Questions	Answers and action	Timing of action and evaluation
1 What sources of recruitment are being or should be used?		
2 Do all advertisements contain the five basic factors? (See Figure 6.2)		
3 Should telephone-in advertisements be tried?		
4 Has current sales force been analysed to identify characteristics of successful men?		
5 Is current application form sufficient? (See Figure 6.3)		
6 How are applications currently reviewed? (See Figure 6.4)		
7 Should telephone Reference Checks be used? (See Figure 6.5)		
8 Should psychological tests be used?		
9 Should Structured Interviews be used? (See Figure 6.6)		
10 Who should do the interviewing?		
11 Are candidates fully analysed and interpreted? (See Figure 6.7)		
12 Where can the recruitment selection and assessment processes be improved by adoption of these concepts and techniques?		

CHAPTER 7

How to Develop Job Skills

Whatever kind of man is recruited, he will need some training to fit him for the job he has to do. Some companies try to avoid this responsibility by arguing that as salesmen are born and not made, accurate selection is all that is required. Brief analysis of the salesman's performance factors described in the previous chapters quickly shows that this belief is not valid in the vast majority of cases. Even where born salesmen are employed, they still need orientation to their new company, its products and its customers.

Another common fallacy is that all the new men need is "to know the product from the ground up." Thus all training time is devoted to studying the technicalities of the product, usually from the viewpoint of manufacture rather than sales. Sales skills are all too often totally ignored as unimportant. This school of thought is found particularly in industrial selling and is a throwback to the days of production-orientation and sellers' markets.

The third popular misconception about the development of job skills is that the new man can learn by accompanying and observing experienced staff. This is the so-called "sit by Nelly" technique, in which the training process consists simply of sending the man out on a territory with a senior representative, in the hope that he will pick up the techniques of the trade. It can be demonstrated very easily that observation alone cannot inculcate skills. One cannot learn to drive a motor car, ride a bicycle or become an actor simply by watching exponents of these arts.

Planning skill development

The art of selling is the presentation of product benefits in such a way that the buyer is persuaded that his needs will be satisfied. If the salesman is to be successful he must not only be knowledgeable about his product and his customer but also skilful in the presentation of this knowledge. Otherwise, the most knowledgeable men would be the most successful salesmen. Increasingly, companies are discovering the lack of correlation between technical knowledge and sales results. For example, for many years it was traditional in the drug industry to employ pharmacists, rather than salesmen, to call on doctors. Both here and in general, an increasing number of firms are finding that staff who are basically salesmen tend to be more successful. Obviously they must be given some technical training but the emphasis is now firmly on the sales aspects of the job.

The training programme must aim to achieve the objectives of giving knowledge and developing skills. The nature and scale of both areas should be specified in advance so that the programme can be directed towards definite goals.

Only when such objectives are identified can the subsidiary questions be answered:

1 What should be taught?
2 Where should it be taught?
3 By whom should it be taught?
4 How should it be taught?

Setting development objectives

This should be approached by identifying the gap between the level of performance expected of the salesmen and their current standards. The level they are supposed to achieve can be defined by analysing the requirements of the job specification. For example, if it is noted in the job description that the salesmen will make presentations at trade conferences or that he is responsible for in-store promotions, the development programme must include training in public speaking and merchandising. Figure 7.1 shows extracts from typical job descriptions and the knowledge and skills required to fulfil the defined tasks. The individual goals of particular parts of the training programme can be derived from this.

The current levels of skill and knowledge can be identified by observing the salesmen in action, examining them on areas such as product knowledge and, where new men are concerned, by analysing the interview findings and reference checks. The data can be collected systematically on a development-needs analysis form (Figure 7.2).

The development of job skills is basically a learning process and therefore development objectives should be set in terms of what is to be learnt. Obviously the aim of such learning is to improve sales and, in some circumstances, it is possible to demonstrate a direct relationship between training and results. However, in most cases the sales force is only one element of the total communications mix and so the impact of a particular training programme cannot often be separately identified.

Knowledge goals

The difficult problem of evaluating training is made virtually impossible when clear goals are not defined. Objectives should be set by defining what the trainee should be able to do at the end of his training. In the knowledge areas this is relatively simple. Instead of formulating a diffuse aim for a course such as "to give knowledge about fork-lift truck model *A*," specific targets should be constructed. Such a goal might be "to be able to list five major benefits of fork-lift truck model *A* and explain how these benefits are derived from the relevant product features." It is then possible to design the programme to achieve the objective set and, most important, to test the trainee to ensure that he has learnt from the programme.

Skill goals

Skill goals are far more difficult to specify. Even so, improvements can often be made. Instead of setting an objective such as "to be able to demonstrate fork-lift truck model *A*," achievement of which can only be qualitatively assessed, "demonstration ability" should be defined. If it can be specified as, for example, "to be able to start the truck, move forward, pick up and place a pallet within sixty seconds," again it will be helpful in programme definition and evaluation.

Extracts from typical job descriptions	Knowledge requirement (What does he need to know?)	Skill requirement (What does he need to do?)
In conjunction with his area manager, set targets by product group	Customer records Prospect records Market information Sales forecasting technique	Ability to analyse statistics, derive trends and identify opportunities
Must be fully knowledgeable about the products and their applications	Product features and applications in customer circumstances	Ability to relate product features to customer needs Ability to find and interest new customers
Must achieve the targets agreed by obtaining orders from existing customers and prospects	Prospecting techniques Preparation techniques Sales interview techniques	Presentational skills Communication skills Persuasion skills
Must handle all customer queries and complaints	Objection-handling techniques Complaint-handling procedures	Communication skills particularly with irate customers
Must represent the company at trade shows and exhibitions and make presentations when called upon to do so	General company history and background	Public speaking Visual aids
Must monitor and report on competitive activity and state of trade in his area	Market research techniques Information sources	Ability to ask fact-finding questions and analyse answers Report-writing
Must ensure the company's products are displayed to best advantage	Merchandising techniques In-store promotions schemes	Display-building Selling merchandising ideas

Fig. 7.1   Knowledge and skill requirements analysis

Sales knowledge and skills are even more difficult to analyse into measurable elements. However, some progress can be made away from general objectives such as "to improve ability in salesmanship." The stages of the sales presentation should be identified and the factors of each stage listed. Thus a goal could be formulated "to be able to answer price objectives by using and proving arguments of longer life, greater reliability and faster operation." Admittedly there is still plenty of room for qualitative judgement in assessing the achievement of such an objective. However, it specifies at least some of the major elements of the objection-handling process, without which the salesman will be unable to develop skill.

There is another danger that must be guarded against in the training of salesmen with some experience. Because they have some knowledge and skill when they start the programme, any testing at the end of it cannot separate the impact of the training from their prior experience. Thus, the fact that they know the twenty eight features of a particular product will not prove that they learnt them on the course. In such a situation tests should be administered at the beginning as well as at the end of the training. The effectiveness of the teaching can then be assessed from the difference between the two scores.

Criteria of good objectives

The criteria of good development objectives are that they should describe:

1 What the trainee should be able to do at the end of his training.
2 The conditions within which he should be able to do it.
3 The standards of performance that he should be able to achieve.

Thus a general statement that he "should be able to build merchandising displays" can be refined into an objective of:

Be able to build cut-case displays } What he should be able to do

Suitable for small counter-service stores } Conditions within which he should be able to do it

Using four cases displaying at least 24 cans and built within five minutes } Standards of performance that he should be able to achieve

What is to be taught?

From Figure 7.2 it can be seen that there are five major areas of knowledge and skill:

1 The company and its policies and procedures.
2 The products and their competitors.
3 Sales techniques.
4 Work organisation.
5 Reporting.

The first two are basically knowledge areas, where information must be imparted to the salesmen. What is so often forgotten is that the knowledge they require needs a particular orientation. For example, they must understand the commission system from the point of view of how it affects their earnings and why it is so constructed, otherwise it will not act as an incentive.

Product knowledge must be taught to the sales force in terms of its application and the benefits that are conferred on the customer. It is not enough to know the technicalities of how to can beans. The salesman must know the impact of this process on product quality and shelf life and why this makes his beans more saleable than those of the competition.

The industrial representative may be fully conversant with the mechanical aspects of his machine tools but unless he can translate these features into benefits to the customer, such as shorter process time, less maintenance and ease of servicing, his knowledge will be useless.

Item 3, sales techniques, even when taught, is often restricted to a study of the sales interview alone. If the salesmen are to appreciate fully their role in the business in general and marketing in particular, these subjects must be added to the training programme, as must such topics as pre-sale preparation and after-sale servicing.

Item 4 is listed separately as so often sales training concentrates only on the qualitative aspects of the job. The amount of selling done can be equally important to the level of sales skill achieved. It is an old cliché of selling that the man who spends most time with customers tends to do most business. Many surveys have shown that the average salesman spends only about a quarter of his day actually face-to-face with customers. For example, a survey of 1954 companies representing over 38000 salesmen showed average face-to-face time varying from 17 per cent in repeat consumer goods selling to about 30 per cent in industrial selling with an average across all types of selling of 25 per cent (*Sales Force Practice Today* published by the Institute of Marketing). If by better work organisation techniques, a salesman can increase his time with customers by ten minutes per day, this is an improvement of about 10 per cent on the total time spent with customers.

Item 5, reporting, is often overlooked completely although sales managers are apt to complain about the quality of their salesmen's reports. The reporting system is the basic regular link between the man in the field and the rest of the company. Unless such reports are succinctly and clearly written, with points for action identified, there is a danger that communications will fail. The customers will grow dissatisfied, market changes will pass unnoticed and competitive activity will not be combated.

Depending on the nature of the company there will be other items for which training is required. Some examples are provided in Figure 7.2. This form should encourage sales management to look beyond the obvious requirements of knowing something about the product towards a realistic analysis of precisely what knowledge their men should possess and what skills they should be capable of wielding.

Where should it be taught?

Normally there are four places at which training can take place:

1   The company factory and offices.
2   The company training room (or hotel room).
3   In the field.
4   On outside courses.

Usually the best location for training in basic company procedures and product knowledge is wherever the work is done. For example, to enable the salesmen to understand the order processing procedure, it is usually wise for them to observe the sales office and see how the various documents are processed. Initial sales technique, work organisation and some product applications training are better conducted in a classroom where practical exercises can be undertaken, films shown and lectures and demonstrations given.

However, the bulk of sales skill development, particularly the continuous training, is indubitably best done in the field where the training can be integrated with demonstrations and real-life practice. Outside courses can be used to broaden the salesman's horizon by exposing him to his peers from other companies. This often helps him to put his own performance and problems into better perspective. Moreover, the outside course offers a solution to the problem of training one or two men for whom it is not economic to

DEVELOPMENT NEEDS ANALYSIS FORM

Name and position of
man appraised _____

_____

Length of time with company _____

Training already undergone _____

_____

_____

Knowledge/skill area	Highly knowledgeable and skilled No further training required	Above average knowledge and skill but some training needed	Below average knowledge and skill lengthy training needed	Poor knowledge and skill considerable training needed	Recommendations
1 Company knowledge					
(a) History and organisation					
(b) Marketing strategy					
(c) Ordering procedures					
(d) Complaints procedures					
(e) Expense claim procedures					
(f) Commission procedures					
(g) Sampling procedures					
2 Product, applications and industry knowledge					
(a) Range (i)					
(b) Range (ii)					
(c) Range (iii)					
(d) Competitors					

Fig. 7.2 Development needs analysis form

Knowledge/skill area	Highly knowledgeable and skilled. No further training required	Above average knowledge and skill but some training needed	Below average knowledge and skill lengthy training needed	Poor knowledge and skill considerable training needed	Recommendations
3 Sales techniques					
(a) Customer needs analysis					
(b) Preparation					
(c) Prospecting					
(d) Opening					
(e) Presentation					
(f) Objection handling					
(g) Closing					
(h) Negotiation					
4 Work organisation					
(a) Journey planning					
(b) Day planning					
(c) Call planning					
5 Reporting					
(a) Structure					
(b) Content					
(c) Clarity					
(d) Action requests					
6 Other areas					
(a) Account planning					
(b) Public speaking					
(c) Financial knowledge					
(d) Merchandising					

Overall recommendations _____

Appraised by _____

Date _____

Fig. 7.2   *(continued)*

establish an in-company programme. However, this type of general course has the very serious drawback that realistic practice of sales techniques is extremely limited because the delegates usually come from a wide variety of companies selling different products.

By whom should it be taught?

The training function is often misinterpreted. Even in companies with large training departments the basic responsibility for salesmen development must still rest with the line manager. Training and development of his staff is a basic responsibility of any manager and it cannot be abrogated. Otherwise, the fundamental rule of congruence of responsibility and authority is broken. Thus, if the salesman fails in the field the manager can blame the training department for poor development, whereupon the trainer is likely to defend his programme and criticise the manager's management ability.

Delegated responsibility of the manager

It is not suggested that the sales manager must conduct all training personally. He should understand, however, that when training is handled by others, he is delegating that responsibility and, as in any other delegated task, he must maintain accountability. The parts of the training that can normally be delegated are the initial company, product and sales training and the formal refresher and continuation training. Where these are delegated, they will usually be handled in one of three ways. First, the company's training department can take the responsibility if the sales force is large enough to justify specialised staff. Company trainers normally have the advantages of being skilled in training and knowledgeable about the firm but they may be too narrow in their approach because they are company employees.

Second, consultants can be used, which overcomes the danger of a "blinkered" approach, but obviously their knowledge of the company, even after conducting a survey of it, will be limited.

Third, external courses can be used. This is often the cheapest way of training one or two men but inevitably the training will be of a general nature and will do little to develop skills.

A mix of the three is often a good solution. Internal staff conduct the company and product knowledge training, consultants run the sales technique and work organisation programmes; and external courses are used to develop particular salesmen in specific areas where the numbers are too small to justify either of the other two approaches.

Importance of field training

The most important area of salesmen development is the continuous field training process. This is normally undertaken by the sales manager concerned. It is difficult to delegate because it is interwoven with other aspects of the management function, such as control and appraisal. Some companies, however, do use a field trainer system. For it to be successful, the division of responsibility and authority between manager and trainer must be carefully defined, otherwise the salesmen will become confused about what guidance to take from whom. Too often, it is a system that is introduced for the wrong reasons – that is, to create a promotion opportunity for senior sales staff or to reward an old company servant who lacks real management potential. If the importance of field training is recognised and seen as an integral part of the sales management function, the need for field trainers seldom arises. Where the volume of field training seems to be beyond the line management capability, the first areas to be examined should be the organisation structure and spans of control.

How should it be taught?

It has been mentioned already that mere observation does not cause skill development to take place. In fact many of the traditional training techniques are suspect when it comes to teaching skills. Such methods as lecturing, showing films, reading books or notes and watching others are valuable for the imparting of knowledge and the setting of frames of reference within which learning can take place. By themselves, however, they do not develop skills.

Problems of skill development

Skills are created by practice in trial and error situations, with guidance being given. The salesman training programme should thus be largely participative and based upon the maximum amount of practice in the skill areas. The major techniques that can be used in initial training are concerned with simulating the sales situation either in total or in part in the classroom. The salesman can then role-play his actual job and develop sales skills. Later, when under field training, the practice can be made absolutely realistic with the skills being tested on actual customers.

Trial and error alone, however, will not necessarily teach. Feedback must be given to identify for the trainee the mistakes he is making. The most powerful form of feedback in terms of skill development is self-perception. If the trainee himself can understand where he is failing, he will be better able to correct it. Self-perception is best developed in the initial training process by providing an audio-visual record of the trainee's performance. This can be arranged by using closed circuit television linked to a videotape recorder whereby the man can see and hear an immediate playback of his role-played performance. The necessary equipment can be hired quite readily and cheaply nowadays and provides the single most powerful sales training tool available. Less sophisticated and more limited in its feedback is the ordinary tape recorder. As this gives only a record of what the man has said, vital weaknesses in his visual impact can easily be overlooked.

Where no such aids are available, feedback must be given by the trainer or the other trainees. When these methods are used, either to support and analyse the audio-visual playback or on their own, great care must be exercised when evaluating the role-players' performance to ensure that acceptance of the deficiencies is gained. Unless the salesmen sincerely accept that they still have weaknesses in their sales technique, they will not be motivated to improve.

In the field training situation the only form of feedback is the manager's comments and, again, the acceptance problem must be overcome. Methods for solving this difficulty are described in Chapter 9.

The development of salesmen is a complex and continuous process, as selling is a set of skills as well as a body of knowledge. Likewise, sales management is a mixture of skill and knowledge, and managers must themselves be trained on the lines indicated above if they are to be fully effective.

ACTION PLANNING CHECKLIST

Questions	Answers and action	Timing of action and evaluation
1 Does the company's training philosophy recognise the problems of knowledge giving and skill development?		
2 Is the company training programme derived from the requirements of the trainee's jobs? (See Figure 7.1)		
3 Are the training needs of the individual systematically analysed? (See Figure 7.2)		
4 Are development objectives quantitatively stated wherever possible?		
5 Does the training programme include the five major areas of knowledge and skill?		
6 Who should conduct the training?		
7 Are the training methods used appropriate to skill development?		

CHAPTER 8

How to Conduct Initial Training

When a new salesman joins a company he should be given some form of training. Too often, even when training is given, the whole time is devoted to company and product knowledge in the hope (usually unfulfilled) that the salesman will somehow pick up sales techniques in the field.

This initial training can be critical to the ultimate success of the new man as it will affect both his ability and morale. It must therefore be very carefully planned and skilfully executed. In fact some firms run the initial training programme before the man joins the company, as part of the recruitment and selection process. This technique is found in fields like life assurance, where evening sales training sessions are offered free to suitable applicants. This gives both the company and the candidates a better opportunity to assess each other before making the employment decision. It also enables the men, if selected, to commence sales work earlier.

What should be included in the initial training programme

The programme material will obviously vary from firm to firm, particularly in terms of the company and product knowledge to be taught.

There are, however, some basic areas of the sales job that should be included in most initial training courses, although with specific biases being given by different companies. There are ten major elements that should be covered.

1 *The marketing concept and the role of the salesforce.* The salesman must understand fully the part he plays in the total effort of the company. Otherwise, he will find it difficult to integrate his work with that of other departments.

2 *The nature of salesmanship.* It is essential that the salesman has a clear definition of what selling is, its role in society and the basic requirements of the sales job. It is surprising how many salesmen cannot even define salesmanship and who at root doubt its social worth. It is incumbent on the manager to ensure that these fundamentals are settled before the man is exposed to more detailed training and particularly before he faces the harsh realities of his working life.

3 *Communications.* As selling is basically a question of persuasive communication, the salesman must understand the inherent difficulties of interpersonal relationships and be given techniques for overcoming these problems. He must be skilled in other forms of communication, such as reporting and talking on the telephone.

4 *Preparation for selling.* This is normally a very weak area of sales skill and yet if a coherent, logical approach to the customer is to be made, it has to be structured in advance, and this technique has to be taught. It is not good enough to simply think about the interview while driving along! The subject of planning is particularly important for those sales staff who deal with major accounts.

5 *Prospecting.* Every business depends to some extent on gaining new customers. This is probably the most difficult part of selling and the salesman should be given a systematic approach to the finding of potential buyers. Having learnt how to look for new business, he will also be better motivated and less likely to avoid prospecting, as so often happens.

6 *Opening the sale.* Obtaining interviews with buyers and making the right impression in the early stages of the presentation are areas where skill is required. A casual approach will lead to failure to pass the receptionist or even when that is achieved to curtailed, unsuccessful interviews.

7 *Making sales presentations.* To be effective as a persuader, the salesman must be skilled in verbal presentation, visual aid handling and product demonstration. There is a body of techniques that can be learnt which will help the salesman to communicate convincingly.

8 *Handling objections.* Every sales interview has within it customer objections on such topics as price, delivery, etc. Some of these can be prevented, others overcome. Certainly most objections can be predicted and the salesman trained in the answers to be given and the methods of expressing them.

9 *Closing the sale.* Again, this is normally a very weak area because the salesman fears rejection. He therefore tends to avoid it by never asking for the order. By never asking the buyer to buy, the buyer never has to refuse. Obviously the whole point of selling is to gain sales and the salesman can be encouraged to request orders more often and more persuasively by thorough training in proven closing techniques.

10 *Work organisation.* The major concentration of initial training is on improving the quality of the salesman's skills. Due regard should also be paid to the quantity of selling so that the man knows how to utilise his very limited time to the maximum. He should be taught techniques of journey planning and day planning.

Concept of customer orientation

Throughout the whole of the initial training programme certain themes will have to be constantly emphasised as some of the basic concepts are hard to instil. One of the most fundamental and vital of these is the philosophy of customer-orientation. Without this approach, the salesman will find it very hard to succeed and yet it is difficult to ensure that it will be practised.

Every salesman must recognise that buyers buy to satisfy *needs*, both rational and emotional. These needs are fulfilled by *benefits* of the product and these benefits are derived from product *features*. Thus the fact that a solid fuel central heating boiler has an automatic gravity feed is a purely technical *feature*. It only becomes of benefit when the buyer realises or is shown that he has a *need* for reliable continuous operation with a minimum of physical involvement. In other words, the salesman must perform the difficult psychological manoeuvre of looking at the situation from the buyer's point of view first and analysing with him his needs. Then and only then can he present the relevant benefits to satisfy these needs before proving the benefits with product features. Unfortunately, like most human beings, many salesmen see life from their own standpoint and this view is often reinforced by wrong emphasis during product training. Thus, sales interviews are approached from entirely the wrong direction with a presentation of technical features from which some benefits may eventually be drawn. After which, assuming the buyer is still present and listening, his needs may be analysed. As all of us are basically more interested in ourselves and our problems than anything else it is patent that such an approach will not be very successful.

Because of the mental difficulty of reversing the viewpoint in this way, successful training in this concept can be hard to achieve. It is helped if a product analysis (Figure 8.1) is demonstrated and this technique is inculcated so that the salesmen analyse the needs, benefits and features of a situation before they commence selling.

Much more could be written about the content of the initial training programme but it would turn this book into a volume on salesmanship. There are many good texts available on selling technique and some of these have been listed in the bibliography at the end of this book. More important than any particular methods are the concepts of customer-orientation described above. If these can be inculcated, techniques are readily developed from them.

How to structure the initial training programme

One common problem of initial training is that the new salesman may never have sold before. Prior to any formal sales training, the man must be given a frame of reference into which his learning will fit. He should be sent into the field for a brief period with an experienced man (perhaps his manager) simply to observe the nature of the trade he is entering. This field exposure is not intended to develop skills but to provide a background so that the relevance of the training can be appreciated.

He can then be given a formal training. It is preferable if there is a number of men to be trained at one time, to arrange an in-company course. This can be conducted by the manager, the company training department or a specialist consultant. Being in-company widens the range of participative methods that can be used as well as focusing total attention on the specific products to be sold. Where there are only one or two men to be trained, individual tuition has to be given or they have to be sent on an outside course.

This initial programme will also include company and product information and these should be integrated with the sales training so the correct customer-orientation of all knowledge given is established.

Programme timing

It is difficult to be precise about the length of the first programme but it should not be much longer than two weeks at the maximum. If there is more material than can be covered in such a period it is better to break it into shorter modules with field work in between. Otherwise the trainees will get mental indigestion and the pressure of the course will have to be significantly lowered to avoid this.

Timing within the course is also important. Sessions should never be more than about ninety minutes without a break and by taking a lengthy lunch interval (about $1\frac{3}{4}$ to 2 hours) work can continue well into the evening. Evening work should avoid lectures and concentrate on participative activity so that interest is maintained. Figure 8.2 shows a typical course structure.

Customer needs	Benefits that will satisfy customer needs	Product features from which the benefits are derived
1 Rational		
(a) *Performance* – must be able to work fast with a variety of implements	Plenty of power, particularly at low speeds	65 BHP diesel engine with high torque at low rpm. Wide range of matched implements available
(b) *Versatility* – must cope with a variety of soil and cultivating conditions	Can travel at a wide variety of speeds	10 speed synchromesh gearbox – four wheel drive available for very difficult conditions
(c) *Simplicity* – must be easy to operate	Simple and speedy implement changeover. Easy to drive	Quick-attach linkage with snap-on hydraulic couplings. Ergonomically placed levers and pedals
(d) *Low cost* – must be economical to run	Low fuel consumption	Efficient engine design with improved braking and fuel injector system. Good power/weight ratio
(e) *Reliability* – must be able to operate continuously and be serviced quickly	Well proven design with all basic snags removed. Local dealer with 24 hour parts service	More than 10 000 units already in operation. Wide dealer network with factory-trained mechanics backed by computerised parts operation
2 Emotional		
(a) *Security* – (fear of making wrong decision)	Most popular tractor on the market – 10 000 farmers can't be wrong	Largest company in the industry with good reputation for reliability and value for money
(b) *Prestige* – (desire to gain status in the eyes of others)	Chosen by those engaged in best agricultural practice	Favoured by agricultural colleges and large farmers

NOTES

1 The product analysis should be completed from left to right. Only when the needs have been identified can the appropriate benefits and the relevant features be selected.

2 If the salesman works from right to left not only will he lose his buyer's interest as he talks about items which may not be of interest, but also he will have no basis for selecting which benefits to stress.

3 This example is not intended as a complete analysis. That can only be done with a specific buyer in mind as each person has an individual need pattern. Performance will be most important to one farmer, low cost to another.

4 It will be noted that some of the product features are so technical as to be almost meaningless to the layman. This is one of the greatest dangers for the industrial salesman. Unless he translates his trade jargon he will fail to achieve understanding and thus cannot be persuasive.

Fig. 8.1   Product analysis
Agricultural tractor example

Learning curve

It should be recognised that learning does not take place at a consistent rate. Studies show that the learning process consists of periods of rapid assimilation interspersed with plateaux during which the learnt material is digested. During such static spells, however, the trainee's morale can easily fall as he feels he is making no progress. He should be reassured by an explanation of this phenomenon, which is known as the "learning curve." Also, during each course, there will be a curve of interest which, typically, will rise towards the midpoint of the programme and then tail away if left unchecked. The trainer should therefore include items of great interest near the end of the programme to ensure the trainees leave at a high point of the interest curve rather than allowing their enthusiasm to decline.

Methods of training

The general problems of knowledge giving and skill development were discussed in the previous chapter. Because of the need to develop techniques, the initial training programme should be highly participative with ample opportunities for presentation exercises, discussion, study groups and particularly role-playing of simulated sales situations with some kind of audio-visual feedback.

Role-playing

Role-playing is sometimes criticised by sales management as being artificial and dependent upon acting rather than selling ability. However, if it is properly organised these objections are not valid.

Assuming there are six men to be trained, they should be divided into three teams of two. Each team is then asked to devise a typical sales situation, preferably from its own real-life experience, and to write down the kind of information a salesman would have in the circumstances. This brief will contain usually the name and address of the buyer, his company details, the nature of the problem and some realistic background on the competitive situation, the buyer's interests, etc. A typical example is:

> Jim Smith is the assistant buyer for Williams of Watford, a medium-size engineering company. They have been good customers in the past, buying an average of £5000 a year of gearwheels and chains from us. One of our competitors has capitalised on our poor delivery situation last year and has got the business although we can now deliver Williams' requirements.

When all three teams have written up their situations these are exchanged, Team *A*'s to Team *B*, Team *B*'s to Team *C*, Team *C*'s to Team *A*.

Each team is then asked to prepare a sales presentation on the brief they have received.

Finally, each team elects a "buyer" and a "salesman." The "salesman" from Team *B* sells to the "buyer" from Team *A* and so forth.

After the sales presentation, each "salesman" is asked to comment on his own performance after which the "buyer" is asked for his evaluation of the "salesman's" efforts. Discussion is then thrown open to the group as a whole and finally the trainer remarks on any aspect that has not been identified by the other means (or not revealed by the trainees when questioned by the trainer). The process is then repeated so that all trainees have at least one opportunity to be the "salesman."

Adopting this sequence removes much of the criticism of artificiality as the trainees devise their own situations, attempt to sell in them and then appraise their own performance. The criticism of play-acting also is invalidated by selecting real-life

---

TRAINING PROGRAMME

Day one	*Timetable*	*Notes*
09 00	Welcome and introduction	Introduce those who have not met
09 15	The salesman's role in XYZ company	Stress role of salesman in company in general and marketing in particular. Also function of selling in company history and development
10 15	Coffee	
10 30	The nature of salesmanship	Define selling and its role in society Stress customer-orientation
11 25	Break	
11 30	Product analysis	Introduce product analysis concept and use it to teach product knowledge about company's ranges and competition Use exercises to get salesmen practising technique
12 30	Lunch	Long lunch break to allow evening work
14 15	Product analysis	As morning session but on other products
15 30	Tea	
15 45	Persuasive communications	Stress principles and problems of interpersonal relationships, with demonstrations and exercises
17 15	Break	
17 20	Film "The Art of Two-way communications"	Reinforce and dramatise communication points
18 00	Evening study work on product knowledge	

Day two		
09 00	Product knowledge test	Evaluate not only knowledge gained but ability to translate into customer need satisfactions
10 15	Coffee	
10 30	Prospecting for new business	Stress need for systematic methods of finding new customers
11 25	Break	
11 30	Preparing to sell	Identify need for structure and how a planned call is prepared
12 30	Lunch	
14 15	Case study preparation	Simple case study – given facts about customer situation, develop a planned call structure
15 00	Case study – reports	Each salesman describes his structure and gives reasons for his decisions
15 30	Tea	
16 00	Opening the sale	Give techniques for attracting buyer's attention by analysing his needs
16 30	Film – e.g. "Starting the interview"	
17 15	Break	
17 20	Making a sales presentation	Stress techniques for building buyer interest. Instruct on use of visual aids. First actual sales exercise focusing on opening and presenting only
18 00	Evening case study – prepare role-playing of opening and presentation	

Day three		
09 00	Role-playing	Each session 5–7 minutes. No recording of performance at this stage. Analysed by other trainees and instructor
10 15	Coffee	

Fig. 8.2 Typical initial training programme for six salesmen

Day three – cont. *Timetable*	*Notes*
10 30 Film – "Selling Benefits"	Used as a summary and reinforcement this time
11 15 Handling objections	Identify techniques for preventing and overcoming objections
12 00 Film – e.g. "Dealing with objections"	
12 30 Lunch	
14 15 Product analysis – Part 2	Either more knowledge on products already covered, correction of product errors made, or cover further products
15 30 Tea	
15 45 Closing the sale	Stress need for and techniques of closing
17 00 Break	
17 15 Film – e.g. "Getting the decision"	
18 00 *Evening* – Preparation for full role-playing session	More difficult situation covering total sales interview

Day four

09 00 Role-playing with video-tape playback	Each session videotaped and played back afterwards. Average session length 35 minutes including role-playing, VTR playback and analysis
10 15 Coffee	
10 30 Role-playing	
12 30 Lunch	
14 15 Preparation for role-playing	
14 44 Role-playing with video-tape play-back	Repeat of morning with other cases illustrating different customer situations
15 30 Tea	
15 45 Role-playing	
17 15 Break	
18 30 *Evening* – dinner with senior management	

Day five

09 00 Organising your time Film "Get Organised"	Techniques of journey planning and day structuring – with practice
10 15 Coffee	
10 30 Sales reporting	How to write call reports, use record cards, etc
11 25 Break	
11 30 Commission and expense systems	Stressing rewards from successful selling
12 30 Lunch	
14 15 Final discussion, review and conclusion	Reiterating all major points, answering final questions, stimulating enthusiasm.
End of course	*Allowing time to get home for weekend*

GENERAL NOTES

1   Note wide variety of techniques – lecture/discussions, films, case study, role-playing, videotape, product knowledge test, etc.
2   Note stress on importance of salesman to build morale – for example day 1 morning sessions and dinner with senior management
3   Note emphasis on participation and practice
4   Note commission discussion placed late on last day in order to stimulate enthusiasm and send men away with high motivation

Fig. 8.2   *(continued)*

Method	Notes on uses
Knowledge-giving	
1 Lecture	Requires considerable skill from trainer to be successful Should be supported with visual aids and plenty of discussion
2 Film/ videotape	Useful for portraying dynamic situations – must be discussed in terms of trainee's own situation
3 Slides/sound presentations	Cheaper form of "canned presentation" than film thus can be made specifically for company
4 Reading material	Useful where considerable information has to be absorbed. Particularly valuable if programmed tests used. Otherwise trainees must be tested to ensure material read and absorbed
Skill Development	
5 Role-playing	Most powerful technique of sales skill development especially when supported by audio-visual feedback
6 Effective speaking	More simple form of presentational skill development. Represents only one-way communication, lacks interaction
7 Case study	Useful for developing analytical skills, for example, in identifying customer needs
8 Simulation exercises	Simple management games on territory planning useful for developing decision-making skills. Likewise in-basket techniques useful for demonstrating how to decide priorities

Fig. 8.3 **Eight major training methods and their uses**

	Product knowledge example	*Sales skill example*
Objectives of sessions	"To recognise the three major types of printing which the company markets and to be able to specify the appropriate method for customer needs"	"To be able to use four techniques of getting orders"
Material	Technical and cost information on letterpress, litho and silk screen printing. Customer needs data and how this is used to indicate relevant method of printing	Information on closing methods of – direct request – alternatives – immediate gain – part-by-part
Method	1 Lecture/discussion 2 Examples of different printing 3 Development of Customer Needs Analysis Chart 4 Examination based on different customer needs where salesmen asked to specify and quote	1 Lecture/discussion 2 Film on closing the sale 3 Role-playing of closing situations using the four methods
Personnel	1 Works manager 2 Works manager 3 Sales trainer 4 Sales trainer	1 Sales trainer 2 Sales trainer 3 Sales trainer
Timing	1 Printing Methods 1 hour 2 Examination of different printed matter and discussion 30 minutes 3 Customer needs analysis 1 hour 4 Examination and discussion of results 1 hour	1 Lecture/discussion 45 minutes 2 Film and discussion 45 minutes 3 Role-playing preparation 45 minutes Role-playing of techniques 10 minutes per man

Fig. 8.4   Course planning sheet

situations within the group's knowledge. Thus, instead of the "buyers" having to create characters, they merely simulate real people, which is much easier. The "salesmen" have no need to act as they carry out their normal job. The role of the trainer is a very passive one and therefore he cannot be accused of setting over-difficult problems.

Furthermore, if the presentations are recorded on videotape and then played back, the whole training process gains yet another dimension.

Role-playing is the most important part of the initial training course because it is aimed at skill-development in situations close to reality. Of course there is a minimal artificiality about the proceedings but after the first few seconds of self-consciousness, the participants quickly fall into the spirit of the exercise and both enjoy it and gain from it. Other training methods are shown in Figure 8.3.

Conclusion

The initial training programme ends when the basic objectives as identified on the development-needs analysis (Figure 7.2) are achieved. By this stage the salesman should have a basic grounding in company and product knowledge and have achieved a level of skill in sales techniques. Formal refresher and continuation training should be planned from time to time to develop further his skills and to reinforce his approach to his job. Some firms plan a specific amount of time each year which will be spent by the sales force on such training. Normally, at least five days per annum are allotted for this purpose. This is not excessive when the developing technology of products, the changing promotional support programmes and the increasing sophistication of customers are considered. The refresher and continuation training programme must be supported by continuous field training, otherwise the enthusiasm and abilities developed by the courses will soon be dissipated by the attrition of customer contact.

Thus the necessary investment in training can be considerable and continuous and must be checked regularly to ensure it is productive.

One important result of the search to reduce the time and cost of training incurred by both trainers and trainees has been the development of "packaged" training especially on a self-learning basis. Many training packages are now available, the best of which are based on the latest developments in behavioural science and learning psychology. They normally consist of highly structured manuals supported by audio cassettes and visual material with built-in testing mechanisms so that the trainee can check his own progress. Their effectiveness is usually enhanced when they are supported by more traditional training sessions run by an experienced trainer particularly for interpersonal skills development. A good example of such a training package is "Creating Major Sales", which was developed from research which showed that a significant number of industrial product and service companies had no systematic day-to-day selling processes to build relationships with major customers leading to the clinching of large orders. Furthermore it was identified that salesmen generally lacked the skills to identify clearly enough major potential customers and the decision-making processes and personnel concerned. Sales management was found to be weak in the monitoring of major sales development and control of the sales staff concerned. The package was developed therefore to provide not only training for major account salesmen but also an integrated planning and control system for the salesmen and their managers.

The process of creating major sales is broken down into ten sequential stages from identifying opportunities to building continuing relationships after the sale. (See Figure 8.5.)

The basic "hardware" of the package consists of five self-learning manuals backed by audio-cassette case studies linked to an account handbook to be completed and used by the salesman on each of his major customers. There is also material to brief management on the programme's objective, content and method and an evaluation system for checking results. On a self-study basis, the whole training programme takes between eleven and sixteen hours, no stage taking longer than three to four hours. It is designed so that it can be studied a stage at a time with controls built in to ensure learning takes place. It is therefore much more cost-effective than traditional major account training especially for companies with large, widespread sales forces. Most important of all, companies using the package have found significant improvements in the planning, organisation, selling and control of major deals and thus increases in their results.

Packaged training of some kind is often the only cost-effective situation when large numbers of sales staff have to be trained (e.g. when companies wish to improve the selling abilities of their distributors' staff) or where the sales force is geographically widespread and the costs of bringing them together are prohibitive (e.g. international sales teams). It seems likely that training packages will continue to gain in popularity as they can offer productive albeit partial solutions to many companies' training problems leaving the trainer free to concentrate on skill development.

---

1   How to select major sales opportunities

2   How to analyse potential customers before contact

3   How to gain commitment of decision-makers to conduct a survey

4   How to identify and gain agreement on needs

5   How to develop a solution to his needs

6   How to cost-justify the solution

7   How to obtain agreement to the solution

8   How to prepare written proposals

9   How to present proposals and close the deal

10 How to build continuing business relationships

Fig. 8.5   Ten stages of "Creating Major Sales"

ACTION PLANNING CHECKLIST

Questions	Answers and action	Timing of action and evaluation
1 Are the ten major areas of sales knowledge included in the initial training programme?		
2 Is sufficient stress laid on the customer-orientation concept? (See Figure 8.1)		
3 Is the initial training programme planned correctly? (See Figure 8.2)		
4 Is sufficient emphasis laid on practice particularly role-playing?		
5 Have all major training methods been examined to ensure the best are used? (See Figure 8.3)		
6 Is the course planned to meet the specified objectives? (See Figure 8.4)		
7 Is there a systematic formal continuation and refresher training programmes?		

CHAPTER 9

How to Improve Sales Performance in the Field

When the newly trained man takes up his position in the field, the sales manager must provide for his continuous development. The standards of performance that he has learnt during his initial training must be consolidated and improved. This is one of the prime tasks of every first-line sales manager.

Unfortunately some supervisors seem to believe that an initial training is all that is required. This cannot be so because of the continuous attrition process that is caused by constant customer contact. It is certain that if no further training is given the salesman's performance will begin to decline. Some managers appear to feel that although field training is necessary for new salesmen, the experienced men, particularly those showing good results, need little or no help. Again, this is a fallacious view.

First, there is not always a positive correlation between experience and good performance and senior men should not be left alone simply because they have been selling for a number of years. Second, there are few good men who cannot be made even better by regular training. In fact, it can be argued that the field manager should spend relatively more of his time with his better men. It is usually easier to improve the results of a man who is already doing well than it is to increase even marginally the dismal performance of an employee who should probably never have been selected in the first place. Obviously something must be done about the below average performers but the manager should remember that his prime objective is producing results, and should allocate his precious time accordingly.

The two basic methods of developing field performance are field training, whereby the manager develops each salesman individually during his normal working day; and sales meetings, which are the regular gatherings of the sales team, either national or district, and provide a corporate training and motivational opportunity.

Field training

The objective of field training is continuously to improve the performance of the salesman so that his results become increasingly better. In order to achieve this goal there are five tasks that must be performed by the manager:

1 Field performance must be assessed systematically against known standards.
2 Deficiencies must be identified and agreed and coaching given in the knowledge and skills necessary to correct the identified faults.
3 Guidance must be given on the self-training that is expected from the salesman.
4 Information should be collected about common faults that can be more economically or effectively corrected on a corporate basis.
5 The effectiveness of the initial training should be assessed so that it can be improved in the future.

Assessment of field performance

In order to evaluate a salesman's performance in the field, the manager must have a set of standards against which it can be appraised. The job description should provide such criteria, particularly when the knowledge and skill requirements for each task have been identified. Equipped with these, the manager can accompany the salesman in the field and observe his performance with customers and prospects. Usually, this is on a monthly basis but varies according to the type and experience of the sales force.

Role of the manager during the sales interview

It is absolutely vital that the manager's presence has as little influence as possible on the course of the interview. This can be arranged by ensuring that a normal day's work is selected for observation. There is not much value in the manager watching the salesman deal with his favourite customers, or being taken to impossible prospects. When the manager and the salesman enter the buyer's office, the salesman should immediately take charge of the interview and make it clear that it is he who will handle the discussion. Where necessary, the manager can be introduced but that is all. The manager observes the whole presentation, resisting all temptations to interrupt or, worst of all, take over. Some managers argue that it is impossible to play such a passive role but a large number of managers perform precisely in this way every day. They realise that if they do enter the discussions and even perhaps favourably influence the buyer, they lose the opportunity to train the salesman. This is because the man will always believe that the manager's action pre-empted his own. As the salesman is alone on the vast majority of his calls, it is more important to improve his ability to cope with crises than for the manager to correct one or two unfavourable situations when he happens to be accompanying his representative. Obviously no manager could or should allow an important order to be lost while he passively observes. The possible gaining of a few orders, however, must be weighed against the critical loss of training opportunities. Some managers also find that buyers insist on making conversation with them, which again can make the interviews atypical. Faced with such customers, the manager should simply refer all comments and questions addressed to him back to the salesman. Another technique for dealing with this situation is for the manager to nod at the buyer's remarks and laugh at his jokes. The buyer often comments to the salesman on the next call that the manager is obviously a man of sound judgement with a good sense of humour!

Appraising the salesman's performance

After the interview the manager and the salesman adjourn to a quiet place, usually the car, where the manager can systematically record his assessment of the man's performance. These evaluations should be noted on a format such as the development-needs analysis (Figure 7.2) or on a specifically designed field appraisal form. Figures 9.1 and 9.2 show examples of forms used in consumer goods and industrial product

Salesman _____

Region _____

Ratings 1 Very good
        2 Above average
        3 Below average
        4 Unsatisfactory

Date	Product knowledge	Selling method	Work habits	Mental attitude	Development needs	General comments	Initials of appraiser	SM's comments
	Company	Merchandising	Car	Company	Mental attitude			
	Competitor	Closing	Planning	Promotion	Work habits			
		Objections	Administration	New ideas	Merchandising			
		Presentation	Sales aids		Sales			
		Approach	Industry		Product			
		Pre-approach						

Fig. 9.1 Salesman's field appraisal form – consumer products

	Good	Above average	Below average	Poor	Comments
Systems advisor ———————————— Date of call ———————————— Name of company ———————————— Type ———————————— (customer, prospect etc)					

	Good	Above average	Below average	Poor	Comments
1 Product knowledge					
(a) Company					
(b) Competitor					
2 Systems knowledge					
3 Sales methods					
(a) Preparation					
(c) Appearance					
(c) Opening					
(d) Presentation					
(e) Handling objections					
(f) Closing					
(g) Keeping initiative					
4 Work and time organisation					
5 Surveys					
(a) Content					
(b) Style					
6 General comments					
7 Recommendations (training, self-training, etc)					
8 Appraised by					

Fig. 9.2   Salesman's field appraisal form – industrial products

companies. It will be noted on these forms, as on all others described in this book, that there are an even number of rating categories. This is to avoid the danger of having an "average" classification, which is a judgement of little value when attempting to gauge the appropriate action. In fact the term "average" is mathematically very precise. The average number of children in British families is 2.2. There are therefore no average families. Unfortunately, however, the term "average" is generally used for blanket coverage of wide ranges of performance. It is far more valuable to judge a man to be above or below the norm, as this gives a clearer indication as to the action to be taken.

Kerbside conference

Having rated the salesman, the manager has to achieve agreement of the appraisal with the salesman and take action to correct the identified deficiencies. This process is embodied in what is often called the "kerbside conference" although it usually takes place in the car or at coffee or lunch-time. The structure of the discussion is absolutely vital to its success. A well-tested framework is:

1   The manager shows appreciation of the skills that have been well used by the salesman. Obviously praise should only be given where it can be offered sincerely. It is unusual, however, for a sales presentation to be so bad that the manager cannot find any aspects worthy of favourable comment. Starting in this way creates a balanced atmosphere, so that the salesman does not feel that he is under constant criticism.

2   The manager asks the salesman to analyse the sales interview and identify the facets which were not successfully handled. He helps the salesman by questioning him to probe the nature and causes of the faults.

3   If the salesman still cannot identify all the deficiencies even after the questioning, the manager must tell him. It must be recognised that to a degree the manager has failed if he has to make statements in this way. One of the basic objectives of field training is to develop further the salesman's self-perception. Obviously this facility is not fully developed if the manager has to inform the salesman of his shortcomings.

4   Once the deficiencies have been specified, the manager must ensure that the salesman fully accepts them. Otherwise he will not be motivated to correct them. It is for this vital reason that all efforts must be made to achieve self-analysis of faults by questioning. It is far more difficult to achieve real acceptance when the man cannot identify his own failure despite probing queries and the manager has been forced to inform him. A good approach to this stage is to ask the man to summarise the major errors he made in the interview.

5   The manager must now instruct and, where appropriate, rehearse the salesman in the action necessary to correct the deficiencies. There are several techniques available to the manager. He can describe to the salesman what he must do to avoid a particular difficulty, he can refer to the appropriate section of the initial training programme or training manual, or he can role-play with the salesman to attempt to strengthen a particular skill. The role-playing approach is especially valuable, not only for developing skill areas after the call, but also for rehearsing and preparing important interviews. As with any form of training, field training will be most effective when maximum participation and practice is encouraged.

6   Follow-up action should now be specified by the manager and the review periods laid down. The manager may decide that he himself will handle the next call so that the man can observe a particular technique in action. Alternatively, the manager might ask the salesman to adopt a certain type of approach on the following interview so that the manager can ascertain whether his instruction has been successful.

Longer-term actions should also be specified. The manager may request the salesman to study his product literature more deeply or to practise his closing techniques so that on the next field accompaniment he can check that progress has been made. It is important that emphasis is laid on the self-training that the man is expected to do. He should carry some responsibility for his own development and there is no reason why he cannot improve at least his product knowledge without constant supervision.

7 Finally, particularly with new salesmen, the manager should encourage the man by giving a balanced summary of the discussions, re-emphasising the strong points of the presentation. Because of the step-like shape of the typical learning curve, it can be demoralising for the man who is on a plateau between periods of improvement.

The "kerbside conference" will only be successful if the manager concentrates on specific deficiencies, identifies particular actions to be achieved within defined time periods and achieves maximum participation from the salesman. (See Figure 9.3.)

Much field training time is wasted because the manager is far too general in his analysis, vague in his instruction and lax in reviewing subsequent performance. Under such conditions performance seldom improves and can even decline.

The "kerbside conference" is not a lengthy procedure; the example shown in Figure 9.3, for instance, only takes four minutes. Yet it is one of the most powerful techniques available to the sales manager when it is skilfully used.

Wider aspects of field training

As well as being the fundamental method of improving the individual salesman's performance, the field training process helps to achieve three other goals.

First, it provides an evaluation of the achievement of the initial training programme. The manager can often identify deficiencies in the field resulting from design or implementation errors in preceding courses. He has a responsibility for advising the company's trainers so that the basic instruction fulfils field requirements. It is a constant complaint of training departments, particularly in large companies, that they are given far too little feedback by line management. Often, in the same company, field managers criticise the initial training programmes for being insufficiently related to the needs of the marketplace.

Second, in the analysis of the faults of the individual salesmen, the manager will often identify deficiencies that occur commonly among the sales force. From such information, corporate training can be included in the regular sales meetings that the manager holds. Where the training requirement is too complex and lengthy to be encompassed within such meetings, formal continuation or refresher training should be arranged.

Third, field training constitutes a major opportunity to evaluate the wider aspects of the sales operation. It provides data to help to assess the organisation structure and staffing of the sales operation. It might be that a continuous deficiency that is occupying much field training time is caused by faulty organisation or inappropriate staff. Instead of attempting to develop a particular set of skills by field training, it might be more effective to recruit a different type of individual or to divide the sales force so that each subsection requires only a limited range of techniques. For example, some consumer goods companies have found it more successful to split the field operation into separate selling and merchandising forces rather than attempt to develop both sets of skills in each individual by field training. Some industrial firms have taken similar views over the separation or integration of sales and technical support teams.

The discussion	Notes
Manager: Well, how do you think it went?	*Immediate involvement by questioning*
Salesman: Pretty well. I got the order, didn't I?	
M Yes, well done. That's the major objective, of course. But do you think it was the right order?	*Sincere praise. Manager beginning to probe*
S Well, I don't think he could have taken any more stock of the product. He doesn't have the space	
M What about our other products?	*Manager exposing limitations of call objective*
S I suppose I could have introduced one or two of the new quality lines. But the opportunity didn't arise	
M Is there anything that could have been done to create an opening?	*Showing that call could have been better prepared*
S Quite honestly I was so pleased with the order that I forgot about anything else	*Salesman admits that once he got the order he did not continue (very common mistake)*
M Perhaps if you had planned the call better, might you have built in a mention?	*Manager still questioning – identified call planning weakness*
S I suppose so. But in any case as you heard, the buyer says he has no space for any more products	
M Yes, what about that objection? Did you believe he meant that?	*Manager now probing second weakness*
S His shelves certainly looked full	*Salesman beginning to get defensive*
M But won't he have to stock somebody's quality line. Our research as you know shows that the market is trending that way. 20 per cent of the customers are now in this segment, aren't they?	*Manager identifying possible objection answer*
S Yes, I should have mentioned it. I guess what he really meant was that he's happy with his current supplier of that type of product	*Salesman shifting ground*
M Would you not have uncovered his real reason if you had pressed a little harder there?	
S I've never been very good at that kind of thing. It can only lead to an argument	*Salesman very defensive. This is the third different attempt to justify his failure to press the buyer*

Fig. 9.3   Typical "kerbside conference"

M	Not necessarily. Anyway we can come back to that later. Overall how would you summarise that interview?	*Manager at fault. Should have gently pursued until gained acceptance. He will now have to tell the salesman of the deficiency*
S	Well, on the good side, I got an order but I suppose with a bit better planning I could have got some of the new products in. But I don't know how if the man simply didn't have the space	*More balanced view than originally from salesman. Recognises his planning failure but still defensive over the space objection*
M	Well, let's take those two points of preparation and objection handling. First the basic aim of preparation is to ensure we have specific objectives for each call. This avoids the danger that the call might simply be a rambling conversation. From these defined targets which are derived from a study of the customer record card we can structure the whole interview – how to open, what to present in what order, what objections are likely and how to close. You probably remember we spent a lot of time on this on the initial training programme?	*Manager now instructs* *Links instruction back to initial training*
S	Yes, now you remind me – it's called structuring, isn't it?	*Salesman beginning to remember*
M	That's right. It makes sure we don't overlook opportunities simply because we've got an order for something. It also helps particularly in predicting objections. Knowing this buyer and knowing you wished to introduce new lines, could you not have forecast that he would object that he had no space?	*Back to the space objection. Manager still having to try and gain acceptance*
S	Yes, I suppose so. He's always moaning that he hasn't got enough room. And he gets upset if you push him	*Salesman still defensive*
M	Quite understandably. You must agree with him that his space is limited but you could have brought the research with you and shown him how the market is changing. Perhaps he would have realised then that he cannot afford to overlook this important group of customers. Also as the research was done by an independent agency, it is not you that he has to argue with. Remember – we called this the Third Party Reference or Testimonial technique?	*Manager instructing now. His points are perfectly valid but could lose impact because of failure to really identify nature of salesman's lack of skill*
S	That's right. But I didn't have the survey with me. I don't really understand this research business, you know. The boys and I have often said it baffles us	*At last, salesman admits he does not really understand the research*
M	Right, we will discuss the use of research surveys at the next sales meeting. But before that meeting, which is a week on Tuesday, I want you to read the latest survey and make sure you always have it with you. It contains many good sales points. Also I want you to re-read the training notes on preparation and objection handling techniques. In fact, it would be valuable if you could give a session at the meeting after next on "How I plan my calls." Pop in next time you are in the office and we will discuss it in more detail. Now for the next call, let's start practising some preparation. Get out your record card and let's see if we can set some specific goals. You did very well to get an order at all. You can do even better next time and get a bigger one	*Manager specifies action and time periods. Note linking of field training to sales meetings as research problem probably common in sales force. Manager should also note for possible inclusion in initial training. Self-training specified and linked to action.* *Delegation but with accountability. Training continues on call preparation. Probably to be followed by rehearsal and role-playing of handling space objection.* *Final words of encouragement*

Fig. 9.3 *(continued)*

Sales meetings

The regular gatherings of the sales team create the other major opportunity for developing sales force performance. In all but the smallest sales forces, these are held at local level, where the regional, area or district manager meets with his salesmen. Where there are no intermediate supervisory levels between the national sales manager and the sales force, these gatherings have to be held on a national basis.

Objectives and planning

The objectives of such meetings should be:

1   To administer corporate training and development.
2   To inform and get feedback from the sales force.
3   To stimulate and if necessary rekindle the salesmen's enthusiasm and motivation.
4   To provide a meeting place and forum for all the salesmen.

Their importance should not be underestimated. A sales force by its nature is usually geographically dispersed. Although the manager might see each individual regularly, he only sees his men as a team on such occasions. Each salesman is unlikely ever to meet all his colleagues except at sales meetings, training programmes, conferences and so on; and he probably sees very few regularly, particularly if he is in a distant territory.

It is unfortunate, therefore, that so many sales meetings are badly prepared, deal only with administrative matters and are regarded as a complete waste of time by the salesmen, whom they are supposed to help.

To be successful, the manager must recognise the importance of the meeting and schedule it accordingly. The normal frequency for such meetings is about once a month. This again varies according to the nature of the trade, the spread of the sales force and the amount of material to be covered. Certainly a manager would be very foolish to run a meeting where there was very little to cover simply because it was four weeks since the last one. On the other hand, a manager is certainly neglecting his duty when he allows months or, in some cases, even years to elapse between meetings. In most well-organised companies it is possible not only to hold regular valuable meetings but also to schedule the dates well in advance, often up to a year ahead, thus emphasising their importance and allowing plenty of time for preparation. The length of each meeting will vary according to content. Most successful companies take between half a day and a whole day. It is often not worth while assembling the salesmen for a shorter period. The sales manager must prepare his meetings carefully and run them skilfully if they are to be successful. There are five basic elements that he must organise:

1   The location.
2   The audience.
3   The agenda.
4   The activities.
5   The chairmanship.

Location

The environment of a meeting can be critical to its success. The room itself should be large enough to accommodate tables and chairs for all attending. It should be well-lit and ventilated and possess the necessary electrical sockets, window blackouts and so on to enable the desired activities to be carried out. If there are windows or low lights, care must be taken to ensure that these do not dazzle the delegates; if forced to choose, the speaker not the audience should face the window. The room should be laid out according to the nature of the activities. If these are largely of a lecture/discussion type, a classroom style is best. All the audience then face the speaker without sitting awkwardly and the members do not distract each other. If a full discussion is intended, a round table or horseshoe layout is preferable so that each member can readily see and talk to his colleagues. Ample space should be provided for writing, storage of papers, etc.

If suitable offices are not available, a room should be hired locally. The additional cost, which is usually only a few pounds, is more than offset by the impact of surroundings conducive to a fruitful exchange.

Audience

The size and nature of the audience will determine to a degree the activities that can be undertaken. For example it is difficult to run successful role-playing sessions with video-tape playback with more than about six to eight salesmen. With a greater number, boredom rapidly sets in as interminable interviews take place before each individual has his turn. The levels of intelligence, education and experience of the salesmen attending will also affect the type of activity. It is dangerous to use participative exercises where there is a correlation between success and intelligence with a sales team consisting of junior but very bright men and senior, but less well-educated representatives. The motivational effect can be the reverse of what is planned if the experienced men feel they are being made to look foolish. Likewise, in meetings where there are significant differences in status and job level, subjects must be chosen carefully. At regional meetings of district managers, field supervisors and salesmen, it might be difficult to stimulate full and frank discussions. The managers, particularly the more junior ones, may fear exposing themselves in front of their subordinates; the salesmen may be nervous of being too honest in front of their superiors, especially with the regional manager present.

Agenda

Every meeting should have an agenda so that everybody knows what is to be discussed, preferably within what time limits. The agenda should be carefully planned to ensure that variety and interest are maintained and that the meeting rises to its peak at the end instead of tailing away. If administrative matters have to be covered, or the salesmen want to air complaints on, for example, product quality or deliveries, it is wise to allot a specific time for these at the beginning. They can thus be cleared before the more important aspects of training and development are tackled. For the same reasons it is often better to cover the "any other business" section at the beginning rather than the end of the meeting. Such a period, however, is usually unnecessary if, as should happen, the agenda is circulated well in advance so that every salesman has a chance to register topics of interest.

If possible a theme should be found for the meeting to give it coherence. Even when a variety of topics are being discussed, such as market research, results to date, closing techniques and product knowledge, their impact will be enhanced if they can be integrated by themes such as "Selling in the 80s," "The Salesman as a Marketing Man" or "Professionalism in Selling." Obviously nothing is gained by using such titles spuriously but if the appropriate aspects of each session emphasise the theme of the meeting the total impression left in the minds of the delegates will be strengthened.

Activities

These need the most careful thought of all. Obviously the type of presentation that can be used will in some cases be limited by the objectives and material of the session. However, the manager must recognise that he faces the same problem at his regular meetings as his salesmen do with regular customers. It becomes increasingly difficult to gain attention and maintain interest. Similar solutions apply in both cases, too. The more participative and visual the presentation can be made the more impact it will have. .

Therefore the manager should use a little creative thought and avoid the standard format of so many meetings, which is that the manager spends most of the time talking to his men, often with little or no impact. Where new information has to be imparted or new policies explained, the normal lecture/discussion approach may have to be used. This can be strengthened by inviting other members of the company or even outsiders to make presentations to the group and ensuring that such sessions are well supported with visual aids. Charts, slides, felt boards, magnetic boards, overhead projectors, models, epidiascopes are all useful and generally readily available. Of all of these the overhead projector is worthy of special mention. Slides can be prepared for it, it can be written on during a session, it operates in daylight and the speaker while operating it faces the audience. No other aid combines all these advantages and it adds interest and professionalism to virtually any presentation.

There are many participative techniques that the manager can use to add variety and impact to his meetings. Case studies and role-playing, particularly with sound or video-tape playback, have been discussed earlier in the chapters on training. Short talks from the salesmen on aspects of their jobs are particularly useful to strengthen the individual in public speaking and to disseminate successful sales techniques. The briefing for such sessions should stress that the salesman should discuss, for example, how he himself closes sales not closing techniques generally. This encourages him to analyse his own performance rather than simply to repeat a section of the notes from his initial training course. It is surprising how often in these short talks (usually only ten to fifteen minutes long) the speaker mentions a particular approach or method that he has developed and used effectively which has not occurred to any other member of the force.

The constant reinforcement and development of product knowledge, although necessary, can be boring if tackled by traditional methods. One highly stimulating approach is to run a quiz. This is done by dividing the salesmen into two teams, each asking questions of the other on particular aspects of product detail. The manager acts as chairman and scorer and the losing team buys drinks for the winners! The advantages of this approach are that in order to prepare the questions to be asked and answered each team must study the products intensively. Second, a man working in a team will often strive harder than for himself, as he will not want to fail his colleagues. Third, it is a totally participative exercise where both questions and answers are set by the salesmen, thus involving them and saving the manager's time. Fourth, the quiz format is different from the normal run of meetings and creates an interesting and competitive situation.

For the more lengthy study of products or markets, the individual project approach has been used successfully in many companies. Here the manager and the men together analyse their expertise deficiencies and allocate a section of the business to each man to study. For example, in a transport firm, the sales force were concerned to develop their knowledge of their various markets and identified a number of areas for research. One aspect was the particular transportation problems of sand and gravel, and the salesman covering the Leighton Buzzard area, the centre of the industry, volunteered to examine it in depth. Each man then, in his own time, researched his subject, visiting customers, industry experts, libraries and so on and prepared a report, which he presented to his colleagues at a sales meeting. The motivational influence on each individual was very strong as he became fascinated by his subject. From the company's point of view, the market knowledge of the sales force increased generally and each man developed a particular expertise which could be used in appropriate situations.

General facilities	Room	Delegate requirements	Agenda
Location Overnight accommodation Eating arrangements Charging and invoicing arrangements Telephones Cloakrooms Lavatories Message handling	Size Layout Chairs Tables Lighting Ventilation Electrical sockets Window blinds Ashtrays: Water and glasses Microphone	Notepaper Binders Pencils Rubbers Name badges *Refreshments* Morning coffee Lunch Afternoon tea	Items requested Theme Finalised Circulated *Audience* Selected Notified Briefed Visitors

PROGRAMME

Session objectives	Content	Method	Visual aids	Hand-outs	Timing	Speaker	Chairman
Example: to increase knowledge of research technique; to improve ability in use of research in selling	Definition of market research Basic methods Interpreting surveys	Lecture/discussion	Overhead projector with prepared slides	Session notes Copy of latest survey	90 minutes	Market research manager	Sales manager
Example: improve objection-handling skill	Résumé of techniques practice	Film Role-playing	16 mm projector and screen	Notes on major techniques with examples	Film – 30 minutes Discussion – 30 minutes Role-playing – 60 minutes	Sales manager	

Notes: Notify salesmen to read survey before meeting
Ask training department to advise on best film available on objection handling

Fig. 9.4 Sales meeting planning form

Chairmanship

The success of any meeting is largely dependent on the quality of the chairman. If the manager takes the chair he must professionally execute his duties. These include keeping the meeting to time, not allowing interruptions or digressions, controlling discussions, ensuring that all who wish to can contribute, summarising points and registering action to be taken.

It is useful to allow members of the sales force to take the chair from time to time. It is an opportunity to develop and test their management potential and again underlines the point that it is their meeting.

Conclusion

Sales meetings can easily fail and many unfortunately do. However, if the sales manager recognises their importance, plans them carefully and runs them creatively and skilfully, they can provide an excellent training opportunity. (See Figure 9.4.) Moreover, they act as a major motivational influence and an occasion when the manager can sell company policies and himself to his team. The key to success is participation. It is the salesmen's only regular opportunity to meet. Every manager should remember the story of the salesman whose wife asked him when he arrived home whether he had enjoyed the sales meeting. He replied: "It was a very good meeting – I spoke."

ACTION PLANNING CHECKLIST

Questions	Answers and action	Timing of action and evaluation
1 Have standards of field performance been identified?		
2 Is each salesman regularly and systematically assessed against these standards? (See Figures 9.1 and 9.2)		
3 Is there a structure for the kerbside conference? (See Figure 9.3)		
4 Is the field training process linked to the other training activities of the company?		
5 Are sales meetings held regularly?		
6 Are they carefully planned? (See Figure 9.4)		
7 What objectives do they achieve? What should they achieve?		
8 Is a sufficient variety of activities used?		
9 Do sales meetings act as a motivational influence?		

CHAPTER 10

How to Motivate the Sales Force I: Financial Incentives

The motivation of salesmen is probably the most common topic of conversation whenever sales managers meet. Every manager has his own pet theories on how to get the best out of men. The reason why it is such a popular discussion point is because salesmen can be directly supervised only intermittently. It is therefore vital to success that they are deeply motivated to work on their own. Moreover, the nature of the sales job inevitably involves loneliness and certain customer contacts which can depress the morale of any but the most enthusiastic salesman.

Nature of motivation

Because of the geographical separation and the wearing aspects of the job, it is vital for success that the sales manager possesses or develops the ability to motivate his men. In order to do so he needs a clear understanding of why people work and what they wish to gain from their work. Only then can he create an environment which will cause his men to employ their full abilities in their jobs.

He must also recognise the difference between motivation and manipulation. If he treats his men as some kind of mechanical devices who will automatically react to given stimuli, as a puppet reacts to the pulling of its strings, he will inevitably create vast problems for himself. He must at all times remember that he is dealing with human beings, whose motivational patterns are excessively complex and who react emotionally as well as physically. Thus, although the cynical manipulation of a man's needs might, in the short term, cause a defined reaction, it will be recognised as such by the man concerned, who will resent being so treated.

Perhaps many of the industrial relations problems spring from this mechanistic concept. For years workers on the shop floor were regarded as units of manufacturing whose output of production was directly geared to the input of wages. Despite substantial pay rises, however, production is increasingly disrupted by strikes, working to rule, and so on; and it does seem that such oversimplified views of why people work are neither valid nor successful in practice.

Of course it is rare for a sales force to go on strike although increasing numbers are becoming unionised. They have no need to take such obvious action even when they deeply object to the way they are treated. Because they are not under close supervision, it is simple for them to avoid working hard at least until their results begin to reflect their lack of effort. To prevent such situations, the sales manager must develop a far more sophisticated view of the nature of motivation than simple beliefs that all that men want is more money or a kick up the pants. In certain circumstances such actions may be correct but they are unlikely to be total solutions.

Incentives and disincentives

The process of motivation is the provision of incentives which encourage salesmen to give of their best and the removal of disincentives which prevent them from devoting their whole energies to their work. Unfortunately, far too often, motivation is equated with incentives only, although it is common to find that the elimination of disincentives – for example, injustices, unfair treatment – is the more powerful influence.

It must also be recognised that virtually every incentive brings with it a disincentive, either for the same person or for his colleagues. For example, while a commission system may provide a strong incentive for a salesman, it may also be a disincentive for him if he feels the payments are unfairly calculated. Likewise, a competition may be a strong motivator for the winners; but it can be demoralising for the losers, particularly if they believe that because of the construction of the contest they never had a real chance of winning.

The task of the manager is therefore to consider the needs of his men, both individually and as a group and arrange a balance of motivational influences that will encourage them to achieve the company's objectives. In essence, this is best done by ensuring that the individual's own goals in life are consistent with the aims of the firm. For example, there is little point recruiting men who are highly money-motivated into a company which offers security as its major satisfaction. Similarly, if the company pays commission as a standard percentage of all turnover achieved, it can hardly complain when the salesmen concentrate on those products which are easiest to sell in volume although they may be the least profitable.

Perhaps the most amusing contradiction is the manager who bemoans the decline of company loyalty as a motivational influence while regularly poaching salesmen from his competitors.

Although recognising that each man has his own individual need pattern, there are five major motivational influences that the sales manager must fully understand. These are:

1 Remuneration.
2 Direct incentives.
3 Job satisfaction.
4 Security.
5 Status.

Remuneration

The most common question raised in the lengthy discussions on motivation is what and how to pay salesmen. Many managers believe that if only they could construct the "right" remuneration scheme, all their motivational problems would be solved. Others feel that pay is unimportant in relation to the other incentives of the job. Sometimes it is difficult to separate remuneration from some of the other influences; for example, a man's ability to satisfy his status or security needs may depend largely on his financial position. Money is important but it is not as overwhelmingly important as is generally supposed.

Conditions when pay is vital

There are, however, three situations in which pay is vital. First, when the remuneration level is below subsistence standard. This is very rare in the UK, particularly in sales jobs; it does however occur in some parts of the world. In such circumstances all the man's attention will be focused on getting more money simply to survive. Second, and far more common, pay is a critical factor when it is below the man's established standard of living. Every man needs a certain level of income to support his living standards. These levels vary, of course, from individual to individual. One man may be happy on £5000 a year, another unable to maintain his customary standards on £10 000 a year. If a man finds himself with regular commitments of, say, a mortgage, school fees and hire-purchase repayments which are near or beyond his income level, he will become obsessed with the financial aspects of his job. It is therefore most important that such relationships are identified at the selection stage whenever possible.

It will usually create motivational problems if a man is employed whose habitual living standard demands an income higher than he can reasonably expect to earn with this company even though he is willing to accept the job at the time. In fact one or two companies use this type of situation to force the salesmen to work harder. In such firms the management deliberately encourages the salesman to spend beyond their means so that they have to earn more by selling more. The most devious form of such manipulation is the sales competition where the prize is the deposit on a yacht or large car! Thus the winner is encouraged to even greater efforts in order to maintain the rest of the payments. Such managerial practices must be frowned upon as representing a most cynical view of staff motivation and they are likely to lead to a rapid deterioration of relationships.

The third situation in which pay is vital is when it is seen or believed to be unfair. Nothing causes more resentment among a sales force than when salesman *A* is paid considerably more than salesman *B* for reasons other than merit. Such situations arise when increments are given not to those who deserve them but to those who complain most or when new men are employed at higher levels of salary than existing staff simply because the current personnel to a degree are insulated from their true market value. Such unfair discrepancies in levels of remuneration create strong disincentives. One of the commonest factors that staff identify in bad management is that of unequal treatment, particularly in terms of pay.

Setting salary levels

The best way to avoid the above situations is to ensure that the remuneration structure is based upon established principles of salary administration. First, management should define the salary grades appropriate to the job level. This grade will represent the market value of the position as well as the worth of the job to the company. The bottom of the category will represent the remuneration of a man entering the position exhibiting minimum standards of performance, the upper limit being paid to a man who can achieve completely all the criteria of the job.

Second, the position of any individual within his grade should be determined by his performance against the job standards. An average performer would therefore be paid at the mid-point of the grade. Such a system prevents management from being tempted to make special arrangements with particular individuals. Justice will be seen to be done even further if the salary grades are published and each man's performance is systematically appraised at least annually to determine his position within his category. The concepts and techniques described in Chapters 5 and 6 for the recruitment and selection of new men can be readily modified to form an assessment system for existing personnel. Thus, the basic salary philosophy will reflect the two major bases of a logical payment structure; the degree of responsibility carried by the position, and the effectiveness with which the man discharges it.

Payment-by-results system

Such an approach to job grading and man appraisal presupposes that the salesmen will be remunerated at least in part by salary. Many sales forces are of course paid in addition to some degree or another on results. In a relatively small number of companies the salesmen are paid entirely by commission. The choice of remuneration system, salary only, salary plus some form of commission, or commission only will depend upon the desired mix of security and incentive. The greater the percentage of remuneration that is guaranteed as a salary, the greater the security offered. Moreover, it is generally easier to recruit, train and control sales forces paid in this way. It is hard to find men who are prepared to work on a payment-by-results basis only and when such men are employed, managerial control is difficult as any time that they are removed from their sales work for conferences, training programmes and the rest literally costs them money. Moreover, it is difficult to ensure that commission-only men perform those tasks, such as customer servicing, which do not directly generate orders. On the other hand, if these problems can be overcome, paying salesmen entirely by results is a tempting method for management. Not only does it ensure that the sales force is self-motivating to a large degree but it also maintains a direct relationship between sales volume and cost. Thus, if revenue declines so does sales force expenditure. (See Figure 10.1.)

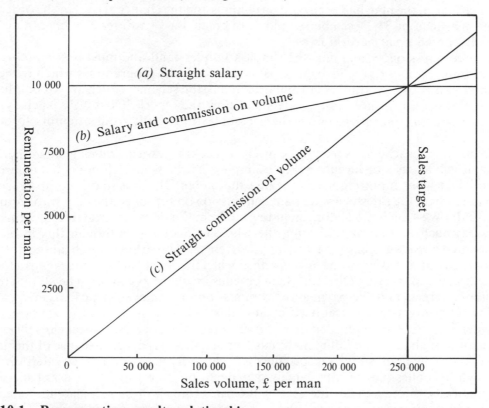

Fig. 10.1 Remuneration–results relationships

Assuming sales target of £250 000 is achieved precisely, remuneration costs of all three systems exactly the same, that is £10 000. If sales target is under-achieved by 20% (that is £200 000) remuneration costs differ as follows): a) £10,000, b) £9500, c) £8000. If sales target is over-achieved by 20% (that is £300,000) then sales costs are: a) £10,000, b) £10 500, c) £12 000. Only in (c) does the volume remuneration relationship remain constant despite differing volume levels

Most companies find that a balance of salary and commission is the best compromise. Usually the relationship is that about two thirds of the total remuneration is salary, the remainder is some system of payment by results. It is not always possible, however, to pay commission.

Preconditions for successful payment-by-results systems. Usually, there are five conditions which must be satisfied.

1   The sales results from a territory must be directly related to the salesman's efforts. If there are overriding factors, such as heavy promotional expenditure or production shortages, which influence the sales level more than the man's work and which are totally beyond his control, it is difficult to remunerate him by commission. It could well be that in a particular period sales may be vastly inflated or deflated by these other elements, which would influence his earnings out of all proportion to his individual effectiveness or lack of it.

2   The sales results from a territory must be related to the *individual* efforts of the salesmen. In many industrial situations, for example, building materials, a sale to a local authority in Lancashire may result from one salesman calling on an architect in London, another persuading the contractor in Norwich and the third influencing the local authority who actually places the order. In such circumstances, it is difficult if not impossible to split fairly the commission between the three men concerned.

3   The number of orders received for each territory must be high, otherwise the coincidental timing of a single order may affect the man's earnings out of all proportion. For example, in one capital equipment company, the sales target was one machine per man per year. If the man had been paid on commission the chance arrival of the order on 1 January instead of 31 December would have created a vast difference in earnings and possibly caused great hardship.

4   The commission system must be simple to understand and must be seen to be fair. Some companies, in trying to arrange payment-by-results programmes which reflect the complex nature of their trading, formulate commission schemes which are so complicated that the salesmen do not really understand how they work. Obviously, such systems cannot act as an incentive. Often these complexities result from attempts to ensure fairness.

Again, when a scheme is seen to be unjust because it rewards on elements other than effort, it will act as a disincentive. For example, territories are seldom equal in terms of potential or work input required to realise that potential. Thus in one company selling garments where the salesmen were paid commission on turnover, the man who happened to have the West End of London, including all the major departmental stores, earned five times as much as the man covering the whole of Scotland, although this in no way represented a real difference in effort or effectiveness. It is perhaps significant to note that this patently unjust system was only changed when the West End salesman began to earn more than the Marketing Director! Such obvious inequalities can often be eliminated by the use of targets and the payment of commission on achievement of target.

However, target-setting can itself create injustices, as it is difficult to set targets for every territory that are equivalent in effort required. Moreover, injustices can still exist in companies, such as the building materials firm mentioned earlier. Because of the nature of the trade, the man calling on specifiers will generally receive very few orders directly, although his colleagues may be largely dependent on his efforts. If he is not successful automatically the success of the rest of the sales force will be seriously inhibited. To arrange fair commissions in such circumstances is extremely difficult.

5   The commission earned must be paid as soon as possible after the effort is made to generate it. The longer the lead time between the sales activity and the payment on the results, the less the incentive. Thus, annual bonuses do not really constitute direct incentives. Although they may be related to the sales performance of the man throughout the year, they will not act as a conscious spur to make that extra call on a wet Monday in February.

If payment by results is to work as a motivational influence, the salesman must feel that the efforts of today will be directly rewarded in the very near future.

Effectiveness of different payment-by-results systems. Despite the difficulties of constructing effective fair payment-by-results schemes, it is still worth while trying to do so. Although little research has been conducted into the relationship between payment schemes and results, the findings that do exist demonstrate clearly that salesmen paid at least in part by commission tend to generate far more volume and profit for their companies than men paid by salary alone. This, of course, might be due to some extent to the fact that different payment systems will attract different types of individual.

Nevertheless, the conclusions of one piece of unpublished American research did show clear profit advantages to the company in paying salary and commission on turnover, as opposed to any other form of remuneration system. This survey is particularly interesting, as it covered salesmen employed in construction equipment dealerships who were selling very similar and, in some cases, exactly the same products. It was therefore possible to compare the sales results and payment systems without too many other variables confusing the picture. Another significant conclusion that emerged was that the range of total remuneration was such that the highest paid salesmen in the industry received about three times as much money as the lowest paid. However, these highly remunerated men sold on average about five times as much as the lowest paid. Furthermore, the highest sales expense, sales ratios, were exhibited by the lowest paid salesmen. These two facts confirm that it is more economic to pay highly for good men than to pay little for poor performers.

Remuneration and its effect on motivation is a vast and complex subject. Little research has been done, particularly in Britain, into the effects of different forms of payment systems. Nevertheless, certain principles can be identified.

1 That pay, although important, is certainly not the only and may not be the prime motivational influence.
2 That most companies will have to pay at least in part by salary and that salaries should depend upon an assessment of the grade for the job and an appraisal of the man in order to position him within the grade.
3 That where it is possible to pay in part by results, this will have a beneficial effect and lead to the achievement of better sales results; but that in order to administer commission schemes successfully, certain preconditions must be met.
4 That the most likely form of commission system to be most effective is payment on the basis of turnover, probably because it is the easiest to understand.

Direct incentives

This term is used to cover all the many systems of payment in cash or in kind other than basic remuneration. It includes fringe benefits, merchandise awards, points schemes and competitions. Apart from fringe benefits, such schemes do not usually make a significant difference to the man's total earnings and their basic intention is motivational.

Fringe benefits

Fringe benefits include pension plans, life assurance, private medical care, school fees, etc. The majority of such schemes aim to enhance the man's security by providing for his old age, ill health and family. Although they are important motivations when a man is selecting a job and certainly help to keep him tied to a particular company, it is doubtful whether they operate as a day-to-day incentive. Moreover, there is a limit to the fringe benefits that can be offered and there is nowadays little to choose between most companies, particularly large ones. Perhaps the major contribution of fringe benefits is to avoid the creation of disincentives, such as worry about retirement.

Payment-in-kind schemes

Merchandise awards and other forms of payment in kind are particularly attractive because the winning of a suite of furniture or a holiday is likely to be remembered longer, as it continues to exist as a physical reminder. The equivalent amount of cash is likely to be swallowed up in the general expenditure of the man and his family.

A devious approach by some companies operating such schemes is to ensure that the man's wife knows the kind of awards that can be won. This is achieved by sending the catalogue to his home address, sometimes addressed personally to his wife. The theory is that she will decide that she would like a mink coat or that the family needs some new garden equipment and will "encourage" her husband to greater efforts to acquire these desirable items.

It has never been shown that such approaches stimulate universally good responses. Some salesmen, and their wives, object violently to what they regard as intrusion into their privacy. It is probably wiser simply to give the catalogue to the salesman. In any case the majority will undoubtedly discuss it with their wives.

Operating a merchandise award scheme

The normal method of operating merchandise award schemes is for the company to employ a firm which specialises in this activity. Jointly, they prepare sales targets and allot a points goal to each sales objective. Thus a company might decide that every unit of product *A* sold within the period of the scheme is worth ten points. The specialist firm provides a brochure of products which normally they have bought in bulk, not unlike a small mail order house catalogue but instead of each item being priced in money terms, it has a points value. Thus a refrigerator might cost 3000 points. The salesman can then easily calculate that if he sells 300 units of product *A* he can obtain the refrigerator.

Of course merchandise awards can be given by the company itself for achievement of targets or as prizes in a contest. The advantage of a points scheme, however, is that all the salesmen can usually amass enough points to gain at least some award. As there are no winners or losers as such, it operates as an incentive for everybody.

Competitions, sales force "league tables," "salesman of the year" awards all have the common disadvantage that only one or, at most, a few members of the force will win. This can demoralise the losers, particularly if the structure of the contests does not give absolutely equal opportunities. It is very difficult to ensure that such schemes are fair to all the salesmen. In practice it is often rapidly obvious who will win and at that point the incentive for the majority is destroyed.

Use of direct incentives

Merchandise awards and competitive schemes are best used to focus short-term attention on particular aspects of the business. They are a tactical rather than a strategic motivational weapon. When employed in this way, they can be very effective to concentrate sales force attention on, for example, gaining new accounts, increasing sales of lower volume products, or even submitting call reports on time.

ACTION PLANNING CHECKLIST

Questions	Answers and action	Timing of action and evaluation
1 Is it known why men wish to join and remain with the company?		
2 Has any study been made of the disincentives of the job?		
3 Is the remuneration system logically and fairly based on job grading and personnel appraisal?		
4 If there is a payment by results scheme does it satisfy the five essential preconditions?		
5 Has any check been made to evaluate the motivational effectiveness of the remuneration structure?		
6 Does the remuneration structure motivate the sales force to achieve company objectives?		
7 Can direct incentives be used more effectively particularly as a tactical weapon?		
8 Is there a long-term plan of financial and direct incentives so that the motivation is continuous?		

CHAPTER 11

How to Motivate the Sales Force II: Job Satisfaction

Direct incentives in either cash or kind are important elements in any motivational scheme. The so-called "psychic wages" of the job however must be given at least equivalent priority. Salesmen spend more than half their waking life working. It is not surprising therefore that they seek fulfilment in the job as well as rewards for the job. It is a fundamental function of any manager to ensure such satisfactions can be gained by the sales force from their work.

Job satisfaction

In most surveys of salesmen's attitudes job satisfaction is rated as the highest motivating influence. It certainly does appear that in an affluent society, where at this level, at least, there is little or no unemployment, the major reason a salesman chooses and remains in a company is because he finds his work enjoyable and fulfilling. It is therefore, at least in part, the responsibility of the manager to create a satisfying environment.

As was mentioned earlier, however, each man has his own particular need pattern and therefore what constitutes job satisfaction will vary from individual to individual. Some men enjoy achieving perfection in the detail of their work, others are motivated by the opportunities of working with a wide cross-section of people. Many different satisfactions can be gained from similar jobs and the manager should emphasise particular aspects for each individual. Likewise, what one salesman finds enjoyable, another dislikes. Again, the incentive–disincentive equation has to be handled with some care by management.

Although there are individual differences in concepts of job satisfaction, some common elements exist which form the basic framework of worthwhile and satisfying sales positions.

Social worth of selling

For any man to gain satisfaction from his career he must believe that it is a worth-while pursuit. The problem of selling is that society at large still seems to hold the view that it is not a desirable endeavour. This stigma appears to spring from several different sources. For many years classical economic theory held that as the sales activity did not add any value to the product it was thus uneconomic. It was even regarded by some academics as "the carbuncle on the neck of industry." Moreover, the historical origins of selling can be traced to the pedlars and travellers of the eighteenth and nineteenth centuries, who were viewed, probably rightly, as rogues, although they performed an essential service of goods distribution. Today, the salesman is still often stereotyped as a glib talker who persuades unwilling customers to buy products they do not want with money they cannot afford. Perhaps a deeper and more significant reason for the social distaste for selling in Britain is that the work of the salesman contravenes many of the value standards of reserve and understatement that still exist and are admired in this country.

However much sales management may protest about the status of selling or pretend that the stigma is disappearing, their actions reveal the truth of the situation. For example, very few salesmen are actually called "salesmen." A whole new nomenclature has been invented, ranging from representative through technical advisor to the extreme of regional sales director. An engineer, however, is still called an engineer.

Sales management must appreciate the nature of the problem and realise that as salesmen are members of society, they too will question, albeit secretly, whether a life spent selling soap powder is a life well spent. Moreover, the sales manager should be able to recognise that the answer to such a question is emphatically affirmative. One of the major contributions that can be made to the basic job satisfaction of any salesman is to explain to him his vital role not only in business but in society as a whole.

A democratic society depends for its survival upon the ability of its members to choose between alternative courses of action. In order to make good decisions, the members must be presented with all possible information about each alternative. The basic system of disseminating facts that has evolved in society is the granting to the proponents of each alternative the right to put forward their case as strongly, as competitively and as persuasively as possible. Having examined the conflicting presentations, the members of the society can then decide. Thus the legal system is based upon each side of a case being argued as convincingly as possible by prosecution and defence counsels. Having heard all the reasons for and against, the jury is in the best position to decide.

An analogous situation exists in business. Competition is preserved by law, so that the consumer has the choice between two or more alternatives. In order to exercise that choice meaningfully, the customer must be presented with information on which to base it. The buyer is given the necessary data by granting the right to each supplier to argue his case as best he can. One of the major forms of such presentations is, of course, the sales function.

The salesman therefore performs a basic and vital social task. If he fails in this duty, he not only fails himself and his company but also, and more important, he weakens the whole fabric of the social structure. Such high responsibilities should be enough to make any salesman feel a sales career worthwhile. The tragedy is that far too few salesmen understand these social duties and even fewer managers ever bother to explain them. When the sales manager takes the time to develop rationales such as this and discusses them with his men, the effect on motivation can be considerable.

The worthiness of a job is a major incentive to those who perform it. In fact, it is evident that when people feel that a particular task is really worth performing they need no other incentives. Their motivation will be so high that even personal danger or discomfort will not deter them. No one ever talks about designing commission systems for revolutionaries, or running competitions for civil rights demonstrators. Because of the power of self-motivation, when a man is not devoting his full energies to his work, the question the manager should ask himself is not "What can be done to make him perform?" but "What is it that is preventing him from working?"

Need for goals and results

Another major element of job satisfaction is the need for salesmen to feel that they are moving purposefully towards goals. This presupposes, of course, that clear and challenging targets have been defined. Research demonstrates that man is an objective-orientated animal. He works most efficiently when he has a precise idea of what he wishes to achieve. If the sales manager can continuously set specific aims to be reached within specific time periods, this will enhance job satisfaction and thus motivation. However, for a goals system to work most effectively it must be complemented by the continuous relaying of results so that those concerned can evaluate their progress. Most sales forces work towards some system of sales targets and certainly these help fulfil the requirement for clear objectives. If these can be amplified to include other aims such as call rates and new business targets, the sales force will be even more highly motivated. Results must be given at frequent intervals so that each man can see how he is progressing and the very act of being able to evaluate his progress will help him improve his performance. Conversely, when results are not made available, frustration will build up and disincentives will be created.

Motivational effect of training

Job satisfaction will be further heightened by the training programmes. One of the basic effects of initial courses is that they make the salesmen realise that there is a body of knowledge and skill to be assimilated. This in itself makes any job more worth while. As the training progresses it is apparent that the learning process has a profound motivational influence. Any experienced trainer is well aware of this situation. It is common to find on a well-conducted programme, men forgoing all leisure time in order to study and discuss the course material. Usually they have to be prevented from staying up half the night. (In one extreme case, a salesman, totally of his own volition, preferred to forgo his honeymoon in order to attend a refresher course!) Yet the direct rewards of such efforts are small. There is no immediate financial incentive, no competitions to be won. If only part of this motivational atmosphere can be transferred to the work situation, the sales manager has little difficulty in achieving results.

Job satisfaction for some salesmen is constituted by the achievement of increasingly higher levels of responsibility. Ambition to progress is certainly a strong motivational influence with many men and overrides all other considerations. It is dangerous to assume, however, that all salesmen are ambitious, although the value standards of society tend to denigrate those people who do not at least profess to desire higher positions. The structure of most sales organisations is such that promotion implies a change not simply in the scale of responsibility but also in its nature. Thus an ambitious, successful salesman when promoted has to work at a level where a totally different range of skills must be used, and where the application of his expertise as a salesman might be lost to the company.

From a managerial viewpoint, therefore, it is essential that promotability is judged on the fitness of the man to perform his new tasks rather than simply on his success in his current position. Remember that the best salesman often makes the worst manager. As the two jobs differ fundamentally in nature, there is no reason why good salesmen should make good managers.

Some companies have dealt with the problem of ambitious, successful salesmen who are unqualified for managerial positions by reorganising the structure so that they can shoulder higher sales responsibilities without any administrative burdens. In effect, these firms have created two promotion ladders. One is the normal progression to management (Figure 11.1*a*); the other enables successful salesmen to be promoted to positions where their sales expertise can be more profitably employed (Figure 11.1*b*). Their salaries and status must obviously reflect their increased responsibility. Having twin promotion systems confers major advantages on the firm, as it provides a means of recognising and handling the customer hierarchy. (See Chapter 4.) It adds to the man's job satisfaction as he can progress within a sales career even though he is unqualified for management.

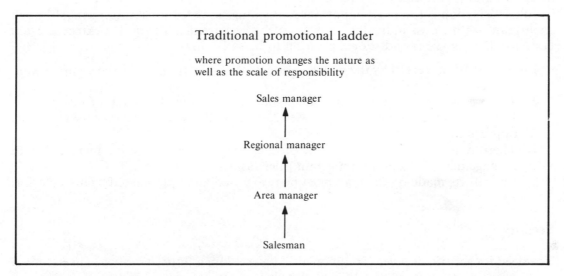

(a) A traditional promotion ladder showing changes in the nature as well as in the scale of responsibility

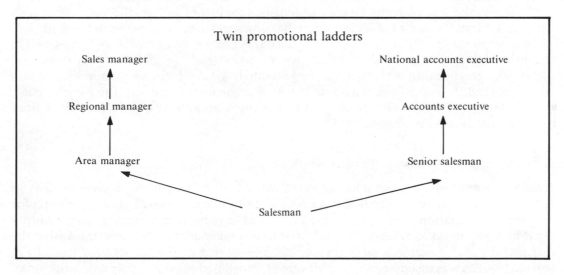

(b) Twin promotion ladders, one of which preserves the necessary management replacement process, while the other enables salesmen to progress to positions of higher sales responsibility, even though they lack true managerial potential

Fig. 11.1 Promotion prospects for salesmen

Need for recognition

Finally, every human being likes to feel his efforts are recognised by other people. The salesman is no exception. His job satisfaction is enhanced when his manager appreciates the work he is doing and especially when he praises him for it. Sincere praise is a strong motivational influence and it is not uncommon to find even the most hardened salesmen carefully preserving notes that they have received from their superiors thanking them for particular achievements. Fair constructive criticism likewise has an incentive value. Most salesmen react well to evaluation as long as it is balanced with recognition of their successes and it is not destructive or unjust.

Job satisfaction is the most important motivating force for most salesmen. Although each man has his own individual concept of his requirements from his career, certain common factors are found. For a position to be satisfying:

1 It must be perceived by the man as being worth while to himself, the company and society.
2 There must be clear and challenging goals with regular feedback of results.
3 It must contain a body of knowledge and skills which the man is given the opportunity to learn.
4 There must be an opportunity of progression, at least for some men, either to management or to more important sales tasks.
5 The efforts made by the man must be recognised and appreciated by his superior.

Security

The need for security is a very common although seldom admitted motive. The nature of the remuneration system and the relative importance of salary and commission will obviously affect job security and must be considered from this aspect.

However, the less obvious facets of security should not escape the sales manager's attention. First, the degree of security that the company wishes to offer must be identified. If the salesmen's jobs are too secure there is a danger that the sales force will stagnate. On the other hand, a high level of insecurity normally leads to high staff turnover and although a great deal of activity might be generated, it is doubtful whether much of it will be purposeful. In companies where insecurity is a constant feature of the environment, morale tends to be low and although there is often an appearance of frenetic action, achievement is usually very limited.

Need for clear performance standards

Ideally, the sales manager should aim to provide an environment which gives security to those who perform up to standard but which identifies men who are below the criteria for the job. This situation presupposes that clear goals have been set so that each man knows what he is supposed to achieve. A man's morale is weakened if he does not know what the satisfactory performance level is for his job. This is one of the reasons for loss of job satisfaction, as was discussed above. Moreover, most men need not only a description of what to do but also of how to do it. Job descriptions and work structuring both help to give security and confidence, and confident salesmen are far more likely to be successful than fearful men are.

Need to belong

Another element of security is the need to belong. Man is a gregarious animal and in a sense salesmen are selected as being those best capable of mixing with a wide cross-section of people. However, a salesman can never really belong to his customer group. He can only feel a member of the team consisting of his colleagues. Again, there is much the manager can do to encourage group spirit by sales meetings and the regular interchange of news and information. Some firms use house magazines or sales bulletins for this purpose.

Need for leadership

The most important element of security comes from the leadership of the manager. There is a vast literature on leadership qualities and styles and an eternal debate as to whether leaders are born or made. It seems likely that the answer is that some of the characteristics of leaders are innate but that these usually need developing. Most managers can improve their performance as leaders if they ponder not the qualities of the great leaders throughout history and then attempt to copy them, but the true nature and meaning of the leadership function.

The purpose of leadership is to unite a body of people so that they can achieve common objectives. It is apparent from studying the great military, social and religious leaders that there is not one single successful method. The key to interpreting why different leaders are successful despite vast differences in their character and actions is to analyse the relationship between the leader and the followers, not simply to identify the personality traits of the leader. Leadership is an interaction between the leader and the led. This helps to explain why, despite the gratitude felt by the nation, so great a leader as Winston Churchill was discarded by them in 1945. The nation's concept of the leadership necessary in peacetime was different from that required in war. It is unlikely that Churchill's personality suddenly changed in 1945. He still possessed the qualities that had made him successful. The leadership needs of the country were suddenly different.

In this sense leadership is akin to salesmanship. The salesman stimulates the customer to buying action by satisfying the customer's needs. The leader stimulates his followers to achieve the objectives by satisfying their needs. Just as every customer has a unique need pattern, which to a degree requires individual satisfaction, so every subordinate requires a particular style of leadership from his manager. This is why it is so dangerous to generalise about the qualities of successful leadership. One man will strive to reach a target when he is given precise and firm orders to do so. Another will work harder if he is not told what to do but rather consulted on the goals to be achieved.

There is a whole spectrum of interactions that can take place between the manager and his team, ranging from the authoritarian situation where the manager orders his subordinates with little or no prior consultation, to the democratic environment where the manager acts as a kind of adviser to the group, which itself makes the decisions. Each type of interaction has its advantages and disadvantages and is to be preferred in particular situations. There are four major stages that can be identified: dictatorship, benevolent autocracy, democracy and *laissez-faire*. (See Figure 11.2.)

Dictatorship, where the manager decides on his own, works well in a command situation where decisions have to be taken and implemented quickly. It is the basis of military decision making, particularly in times of war, when to allow questioning and discussion of orders could literally be fatal. However, it depends on the manager always being right and the discipline of the group to implement what he commands. The business manager obviously lacks the sanctions of the army officer and cannot court-martial a salesman for refusing to obey orders. Also, as there are few business situations that have the urgency of the battle-field, the need and acceptability of this kind of leadership is far less. Certain pioneer sales groups, however, react well to the authoritarian style, but most sales forces find this kind of management intolerable.

Benevolent autocracy is still authoritarian in the sense that the manager takes the

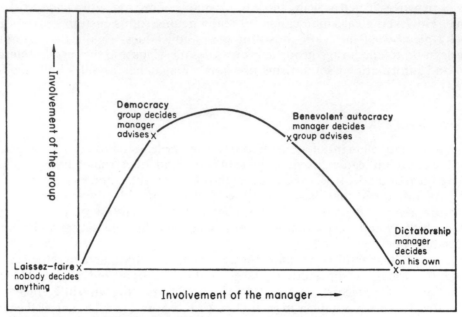

Fig. 11.2   Manager–group interaction

decisions but is benevolent in that he consults sincerely with his group before he decides. Such an approach combines the effectiveness of individual responsibility for decision making with the motivational and advisory impact of involving the total team. This is probably the most commonly successful form of leadership.

Democracy obtains when the majority of the group concerned takes the decision, usually with the manager acting as an adviser or representative. Although it conforms to some of the ideals of our society, it has the inherent danger that to reach any decision at all can take a long time as so many people are involved, and even then the decision may have to be a compromise in order to gain majority support. However, if it is imperative that the majority is committed to a particular course of action, or if it does not matter what decision is made as long as some view is taken, the democratic approach can work well and has a high incentive value

Laissez-faire management is typified by no decisions being taken by anybody and is often a degeneration from the worse excesses of the democratic style. In the attempt to ensure that all concerned are involved in the decision, it is easy to fail to decide anything, thus not offending anybody. This type of management has nothing to commend it.

From an understanding of the nature and range of leader-group interaction, the manager can develop the leadership necessary for his sales force as a whole and individually. He may well come to the conclusion that in total his men are well-experienced, responsible individuals who will respond best to being consulted before decisions are taken. On the other hand, the nature of business pressure may demand a rapidity of decision-making and so a benevolent but autocratic style is generally the most appropriate. There may be a particular individual, however, who is relatively inexperienced and by character insecure and uncertain. He will probably react best to a firm hand with clear orders being given. Anything other than a fairly authoritarian approach will probably make him even more insecure. Particular situations might arise such as the annual decision on the holiday rota. From the manager's point of view it probably does not matter who goes on vacation when, as long as basic criteria are observed, such as no two salesmen to be away at the same time and all holidays to be taken between May and October. Such decisions are often best left to democratic processes.

It is a mark of a good manager that he can satisfy different leadership needs by different approaches. As long as the real nature of leadership is recognised in terms of manager-group interactions, it is perhaps not too dangerous to analyse other general characteristics. When surveys have been conducted of salesmen asking them to list the prime traits of the best manager they have ever had, certain factors occur repeatedly. These include:

1 Not afraid to take decisions.
2 Gave sincere praise and criticism.
3 Did not play favourites.
4 Took the responsibility himself when things went wrong.
5 Could do what he asked us to do.
6 Worked harder than he asked us to work.

In other words, salesmen generally want decisive, honest, fair, professional, hard-working managers. Any manager can test the requirements of his own men by asking them the same question. Obviously answers should be collected anonymously. Even small surveys such as this can give valuable insights into the vital tasks of leadership that the sales manager must be able to perform.

Finally, the manager must remember at all times that he is the manager. While working *with* his team he must not try to be a member *of* his team. Many recently promoted managers make the fatal mistake of trying to be "one of the boys." Salesmen neither want nor respect this attitude.

Status

The social status of selling has already been mentioned in the earlier discussions on job satisfaction. As the manager explains the social worth of the sales function, he will also be up-grading its position in society. He can also help to improve its status within the company and the market by ensuring that the job titles given carry as much prestige as possible without going to the extremes of "regional sales director." He should ensure, too, that the rest of the company realises the importance of the function so that when a customer telephones and asks for one of the field force by name, the switchboard operator does not reply that as Mr Smith is "only one of our salesmen" (or, worse still, "travellers"), he is not in the office. Likewise when the caller is eventually put through to the sales department, he should be greeted by a girl who says she is Mr Smith's secretary. She can, of course, be "secretary" to a number of other salesmen as well.

The salesman should be provided with the best possible equipment for his job. Well-printed visiting cards with his name in the middle, a well-made briefcase or sample case and good literature all contribute to his status in the eyes of his customers. His car is perhaps the most significant symbol of all, not only to his buyers but also to his family and friends. The price difference between the standard and de luxe versions of cars is usually well worth the extra values conferred. Vans should be avoided whenever possible as they cause great recruitment difficulties. There is not much prestige in spending Sunday morning washing down a commercial vehicle, blazoned with the company's name, in front of the neighbours.

The man's status within his social group is important to his motivation. By the nature of the function, the salesman's social life is likely to be more disrupted than that of his friends in other careers. He is expected to work long and irregular hours, to spend time away from home, to use his wife as a telephone answering service for customers, to fill his garage with stacks of promotional literature, etc. If these demands are known to be appreciated by management and perhaps occasional dinners are held for the men and their families, this social contact helps again to stress the importance of the task. Some sales managers make a point of sending personal Christmas cards to the wives with a note of thanks for the support they have given throughout the year. Others go even further and send presents, arrange staff outings, etc. Such practices must be done sincerely to be effective, not as an automatic technique.

It is popular at present to mock the status needs and symbols of society. The key to the executive washroom has become a joke and perhaps rightly so. The sales manager must not forget, however, that, whether it is amusing or not, most men have a need for status. To some, status is more important than any other motivation. In one extreme case a salesman begged to be given the title of area manager and offered to take a salary reduction to compensate for it. The manager, disturbed by such a strange request, probed the reasons. He discovered that the man's wife had been employed as a demonstrator with another firm and had been recently promoted to area supervisor. The difference in their status levels caused difficulty at home and particularly in their social life. The man felt that his friends and acquaintances thought less of him now his wife had the job with more prestige value.

Most people are conscious of their standing in business and society at large. The salesman is in a unique position in that the traditionally low status of selling in no way reflects its high importance as an industrial and social function. If sales management appreciates this paradox and does all it can to enhance the status of the sales career, not only will individual salesmen benefit but also, perhaps, in the future, the real values of selling will be more widely recognised.

Identifying motivational influences and planning motivational schemes

Motivation is the business of management. "Getting things done through other people towards economic objectives" implies quite rightly a leadership function.

The sales manager's motivational task starts when he sets the job specifications and salary grades of his sales force. In formulating these, he will begin to set the framework of motivational satisfactions that the company can offer in order that its objectives are reached. It is extremely important that conscious thought is given to ensure compatibility between the goals of the firm and those of its employees.

In staffing the organisation, again the motives of applicants have to be evaluated. Chapter 6 described how this can be done. It has been stressed continually that each individual has his own unique need pattern and that although some generalisations can be made, the manager must never forget to treat each salesman as an individual. The true motivations of each man can be identified by careful analysis of his behavioural traits both before he joins the company and while he is an employee. Care must be taken to ascertain which of his motivations have to be satisfied from the job and which from his other pursuits.

Employee opinion polling

It can be informative from time to time to establish a more objective picture of sales force motivation. Although a good sales manager will have a deep understanding of his force, nevertheless they may not all be completely open and frank about their feelings towards the company and the job.

Some companies therefore use employee opinion polls (which have to be conducted by outsiders and guarantee anonymity to the participants) to identify the real motivational patterns. By the use of questionnaires and discussion groups, such surveys can uncover attitudes which are not conducive to fully productive work, often caused by apparently minor items. In one company the sales force was disgruntled by the fact that the amount allowed for postage of daily reports had not been increased in line with the increasing cost of stamps owing to administrative oversight. In another firm positive suggestions from the sales force via an opinion poll resulted in the saving of about an hour a day on unnecessary form filling. It is often apparently unimportant aspects of the job such as these which if left uncovered and uncorrected can be magnified by people in the field into a feeling that management does not care about their daily activities.

Regular objective checking of the motivational temperature is thus a wise precaution particularly in those companies whose sales forces are widespread and have insufficient contact with each other and even with their management! Opinion polls can give a sound basis, particularly in such circumstances, for positive and visible managerial action.

Having analysed the needs of each of his subordinates, the manager can then judge which general schemes will be applicable. He will no doubt consider the likely value of payment by results and other direct incentives, while remembering the need to avoid and remove disincentives. Certainly the area of job satisfaction will require careful study as it is such a major motive. The provision of security and status satisfactions will also be high on the list.

General schemes, however, will never fulfil the total motivational requirement of a sales force. The individual need patterns have to be satisfied to a large degree individually by the leadership of the manager. The style of leadership that he will offer will depend upon his analysis of the needs of his staff, as he will recognise that leadership is an interaction between himself and his subordinates.

The process of identifying and satisfying motivational needs must be a continuous and integral part of the management function.

ACTION PLANNING CHECKLIST

Questions	Answers and action	Timing of action and evaluation
1 Has any study been made of the satisfactions that can be derived from the job?		
2 Has the social role of selling been carefully explained to the sales force?		
3 Do the salesmen have clear goals with regular results?		
4 Are the motivational effects of training clearly recognised?		
5 Does the company promotional system allow progression to higher levels of sales responsibility?		
6 Are they regularly praised and criticised on their work?		
7 Are all opportunities taken to create team spirit?		
8 Have the leadership needs of the sales force been recognised and satisfied?		
9 Has action been taken to improve the status of the job within the company and social group?		
10 Is the motivational environment regularly reviewed to ensure that all the sales force are devoting their full abilities to their work?		

CHAPTER 12

How to Control the Sales Operation

In order to control any activity, there must first be an objective and a plan. Unless it is known what is to be achieved and how, whether it is being achieved cannot be assessed. Conversely, there is little point in setting goals and defining actions unless there is an evaluation procedure.

The integrated nature of the objective–planning–control continuum was stressed in Chapter 3. It has been reiterated here because it is apparent that some companies regard control as a separate process. For example, in one business equipment firm, the sales manager developed a system whereby he could analyse the monthly performance of every salesman under eighteen different categories of activity. Thus he could identify how many hours each man had spent on each facet of his job. He could ascertain for instance that salesman X had spent seven and a half hours on prospecting, salesman Y eight hours on report writing. He obviously believed that control was constituted by the collection of detailed information. Such attitudes are common among sales management and one of the impacts of computerisation is that data suddenly becomes available in vast quantities, thus apparently giving even more minute control.

Concept of control

It must be realised that the provision of information, however accurate, up to date and detailed, in itself in no way constitutes control. This is for the very basic reason that there is little point in knowing what has happened unless there is a clear conception of what should have happened. Control can then be exercised by comparing actual performance with planned performance and deriving variances. It is on these variances that corrective action should be based. Control can be summarised therefore as:

$$A - S = \pm V$$

– where A is the actual performance, S is the preset standard and V is the variance between the two. To know that salesman X spent seven and a half hours prospecting is meaningless by itself. However if the standard for this activity is ten hours then there is a minus variance of two and a half hours and it is this figure which should cause the manager to take corrective action. If, however, the standard were seven and a half hours, as the actual performance is equivalent to the desired standard, no managerial action is required. Only by adopting such a concept can management time be economically utilised.

Management by exception

The basic problem of any manager is that he has to achieve results from resources which are scarce. He has only a limited amount of manpower, money and facilities. In particular, he has the most severe constrictions on his own time because although other resources can be expanded where necessary, the number of hours in the day cannot. It is essential, therefore, that his time is used efficiently. One of the prime methods for ensuring this is to devote time only to those parts of the business which are not running according to plan.

The analysis of facets which are not up to standard implies a control system which indicates such variances. This whole process is known as "management by exception" and can be operated wherever a control mechanism of this kind has been constructed. For example, if the standards set are costs, the result is a standard costing system; if they are budgets, a budgetary control system. To operate such control systems in this way requires that:

1 Standards are set.
2 Actual information is collected.
3 Variances are produced and analysed.
4 Corrective action is taken.

Setting standards of field sales performance

In order to identify appropriate standards for control, the manager should ask two questions:

1 What constitutes success?
2 What affects the achievement of success?

Absolute standards

In a sales operation success can usually be defined as the achievement of the sales targets. These serve as the prime standards of control. By themselves, however, they are insufficient. The achievement or otherwise of the annual sales target constitutes an *absolute standard*. It measures what has happened but it is then usually far too late to redress the balance. Moreover, it does not indicate why the performance has been poor. In a sense it is analogous to the oil pressure warning light on a car. When it glows it indicates that the pressure has fallen below the level necessary for efficient engine operation. It registers this fact after the event has taken place. If the car is being driven at high speed on a motorway, by the time corrective action is taken, damage may well have occurred. Even if that is avoided, the motorist will still not know why his oil pressure has decreased.

Moving standards

A more sophisticated approach is to use *moving standards*. If the sales performance against target is monitored monthly, weekly or even daily, variances can be identified more quickly and trends in the variances will allow future problems to be predicted. Likewise, the oil pressure gauge on a car is a significant improvement over the warning light. By observing the behaviour of the needle, the motorist can register a fall in pressure before danger level is reached and take appropriate action in advance of the problem. Still, however, neither the sales manager nor the motorist will know why performance is falling below standard. It is obviously difficult to decide on the appropriate corrective action when the reasons for the variances are unknown.

Diagnostic standards

Diagnostic standards, which help to identify why performance is varying from target are defined by asking the second question: "What affects the achievement of success?"

The manager must consider in the case of a particular salesman failing to achieve target what are the actions that the salesman himself takes that should lead to the goals being met. Surprisingly, there are only four and these can be identified by the following questions:

1 What kind of people does he call upon?
2 How many does he call upon?
3 How often does he call?
4 What does he do while he is there?

There may well be, of course, other factors outside the man's control that affect target achievement. The target itself may be too high, the advertising campaign might have failed, production perhaps cannot supply, competition may be particularly strong. The concern of the sales manager in formulating a sales force control system must be first to evaluate those factors within the control of the sales force. He should therefore define diagnostic standards for each element of the sales activity.

The type of people to be called upon can be specified either by name and address on a customer list or by a customer profile. For example, an industrial sales force can be instructed to concentrate on light engineering firms with over 100 employees. A door-to-door sales team might be told to call on householders with telephones and cars.

How many people are called upon how often will be determined by the call frequency and call rate standards. For example, if a salesman can average ten calls per day and has 220 working days in the year, he can achieve an annual call total of 2200. If the number of desired contacts is 550, he will have an average frequency standard of four times per year. Alternatively, if the call frequency is regarded as more important and it is necessary that he calls on average five times per annum, he can handle only 440 customers, unless the call rate standard can be modified. (See Chapter 4 for a fuller discussion of organising sales force workloads.)

The first three elements of the salesman's work can thus be defined and measurable standards set. The fourth aspect, what he does when he calls, is far more difficult to quantify. At least his actual sales presentation can be qualitatively evaluated. The field appraisal techniques described in Chapter 9 will help with such assessment. Some companies have attempted to quantify the relationship between what the salesman does and the results gained. One such approach is for the manager, when accompanying his representatives in the field, to note which benefits are stressed in each interview. An analysis can then be made to identify any correlations between what the men said and the outcome of the interviews. In one hosiery company, for example, it was discovered that salesmen who stressed to the buyer the merchandising and advertising support on a range of socks gained more and bigger orders than those who mentioned only product quality, price and delivery. This helped to guide the company in the training and structuring of sales presentations. Such benefits/results analyses can help to quantify what the salesmen should do in the interview.

Refining the standards

Figure 12.1 shows in summary form the overall standard-setting process for the control of the field sales operation. The procedure can be refined to suit the needs of particular situations. The targets themselves can be broken down product by product, by repeat and new business, etc. In some companies the number of orders and average size of order are specified and from these an order: call ratio set. When analysis of this kind is carried out, the sales manager can identify more precisely the area of performance failure. For example, in a company selling pneumatic compressors it was found that the salesmen did not vary greatly in terms of the number of orders gained. There were, however, significant differences in average order size between the best and the worst salesmen. This was because the poorer salesmen, having obtained an order for a compressor, generally then terminated the interview. The good salesmen, having settled the compressor order, continued to sell couplings, hoses and tools. Similar exercises can be conducted on the other standards in order to tighten control. The call rate can be split into effective and non-effective calls defining the difference on the basis of whether the buyer was seen or not. Unless such distinctions are made the manager may be misled by a weak salesman who achieves the call rate standard in terms of quantity but who fails to make contact at the appropriate level. Call rates will probably also have to be split into existing customer calls and new prospect calls. In the absence of a new business standard, most salesmen will fill their day with visits to existing customers only.

Financial standards

Further refinements can be added by setting sales costs standards. Certainly many sales managers would save considerable time if they predetermined an acceptable level of salesmen's expenses. Too much managerial time is occupied in too many firms with microscopic examination of entertainment vouchers to see whether the man has claimed a few pence more than he should. The same amount of time devoted to the analysis of why sales have slumped on a particular product could produce far more significant results. If there is a standard for salesmen's expenses the manager need only concern himself with the exceptions. Obviously studies will be necessary from time to time to ensure such standard amounts are not simply being spent because they are allowed to be spent. This is an inherent danger of standard setting and the management by exception system. Occasional analyses, however, will help prevent this tendency and lead to improved standard-setting without a continual wastage of managerial time.

Identifying future problems

The great advantage of diagnostic standards, particularly when prepared in detail, is not simply that they identify the factors of work that affect target achievement and therefore the nature and scale of salesman failure. In many ways their most significant value is that they identify likely problems before the event. In most businesses there is a considerable lead time between initial contact and order receipt. It is too late to identify when the volume of orders declines that insufficient prospecting was done. If a canvassing standard has been determined, failure to achieve it will help to predict the future order position, usually in sufficient time to take corrective action. For example, in one computer company where the only sales control was achievement of target it was noted that the business exhibited a cyclical pattern about every two years. Analysis showed that this was because the average lead time between initial contact was likewise about two years. The sales force were, for instance, in year *1* making considerable prospecting efforts but gaining few orders. In year *2* the earlier prospecting began to bear fruit and all sales force attention was devoted to survey work and clinching orders. In year *2* the order level was thus considerably higher. In year *3*, however, because of the lack of prospecting in year *2*, orders declined and prospecting had to be recommended. Year *4* again showed an increase as the canvassing work in year *3* reached the end of its lead time, and so on. Management alleviated the situation by setting standards for each stage of the business process so that the sales force each year had targets of prospecting, survey work and orders to achieve. Thus orders were gained in each year while prospecting for next year's business was also maintained.

Question 1 What constitutes success in selling?	Achievement of sales targets
Question 2 What affects that achievement?	
ACTIVITY	FORMAT OF STANDARD
What kind of people are to be called upon?	Prospect list
	Customer list
	Customer profile
How many are to be called upon?	Call rate
	Prospecting rate
How often are they to be called upon?	Call frequency
What is to be done in each call?	Field appraisal
	Benefits/results analysis

Fig. 12.1 Setting standards for field sales operations

How to set standards

Having defined the type of standards required the manager must set the levels of each standard. This is usually best done by analysing past performance, examining other divisions of the company and, where possible, other companies. From this data the manager will derive an impression of the current relationships between the various elements of his sales activity. He can then seek to improve by tighter control on parts or on the whole of the process. To continue the example of the computer firm, it was found that historically the ratios between the various stages of the selling process were as follows.

For every order, three surveys had been completed on which decisions had been made. For every three "decisioned" surveys, five surveys had been submitted. For every five surveys, twenty feasibility studies had been conducted to check whether a survey was worth while. To produce twenty companies worthy of feasibility studies had required about one hundred prospect contacts. (See Figure 12.2.)

	Orders	Decisioned surveys	Submitted surveys	Feasibility studies	Prospect contacts
	1	3	5	20	100
		(a)	*(b)*	*(c)*	*(d)*
Ratios		3:1	5:3	4:1	5:1

Fig. 12.2   Sales activity relationships in a computer company

The sales manager was pleased with ratio *(a)* as it was far higher than the company's market share. He was disturbed by ratio *(b)*, however, because it meant that 40 per cent of survey work, which was very costly and time-consuming, was in effect being wasted. Further investigation showed that some of the wastage was unavoidable. Some surveys had been commissioned and conducted but had been delayed or shelved due to a change in the circumstances of the potential customer – for example, unable to afford to buy a computer, taken over, change of policy, etc. Other firms, however, should either never have been investigated in the first place or more sales pressure should have been exerted to bring them to a conclusion, obviously where possible to the benefit of the computer company concerned. The manager, therefore, could set improved standards for this stage.

Assuming that ratio *(b)* could be improved from 5.3 to 4.3, this would have a significant impact upon the sales activity even though all other ratios remain constant. (See Figure

12.3). A 20 per cent saving on feasibility studies and a 20 per cent saving on prospecting would result, while the same number of orders would be achieved. The time thus saved could then be devoted to getting further orders. This demonstrates how historical analysis can help to set standards and in particular can assist in pinpointing areas for improvement in standards and thus sales force activity.

	Orders	Decisioned surveys	Submitted surveys	Feasibility studies	Prospect contacts
	1	3	4	16	80
		(a)	*(b)*	*(c)*	*(d)*
Ratios		3:1	4:3	4:1	5:1

Fig. 12.3   Refined sales standards in a computer company

Preventing performance failure by planning

One of the aims of setting standards is to control the sales activity at an early enough stage to prevent failure to achieve orders. This aspect of control can be further refined by evaluating planned performance against standard before the activity takes place. In fact it is only by assessing the intended action of the sales force that the sales manager can directly prevent failure. Obviously he must check his own plans to ensure that if achieved they reach the desired objectives. He can go further by assessing each salesman's activity plans before they are put into action. This is normally done by the submission of weekly calling plans (Figure 12.4) on which each man identifies who he is intending to visit, for what reason and when he last saw this customer (if applicable). The sales manager can thus rapidly check that the intended call matches the standards of the customer list or customer profile and call frequency. Moreover, by examining the objectives he can to a degree determine whether it is likely to be a worth-while visit or not. Further evidence will be given by the "appointment" column. It is far more likely to be a non-effective call if made without prior arrangement, particularly in industrial markets. He can also check the projected call rate by totalling the number of calls planned. The salesman can explain in the "remarks" column the reasons for planned variances from standard or make requests for literature to be sent, etc. Finally, the manager can check the whole shape of the week's work to ensure that economic routes have been planned, adequate time has been left between appointments and that generally the man is using his time efficiently.

The weekly calling plans should be submitted no later than the Thursday of the previous week to allow the manager time to assess and where necessary modify the projected activity. Of course there are situations where ample time has to be left for urgent calls and also where the plan will be achieved to the full. Such considerations will limit the effectiveness of the system. They do not, however, negate its value totally and all managers

WEEKLY CALLING PLAN

Representative_____

Week commencing_____

Contact, company name & address	Appointment	Objective	Last seen	Remarks
Monday				
Tuesday				
Wednesday				
Thursday				
Friday				

Fig. 12.4   Weekly calling plan

must be careful not to make perfection the enemy of good.

The calling plans should be constructed by the salesmen from a study of their customer and prospect record cards which are essential in any well-controlled sales operation. Information that should be recorded on each customer and prospect should include the following:

1 Company name, address and telephone number.
2 Name and position of contacts.
3 Call frequency classification.
4 Accounts information, e.g. credit rating.
5 Nature and scale of business activity.
6 Visit record.
7 Buying record.
8 General remarks – for example, best days and times for visiting, whether appointments necessary, personal habits of contacts, travel and parking arrangements, etc.

An example of a combined prospect/customer record card used in a plant hire company is shown in Figure 12.5. Record cards have to be designed to suit the specific situation of each firm but it is not a very difficult process. Some salesmen argue that they are unnecessary as they carry all this data in their heads. Not only is this patently impossible with more than a few customers but also it creates great difficulties when a new man takes over the territory.

The construction of standards is the essential first element in the sales force control system. In order to ensure appropriate standards have been set, the sales manager should check to ensure they satisfy five criteria:

1 That they are quantitative wherever possible so that variances can be measured.
2 That they cover what the sales force is supposed to achieve.
3 That they measure how the sales force is progressing and help to predict the likely outcome.
4 That they help to diagnose the reasons for sales force performance.
5 That they identify likely variances early enough to enable corrective action to be taken.

The secret of effective control is the definition of appropriate quantitative standards. Without them, control is virtually impossible. With them, the manager's task is dramatically simplified and significant amounts of time are saved.

Collection of information

Details of actual performance have to be collected so that they can be compared against standards. The better the definition of the standards, the clearer the specification of the information required. Every manager complains about the ever-increasing volume of paper work, facts and figures that has to be handled. One of the major reasons for the explosive growth of available information is that generally the ability to collect and process data has outstripped the skills to use it. In a frantic attempt to gain some form of control management calls for more and more analyses and because of the sheer quantity of available information believes that it thus has a grip on the situation.

Criteria for information collection

Nothing could be further from the truth. The information collection process should not be started until a clear set of standards is defined. Otherwise, faced with a lack of

Territory _____	National account/local account
	Rates agreed _____
Call frequency _____	Account code number _____

Name	Contacts
Address	
Telephone number	
_____	

| Type of business | Machines owned |

| Hiring requirements (including competitors) | Contacts | | | Date | Who | Results |
| | Date | Who | Results | | | |

General remarks

Fig. 12.5   Prospect/customer record card *(front)*

HIRINGS					
Machine	Start	Finish	Rate	Op/non-op	Remarks

Fig. 12.5 **Prospect/customer record card** *(back)*

definition of what should happen, the manager has to search through thousands of facts on what has happened and must somehow arrive at a judgement as to the corrective action needed. The development of electronic data processing has simply worsened the situation because it has improved information capture and processing. Paradoxically, computers are best used as a tool of managerial control when they give the minimum information not the maximum available data. Once standards have been defined, the computer can be readily used to run a management by exception system pointing out only the variances from plan for management to take corrective action. It is a good rule before any information is ever collected about any aspect of business to query:

1   What decision has to be taken?
2   Within what degree of accuracy?
3   How quickly?

– and then to ask

4   What information is necessary?
5   From whom should it be collected?
6   How should it be collected?

Dangers of the information explosion

Again, the dangers of sophisticated data processing must be avoided. Because it may be possible (at a cost of course) to produce highly accurate information very quickly, this does not mean that the management decision-making process is at all improved.

To be able to discover within twenty-four hours that there are precisely 175 329 companies in Britain who have a potential use for product X is of no great value if the manufacturer can only possibly supply 50 000 within the next three years. An estimate that put the market size between 150 000 and 200 000, although not as accurate, would not change any decisions that are likely to be taken in the short term. Longer-term decisions, such as expanding the production facilities, normally do not depend upon data being produced within twenty-four hours. Moreover, the semblance of precision that is given in a typed print-out can itself be misleading. The accuracy of the answer will depend directly on the quality of the input and analytical process. If the estimates of what constitutes a potential user for product X are themselves inaccurate, then the figure of 175 329 becomes highly suspect.

No criticism is intended of information sources or data processing devices; only of management's ability to use them. With an awareness of all these pitfalls the sales manager can now ponder how to collect the appropriate information.

Collecting the right information

Sales results are the most obvious data for comparison with targets and should be readily available. From the actual sales figures can be calculated many of the details that are needed; average order size, new orders: repeat orders ratio, etc.

The more difficult information to collect is that appertaining to the sales force activity that generates the orders. The prime means for gathering this is the call reporting system. Companies vary in the frequency with which they require salesmen to report. Some sales forces submit reports after each call, others at the end of the day, week or month. There are still sales managers who have no reporting systems, believing that results are the only facts worth knowing. Although orders are the major objective it is surely apparent that failure to collect data on *how* the results are obtained must inhibit the correction of discrepancies between actual sales performance and targets.

The call report is a critical part of the whole sales force control system and it is preferable that each call should be the subject of a report. If the salesman is making five calls a day and his costs total, say, £20,000 a year, including salary, car, overhead expenses and so on the cost of each call is about £20. No sales manager would allow £20 to be spent out of petty cash without supporting vouchers. More important, it is imperative that the sales manager knows what his men are doing and as he cannot accompany all of them all the time, the call report is his basic source of information. The report should include:

1 Who has been called upon.
2 When he was last called upon.
3 Objective of the call.
4 Summary of discussion.
5 Results.
6 Action to be taken by the salesman.
7 Action to be taken by the office.
8 Other information (competitive activity, etc).

A typical call report form is shown in Figure 12.6. Some firms prefer more structured forms to reduce the amount of writing and to remind the man what he should report. Repeat consumer goods selling lends itself to this approach.

The call report should be written immediately after each call so that nothing vital is forgotten. If it is completed then, it takes only a very few minutes. For some reason many salesmen seem to prefer to write all the reports on the day's work in the evening. This should be frowned upon as tests have revealed that inevitably important points are overlooked because of the time-lag. One method of discouraging this practice is to request the men to post the morning's call reports at lunch-time and the afternoon's reports in the evening collection. With the help of this system and some training in writing terse, accurate reports, the salesmen soon find that they can easily complete the form immediately after the call.

Call report analysis

On receiving the reports they should be checked to ensure that the call, the contact and the objective agree with the weekly calling plan and tne salesman should be questioned if they do not. The reason for repeating these items on the two documents is to ensure planned activity is carried out. It has been found that without the prior identification of these factors a call report system alone is open to abuse. For example, some salesmen will make the call first and specify the objective afterwards to ensure that it is appropriate to the proceedings of the interview! Likewise, it was only by checking the actual calls against the previously agreed plan that one manager discovered a salesman planning calls that he never actually found the time to make. Despite the fact that it was planned that an important customer in the east end of London should be visited every week, these visits never took place. The discovery of the discrepancy enabled the manager to probe the salesman and to identify that he was afraid of this customer who could be extremely bad-tempered and rude. The manager could then take the corrective action of retraining the man, building his confidence and accompanying him on the next visit.

Having ensured that the actual call is in accordance with the plan, the manager can then examine the results, the summary of discussion and the actions to be taken. These can be illuminating to the experienced manager. Does the pattern of results show that the salesman is stronger on selling one product than another? Is he obtaining the appropriate size and frequency of orders from this type and size of customer? Do the notes on the discussion reveal weaknesses in his knowledge and skill? For example, if phrases such as:

CALL REPORT FORM

Name and address   Representative _____

                                          Date of call _____

                                          Date of last call _____

Objective of call

Summary of discussion

Results

Action to be taken by representative

By office

Other information – for example, competitive activity, trading situation, etc

Fig. 12.6   Call report form

1   Not the right line for this customer to purchase.
2   Mr Smith said he would think about it.
3   Mr Jones has just ordered from a competitor.
4   Will call back on this customer later.
5   Have arranged to send more information.

– continuously occur it usually means the man is weak in closing technique. Likewise, the actions to be taken can be equally revealing. Are all the salesman's actions fairly negative, such as:

6   Will think about this customer's problem.
7   Will call back in about a year.
8   Will drop in some literature next time I am in the area.

– or are they positive?

9   Will return next week with samples which, if satisfactory, will clinch the deal.
10   Have arranged visit to customer *x* to see machine in operation.
11   Have fixed to build merchandising display first week in March.

The action requested from the office should be examined to check that it is reasonable and a valid use of office time and staff, not simply buck-passing. This in turn constitutes a standard for the control of the sales office. Do they take action on the requests made?

The final comments on the report will reveal how skilled the salesman is in interpreting competitive activity in this area, how well organised his sources of information and, overall, how sound his business judgement. It is often the case that there is at least one man in a sales force who consistently reports depressed trading conditions and vicious competitive activity in his particular territory, despite the fact that such comments are the reverse of those made by the rest of the sales force. This is usually an attempt, of course, to rationalise poor sales results and will not escape the attention of a skilled sales manager.

The information gleaned from the call report system should be supplemented by regular field visits. The field appraisal technique has been fully described in Chapter 9. Other sources of information include sales meetings, conferences and training programmes, all of which add to the manager's data and aid the evaluation of performance against the standards.

Variance production and analysis

Variances are produced by comparing actual results against the pre-set standards. However, this simple method may need refining as high variances may result which reflect the forecast error of the standards. For example, although the average daily call rate is set at eight, there is probably no cause for alarm if this varies between six and ten. Because so many of the standards are produced by averaging past performance it may well be necessary to process the actual results before comparing them against standard.

Smoothing out random variations

There are several methods of smoothing out random variations. First, cumulative totals can be used so that individual monthly variations will tend to cancel each other out. Likewise moving annual totals can be employed by taking the twelve months' performance up to and including the month in question. Because as each month is added, the same month of the previous year is deducted, the trend in the moving annual total will indicate present performance compared with the same period in the previous year. Figure 12.7 will make this clear. The figure shows what is known as a *Z* chart because of its shape.

Such a graph enables three comparisons to be made on a single diagram; monthly performance against target, cumulative performance against target and, via the moving annual total, the present year compared with the previous year.

Second, averaging can be used to smooth out variations. Totals over a time period can be divided to produce for example a man's average daily call rate to compare with the standard. Probably the appropriate period for such averaging is monthly, for most purposes – for example, prospecting rate, effective call rate. Order: call ratios and average size of order figures because of the infrequency of orders may have to be taken over longer periods, such as a quarter, to produce meaningful data.

In circumstances where standards are known to include measurable errors, it may be worth while setting performance parameters in advance. This is analogous to the concept of engineering tolerances. Thus, instead of insisting that twenty-five calls should be made each week, a range of twenty-three to twenty-seven can be set as the standard.

Variance analysis

Having procured the actual results and compared them against the standards, variances will become apparent. These discrepancies may need more careful analysis before corrective action is taken. For example, in one firm it was known from past experience that the majority of the selling depended upon seeing the senior management of the customers, which could only be done by appointment. The results of some of the salesmen, however, were disappointing despite the fact that the percentage of calls by appointments was well up to the pre-set standard. It began to become clear when performance against other standards was examined. It was noted that their overall call rate was below par and thus although the appointment:total call ratio was high, this was due to a smaller number of other calls rather than an over-achievement of appointments. Furthermore, it was discovered that as they increased their number of appointments, their overall call rates decreased markedly.

What in fact was happening was that these men in their enthusiasm to gain appointments had not controlled the timing of such meetings. They had placed them in the middle of the mornings and afternoons, therefore limiting their ability to make other calls. The more experienced men systematically made appointments early in the morning, immediately before lunch, immediately after lunch or late in the afternoon, leaving midmorning and mid-afternoon free to make cold calls which, although not as important, resulted in enough business to make their results superior. It would have been very easy to jump to the conclusion that the less experienced men's disappointing results were due to a lack of sales skill. It was only by careful variance analysis that the real problem of appointment timing was identified.

Taking corrective action

Having identified the true nature of the variance, the sales manager has to decide whether it results from faulty standard setting or inadequate salesman performance. If the former, the standards will have to be modified. If the latter, the performance of the man will have to be improved, usually by some form of training or instruction. If the man is to improve he must be given specific targets to achieve within specific time periods otherwise little or no change will result.

If he fails to improve and the manager is certain that the standards are correct and that the appropriate legal procedures have been followed, there is no choice but to transfer him from the sales force or, more likely, terminate his employment with the company.

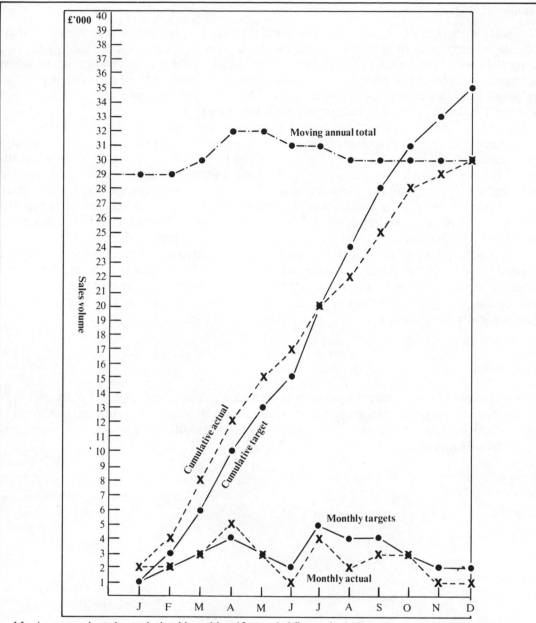

Moving annual totals are derived by taking 12 months' figures including latest month. Thus MAT for June covers period July last year to June this year. MAT for August is calculated by deducting August last year adding August this year. Therefore if total rises, performance is better than last year.

	Actual sales last year	Sales target this year	Actual sales this year	Moving annual total (12 months to date)
J	10 000	10 000	20 000	290 000
F	20 000	20 000	20 000	290 000
M	20 000	30 000	30 000	300 000
A	30 000	40 000	50 000	320 000
M	30 000	30 000	30 000	320 000
J	20 000	20 000	10 000	310 000
J	40 000	50 000	40 000	310 000
A	30 000	40 000	20 000	300 000
S	30 000	40 000	30 000	300 000
O	30 000	30 000	30 000	300 000
N	10 000	20 000	10 000	300 000
D	10 000	20 000	10 000	300 000
Total	280 000	350 000	300 000	

Fig. 12.7 Typical Z chart

Management responsibility for corrective action

The sales manager must not shirk this fundamental responsibility although it can be extremely distressing to have to fire a man who may have been with the company for some years and whom the manager has come to know well. It is almost axiomatic that the worst personnel problems are found in those companies which have tried to pretend that the failures would improve somehow some time. The sales manager can be absolutely certain that staff difficulties of this nature can only get worse.

He must realise that there are four aspects to this basic responsibility. First, he is charged by the company to achieve economic objectives. Second, he has a responsibility to himself to fulfil his task as a manager. Third, he has a duty to the other members of his team to ensure their efforts are not dragged down by retaining below-standard performers. Fourth, and most important of all, he has a critical responsibility to the man to tell him as soon as he is certain that he cannot achieve the standards demanded by the company. No man can be happy in a job that he knows he cannot do. The sooner he finds a position where his talents can be utilised, the better for all concerned. A company is never more culpable than when it retains a man, who is palpably incapable of achieving the desired levels of performance, for so many years that he becomes virtually unemployable when he is eventually asked to leave. Management cowardice or, at best, *laissez-faire* is one of the worst failings that companies ever exhibit. A philosophy of ruthlessness paradoxically is often the kindest and fairest attitude that a firm can have.

Conclusion

The objective of any control system is to monitor performance against plan and take corrective action when variances occur. Unless sales management are prepared to take that action, even when it is emotionally distressing, they will never be true managers and the firm will not prosper.

ACTION PLANNING CHECKLIST

Questions	Answers and action	Timing of action and evaluation
1 Have standards been set for each stage of sales activity?		
2 Have the absolute, moving and diagnostic standards been identified? (See Figure 12.1)		
3 Are weekly calling plans being used? (Figure 12.4)		
4 Are Prospect/Customer Record cards used properly by the sales force? (Figure 12.5)		
5 Is the information collection process geared to the standards that have been set?		
6 Is there a well-constructed call reporting system? (Figure 12.6)		
7 Have the salesmen been trained in report-writing and the manager in report analysis?		
8 Are variances produced and analysed systematically?		
9 Is appropriate corrective action taken promptly?		
10 Is the whole control system seen as an integral part of the fundamental management responsibility?		

PART THREE

SALES MANAGEMENT IN ACTION

CHAPTER 13

Improving Sales Productivity

The preceding chapters have attempted to describe in a systematic and sequential way the principles and practices of sound sales management giving brief examples wherever possible. We know, however, from working with many hundreds of firms and many thousands of sales managers throughout the world that the translation of even the most practical advice into action is difficult. Every company's circumstances are in some way unique to it and that uniqueness changes over time. The goals that enterprises try and achieve have to be modified in the light of their environments. Volume growth though desirable may not be feasible in depressed markets and margin protection may thus become paramount. The methods used to achieve sales results too change with the changing world. Van selling, once a widespread technique, particularly in perishable consumer goods industries, has become an increasingly expensive and decreasingly attractive option and fuel and many other related costs have soared. The rapid development of computerisation and particularly its miniaturisation offers cheaper, faster control possibilities than traditional paperwork procedures.

The accelerating speed and volatility of change in the modern world means that the sales manager must regularly and frequently review his operations to ensure their cost-effectiveness. This focus on productivity is particularly important in those industries which can no longer expect the continuous growth which they have traditionally enjoyed.

A productivity improvement programme starts with an assessment of the current situation using the techniques and methods described so far starting with performance analysis as described in Chapter 3. The second stage is to reconsider the goals to be achieved (ie. volume, revenue, margin, market share, etc) in the context of the current environment before re-evaluating and re-organising the methods by which these objectives are likely to be most cost-effectively reached. Finally, each individual area of sales management activity (i.e. recruitment, selection, training, motivation, control) should be reviewed to check that it is efficient and that full use is being made of current research and technology. Each of these major stages of a productivity improvement programme can be further broken down as is shown in Figure 13.1 'A 14-Step Programme for Improving Sales Productivity'.

Using a checklist like this, the sales manager should be able to review his activity regularly to ensure that it is kept as productive as possible within the changing environment. Most managers, however, find it easier to understand thoroughly the implications of such a programme if they are shown case histories of companies who have applied this kind of principles. The remainder of this section therefore is devoted to a series of examples drawn from a variety of industries which illustrate different aspects of sales management in action. As most of them are in fact cases where we were involved as consultants, professional ethics demand that they be made anonymous and in some instances further disguised to prevent identification. However, the situations faced by the firms and the actions taken are all represented accurately.

---

1   Decide the key measurements in the business in the terms of the cause–effect relationships involved. (See Figure 3.6, Assessing Sales Productivity.)

2   Analyse the current situation against the past, across the sales force and versus comparable situations in other divisions, other companies or other industries.

3   Reasssess the desired and achievable outputs required in terms of what results (i.e. volume, revenue, margin etc.) from whom (i.e. what type of customers).

4   Establish what has to be done to persuade them to buy – using perception surveys where necessary

5   Categorise customers in terms of their "service requirements" (i.e. those actions which will persuade them to buy.

6   Consider how those services can be most cost-effectively provided by, for example, the field force, teleselling, brokers etc

7   Structure the sales activity to reflect the nature, scale and requirements of the customer groups to be served

8   Organise the sales activity on the basis of workload and to maximise selling time

9   Improve the recruitment and selection processes to provide the maximum number of salesmen with the potential to be highly effective.

10 Construct training programmes which accurately reflect the sales task to be performed and consider the most cost-effective means of running them.

11 Check the motivational environment – using opinion polls where necessary – and create appropriate financial and non-financial incentives.

12 Monitor and analyse productivity performance against pre-set criteria regularly.

13 Search for productivity improvement from a better understanding of the buyer/seller relationships checking behavioural research for suggestions.

14 Use technology to free sales force time for redeployment on more creative activities e.g. computerised reporting and ordering procedures.

Fig. 13.1   A 14-step programme for improving sales productivity

Case History No. 1: Establishing Current Sales Productivity

Because of declining profitability INCAP, an international capital equipment group, decided to analyse the productivity of its major European sales operations, each of which sold through a dealer network to the market.

Total sales over the previous 6 years had grown but more in revenue than in volume even at constant prices.

	Volume	*Revenue*
Total Group	+13%	+19%

However, the pattern among the European subsidiaries varied widely and in some cases surprisingly from those figures.

	Volume	*Revenue*
France	-12%	+22%
Germany	+ 5%	+ 1%
UK	-41%	-36%
Holland	+12%	+17%
Belgium	+26%	+50%
Denmark	-46%	-20%

The next stage was to analyse the average sales value per unit sold, again at constant prices, as a guide to how the product mix had changed.

	% change in average sales value per unit
France	+39%
Germany	-4%
UK	+10%
Holland	+4%
Belgium	+34%
Denmark	+48%
Group	+6%

Again, there were some surprising variations – Denmark had lost most volume but gained most in average sales value, Germany had lost most average sales value but gained some volume. This gave rise to questions about pricing and mix policies in these sales operations.

Looking in more detail at the sales operations, productivity in terms of sales per person employed gave the following changes in the period:

	Average Sales per Person Employed	
	Volume	*Revenue*
France	-25%	-16%
Germany	+5%	+1%
UK	-48%	-43%
Holland	-51%	-48%
Belgium	-53%	-38%
Denmark	-53%	-30%
Group	-20%	-15%

These numbers suggested in a number of countries that it was taking twice as many people to sell the same volume as 6 years previously. Only Germany had increased volume and revenue per person.

A more detailed analysis of sales activities showed the following:

	Sales per Salesman (Units)	*Dealers per Salesmen*	*Sales per Dealer*
France	1203	85	14
Germany	399	32	12.4
UK	812	90	9
Holland	1978	40	49.4
Belgium	1114	318	3.5
Denmark (not analysed)			

There was obviously some correlation between the three factors: e.g. Holland has the highest sales per salesman and per dealer and second lowest number of dealers per salesman; Belgium on the other hand has the highest number of dealers per salesman and the lowest sales per dealer. Perhaps more interesting is the range of performance: 5:1 in terms of sales per man, 14:1 in terms of sales per dealer.

Even this brief analysis of overall sales productivity suggested some clear lines of enquiry:

1 How many dealers should there be in each territory relative to volume potential and country characteristics?
2 How many dealers can a salesman optimally handle?
3 What kind and how many support staff should back up the sales force?
4 How can pricing and product mix be better controlled?
5 Are the variations in sales per salesman explicable in terms of recruitment, training, motivation, etc., policies?

Action being taken includes:

1 Building a "model" of the optimum distribution network for the future: ie. analysis of number and type of potential consumers, specification of number of dealers, volume per each dealer, etc., specification of dealer functions as against sales force activity
2 Reducing drastically the number of dealers in certain countries, leading to a reduction in the sales force and back-up staff
3 Improved sales training and management organisation
4 More effective policies on pricing and product mix
5 Developing after-sales service as a profit centre activity to compensate for the volume decline in equipment.

Case History No. 2: Redefining goals and how to achieve them in a changing marketplace

A drawing office supplies company after many years of successful growth was faced with a market static at best and declining in some segments, declining volume sales and inadequate profitability on some of its products due to a mixture of price-cutting and high manufacturing and sales costs.

These problems had been masked in the past by regular sales revenue increases year by year. In fact, the traditional sales forecasting and targeting system had been simply to add on a percentage for "growth" to the previous year's sales across the total market with no real breakdown by major product group or market segment.

The company believed that there was considerable scope for productivity improvement in its sales activity which could contribute significantly to its objective of profit and profitability improvement. However, it was impossible to decide how or where sales productivity could be increased until the structure of the desired outputs was delineated.

The Board started by redefining the corporate profit goals in terms of the return on capital employed mechanism, ie:

$$\frac{\text{Return}}{\text{Capital Employed}} = \frac{\text{Return}}{\text{Sales}} \times \frac{\text{Sales}}{\text{Capital Employed}}$$

From this, it was possible to calculate revenue and margins targets.

The next stage was to analyse the market by segment to identify the most likely areas where profitable sales could be achieved, the structure of each segment in terms of the nature and scale of the customers within it, and the performance of the company in each sector.

It became clear from this study that the company's major market was declining and becoming more competitive. Prices had been reduced to try and retain market share which had led to severe reduction in gross margins. The nature of the market was changing, distributors becoming more powerful at the expense of direct accounts and both the distributive and direct sectors exhibiting strong 80:20 characteristics. 6 per cent of the trade accounts represented 60 per cent of all trade revenue; 14 per cent of the direct accounts represented 94 per cent of the sector revenue. Conversely, 86 per cent of all the accounts represented only 6 per cent of the revenue.

A perception survey of major accounts showed the following rank ordering of purchasing criteria:

1 Quality and consistency of supplies
2 Reliability of delivery
3 Speed of delivery
4 Price
5 Service and maintenance
6 Technical support and advice

which called into question some of the traditional beliefs and practices of the company, especially as regards price.

More worrying were some of the comments from the customers when asked about the differences between competitive suppliers. Broadly, it was observed that the company was not well-organised from the customer point of view, that it was difficult to know who to contact for information and that they did not treat their major customers with the importance that they expected.

The key conclusions drawn from this analysis of "what results should we be trying to achieve from whom" were that:

1 a clearer distinction needed to be drawn from both sales policy and activity viewpoints, between distributive and direct accounts;

2   a distributive strategy needed to be constructed focussed on what the distributors could *sell out* not simply what they were *buying in* leading to more accurate and specific target-setting;

3   there should be a major account activity based on detailed analysis of each major account, particularly its profitability, again leading to more accurate and specific target-setting to be achieved from better service along the lines indicated by the perception survey;

4   there should be a much greater concentration generally on the small percentage of accounts that made up most of the business;

5   it was seriously questioned whether the 86% of the accounts representing 6% of the revenue could ever benefit from or justify direct sales contact;

6   the sales forecasting and targeting process should be improved by being based on better profitability data. (It was impossible to identify profit by sales area or major customer with the existing costing system.)

Following reassessment of the outputs they required from whom, attention was turned to the sales activity where originally it had been felt that there was considerable room for productivity improvement.

The sales force consisted of 62 salesmen organised into 12 branches, the smallest having 2 men, the largest 9. Between them they covered 14000 accounts, but the number per man varied widely as did the sales per man in a range of almost 3:1. Some of the differences were explicable in terms of area potential, geography etc., but by no means all.

The sales force was organised on a geographical territory basis regardless of the different types and sizes of accounts. Not surprisingly their workloads varied considerably as did the average number of calls they made each day by a factor of almost 2:1. In all cases the call rate was far below that experienced in similar companies, partly because of the amount of sales administration with which they were involved.

It became clear from this analysis related to the restructured sales objectives and strategies that there was considerable room for productivity improvement by reducing the sales force and focussing it on the accounts with potential. 14 per cent of the accounts represented 94 per cent of all revenue. Many of these large accounts had several locations, though not all locations were significant purchasers.

Detailed analysis showed there were about 700 accounts requiring constant sales attention and yielding sales at a profitable level.

Work then progressed:

1   to define the overall sales force structure to focus individual attention on the distributive sector and major accounts;

2   to calculate how many salesmen were needed for each task and their activities;

3   to reduce the sales force and its management;

4   to define the marketing and sales support needed for the field sales activity;

5   to decide how the small accounts should be handled in the future (i.e. perhaps through some distributive channel).

So far the total sales force has been reduced by over a third largely by combining branches and eliminating one level of sales management which research showed had little more than a "postbox" function. This action has cut costs dramatically without any loss of sales as the remaining sales activity is much better focused on the key potential areas of the business.

Case History No. 3: Research to the aid of the sales force

It so often happens that sales force effectiveness is inhibited by traditional attitudes of customers particularly against new products and processes; furthermore such resistance to change is often rationalised particularly by trade customers on the basis that their consumers hold the same opinions.

Such a problem faced a manufacturer of sausage casings. Traditionally sausages were cased in gut but for more than fifteen years now collagen, which is a natural protein, has been sold very successfully to sausage manufacturers. The manufacturers changed to collagen because it gives a cleaner, quicker, more accurate fill. However, a significant percentage of the sausage market is supplied by butchers who make their own, and this segment has not adopted collagen to any degree despite its production advantages.

Research was commissioned therefore to establish why butchers did not use collagen. This survey showed that most butchers thought of collagen casings as synthetic or plastic; in fact only 11 per cent knew that it was a natural protein. The majority said that they had continued to use gut because customers preferred it and that collagen casings were difficult to use. However, less than a third of butchers had ever tried collagen and when asked what characteristics they wanted from a casing (e.g. uniform diameter, no holes, etc) their criteria are better met by collagen than by gut. This thus gave a much stronger argument to the sales force in communicating the production advantages of collagen to butchers.

There remained, however, the key question of consumer preference. It was established that consumers judged sausages by their appearance, uncooked and cooked, and not surprisingly by their taste. Consumer research was conducted using sausages identical in every way other than the casing to establish if there was a preference for gut over collagen as the butchers had maintained. The respondents were asked to rate each type of sausage (without of course knowing which had which casing) in terms of its shape, colour, appearance, size, tenderness, flavour, and easiness to chew. On every factor other than flavour there was a marked preference for collagen-cased sausages; on flavour there was only a marginal preference which is not surprising as the flavour comes from the sausage mix used which was identical in both types.

These research findings are of course of key importance to the sales force, demonstrating objectively and quantitatively to butchers that consumers strongly prefer collagen casings and that collagen offers significant production advantages. Obviously when facts conflict so strongly with ingrained attitudes, great sales skill is needed to communicate them unemotionally and persuasively. Conducting and using research in this way, however, does offer an approach much more likely to succeed than the clash of unsubstantiated opinion between salesman and customer.

Case History No. 4: Telephone selling as a cost-effective alternative

Telephone selling has become increasingly popular for handling such tasks as routine order-taking, maintaining customer contact, arranging appointments, etc. It seems to be most productive when used to supplement the field sales force activity rather than totally replacing it. It is cost-effective because commonly 50/60 calls per day can be made by telephone in markets where 8/10 personal visits is the maximum. Telephone sales staff costs and related expenses (eg. no cars) are much lower and the reduction usually more than offsets the actual telephone costs. Because of the cost differentials, profit increases can be achieved even if sales revenue declines. The normal experience however is that a correctly directed and structured telesales operation will at least equal and sometimes surpass the results of the traditional sales activity.

It is always advisable to experiment to test the hypotheses on which the telesales activity is to be based. For example, a soft drinks company concerned about the sales costs of routine order-taking from off-licence and liquor stores decided to reduce the salesmens' call rate from weekly to monthly using telesales girls to collect the regular weekly orders. This would leave the salesman free to concentrate on introducing new products, arranging promotions, opening new accounts, etc.

Objectives	Results	
1 To increase sterling sales to existing customers: – against budget – against base period	Test area: Control area: Test area: Control area:	35% increase 23% increase 11% increase 6% increase
2 To liberate salesmen's time by reducing routine calling activity (against base period)	Test area: Control area:	6% reduction Nil
3 To increase the frequency of customer contact (against base period)	Test area: Control area:	33% increase 3% increase
4 To increase the rate at which promotions are sold in (against base period)	Test area: Control area:	2.8X increase 1.7X increase
5 To open new accounts (against base period)	Test area: Control area:	3% increase 28% decrease
6 To revive moribund accounts which have not ordered for six months (against base period)	Test area: Control area:	41% decrease 54% decrease
7 To introduce new lines to customers (against base period)	Test area: Control area:	4% increase 3% decrease
8 To negotiate more promotions (against base period)	Test area: Control area:	177% increase 67% increase
9 To increase average order size (against base period)	Test area: Control area:	30% increase 14% increase
10 To increase the total numbers of orders obtained per week (against base period)	Test area: Control area:	26% increase Nil increase

Fig. 13.2   Effect of telesales on a soft drinks company over a 3 month period

North London was selected for the experiment, holding South London, a similar area in terms of volumes, outlets, etc, as a control group. After three months sales in North London had increased 12 per cent more than in South London and other objectives in terms of new accounts, new product introductions, arranging promotions, had also been achieved. (See Figure 13.2.) The sales revenue increase more than offset the additional costs of the telesales operation. Moreover, when fully implemented nationally, the telesales costs were compensated for by a reduction in the field force.

Case History No. 5: Redefining the nature and structure of the sales activity in a changing environment

As markets become more competitive, they tend to change in nature as well as in scale. This means that for many companies, their traditional policies and methods of selling have to be radically altered if they are to continue to prosper.

In the supply of industrial components, the historical focus has been for most manufacturers on the needs of the major customers, the original equipment (OE) manufacturers, rather than on the much more fragmented replacement market. One large European manufacturer, having enjoyed years of success when OE markets (eg. automotive, machine tools, farm machinery) were buoyant, found itself in the mid 1970s facing stagnation and often decline in these industries, increasing competition from other suppliers notably Japanese, falling price and margin levels and thus serious threats to its profitability. It had never been deeply concerned about the replacement market with all its difficulties whilst its major OE customers were providing sufficient growth. It was realised however, that the aftermarket although characterised by having to be supplied through distribution networks to a multitude of small customers did offer relatively greater potential as it is not as volatile nor as competitive as the original equipment sector and price levels are significantly higher.

The sales force in each country had been organised on a simple geographic basis focused around the major OE customers with each territory salesman also supposed to sell to dealers for the replacement market.

The nature of selling to the OE customers demands high technical expertise, lengthy contract negotiation, often starting from the design stage and, once the order was obtained, the management of supply to the customer.

Selling via distributors to the replacement market is entirely different. The distributor, like any retailer, largely responds to the demands of his consumers and he only buys in order to resell. The essential problem therefore, was not how to sell to the distributor but how to ensure he sold to his consumers. This involved understanding the distributor's local market, how local sales merchandising and promotion efforts could be mounted, ensuring appropriate stock levels etc; all skills quite foreign to the technical OE salesman.

Thus if this industrial component manufacturer were to redirect his efforts more into the replacement market, the whole nature of the sales effort had to be changed. The first stage was to define more precisely the needs of the various participants (e.g. consumers, dealers, distributors) in this market. The manufacturer, because of the traditional lack of concentration, knew very little in depth about it and research had to be commissioned to identify the buying criteria of the consumer (e.g. why did he go to a particular dealer for particular components?) and of the dealers (e.g. how did they choose which manufacturers to buy from?). This research confirmed in detail that the salesmen's role selling via dealers to the replacement market was entirely different from selling to the OE manufacturer, even though they were selling the same product range.

Even more importantly, from a strategic point of view, this research provided the basis for a redefinition of distribution policy in terms of which of the alternative distribution channels should be chosen, the criteria for selecting individual dealers within each network and the quantification of how many dealers were needed for market coverage, thus indicating the numbers of salesmen required.

The second stage, therefore, was to reflect the difference organisationally by separating the OE and replacement market sales forces. The job of the replacement market salesman was redefined, fundamentally as *marketing through* the distribution network not *selling to* it. This led to a different recruitment profile and to a major training exercise to equip sales management and the sales force with a much larger understanding of how dealers operate so they could help them sell more (and thus inevitably buy more). Training modules were produced covering all major aspects of dealer operations, (e.g. stock planning and control, local advertising and sales promotion, financial management, dealer pricing, etc) as well as the basics of dealer selection and appointment. Training was also given in training so that the manufacturer's sales team could help develop the dealer's staff to sell more.

The result has been that the replacement sector of the business has grown to over a third of the total business in terms of sales and more than that in terms of profit, reflecting both the changing balance in the market and the effectiveness of the manufacturer's response to it.

Case History No. 6: Improving the management of major accounts

Over recent years the trend towards market domination by fewer, larger retailers has been seen in many industries, nowhere more so than the food trade. At the same time most food markets have stagnated or grown only slowly and as the major retailers have wielded their buying power, manufacturers' profits and profitability have suffered.

Traditionally, food company sales forces have been focused on volume and revenue growth but, with the key accounts demanding ever-increasing concessions, it has become vital for the manufacturer to review the profitability of his dealings with his major customers. One large food company recognising this situation realised that he had no means of assessing customer profitability, ie. no system of cost allocation by customer, only by product. This means that he did not know how much profit each customer provided nor how much each could or should provide. Thus the accounts plans produced by the sales teams were limited in their scope, it was difficult to evaluate the financial effect of the concessions traded in the negotiations with major customers, and management had no sound basis for the planning and evaluation of the key account sales activity.

The first stage therefore was to devise a format which could analyse the revenue and costs by major customer and to plot the top accounts on it to see what profits and profitability they each produced. This required considerable work in cost identification and allocation before it was possible to produce the summary format shown in Figure 13.3. Starting off with the list price for the quantities concerned, this deducts discounts, selling, production, distribution and financing costs to arrive at the contribution each account makes to the company overhead and profit. It was immediately apparent that there were significant differences in profitability between the major accounts even where they bought similar volumes. Surprisingly the largest discounts did not go to the largest customer and the discount structure varied markedly. Selling costs ranged from 0.2 per cent to 4.4 per cent of gross revenue, in the latter case largely due to a heavy merchandising input. Many other differences can be seen which had apparently no logical explanation reflecting the fact that there had never been any mechanisms for analysing revenue, costs and profit contribution by account, therefore decisions had had to be made on each individual item on a somewhat ad-hoc basis.

The analysis work continued to ascertain the breakdown of each account's profitability by product group of which there were six. Figure 13.4 shows how each product group contributed to the total and demonstrates an enormous variation both within and between customers: Product Group F, for example, showing only 4.7 per cent profit to gross revenue in Customer 1 and 18.1 per cent in Customer 4, a fourfold difference although overall Customer 4 is only 5 per cent more profitable than Customer 1. The effect of not stocking Product Group C has apparently constrained the profitability of Customers 1, 2 and 3, although Customer 6 is yielding very little profitability on these products compared with the other two stockists.

	Customer 1	Customer 2	Customer 3	Customer 4	Customer 5	Customer 6
Cases sold	600,000	352,000	512,000	146,000	498,000	1,480,000
List price	100.00	100.00	100.00	100.00	100.00	100.00
Discounts negotiated	10.6%	7.7%	8.2%	6.0%	9.4%	9.6%
Retrospective	1.9%	1.3%	2.7%	1.6%		3.0%
Advertising	1.8%	0.5%	0.1%	1.1%	1.3%	0.2%
Account Development		.1%		.1%		.6%
Special Packs	.4%	.1%	.9%	.1%		.4%
Others	.4%	.3%	6.3%	.4%	.2%	.2%
TOTAL DISCOUNT	15.1%	10.0%	18.2%	9.3%	10.9%	14.0%
Selling costs Sales force	1.5%	1.4%				1.5%
Merchandising	2.7%	.6%				1.1%
National Account Mgmt.	0.1%	0.2%	0.1%	0.2%	0.2%	
Damaged Goods Returned	0.1%	0.1%	0.3%			0.1%
TOTAL SELLING COSTS	4.4%	2.3%	0.4%	0.2%	0.2%	2.7%
Production costs Cost ex-factory	55.0%	55.5%	58.0%	55.7%	55.3%	55.9%
Delivery: – Direct from factory – Depot	4.3%	1.3% 3.0%	1.3% 2.8%	1.2% 2.8%	3.3%	5.9%
TOTAL PRODUCTION AND DISTRIBUTION COSTS	59.3%	59.8%	62.1%	59.7%	58.6%	61.8%
Finance costs Early Payment Discount	0.4%	0.4%		0.5%	0.5%	0.5%
Cost of Debtors			0.5			
TOTAL FINANCE COSTS	0.4%	0.4%	0.5%	0.5%	0.5%	0.5%
Profit contribution (% of list price)	20.8%	27.5%	18.8%	30.3%	29.8%	21.0%

Fig. 13.3 Major customer profitability

Obviously these analyses raised many vital questions about account performance, planning, negotiation and control. Work continued to computerise the profitability analysis systems so that this vital data could be produced on a regular basis. A new major account planning system was designed covering analysis of past performance, setting of profit and revenue objectives and detailing the products to be sold, the pricing and discount structure, and the sales, promotion, merchandising and distribution activity. Training was then prepared for all key account managers so that they fully understood the implications of the profitability analysis, how to plan using it as a basis and how to negotiate with their major customers to improve profitability.

Product Groups

Major Customers	A	B	C	D	E	F	Total
1	25.2%	32.5%	—	15.8%	17.1%	4.7%	20.8%
2	37.5%	36.1%	—	25.4%	23.8%	13.4%	27.5%
3	16.2%	30.8%	—	6.8%	13.3%	5.2%	18.8%
4	38.8%	35.8%	31.1%	24.6%	32.7%	18.1%	30.3%
5	24.3%	41.0%	41.5%	21.1%	26.6%	17.8%	29.8%
6	29.7%	32.3%	15.3%	15.6%	18.6%	9.6%	21.0%

Fig. 13.4   Profit contribution by product group for major customers

Case History No. 7: Improving recruitment and retention of good salesmen

It is a blinding glimpse of the obvious that sales force success is primarily determined by the quality of the people employed. Yet most sales managers seem dissatisfied with their recruitment and selection procedures as was evidenced by the Institute of Marketing study *Sales Force Practice Today*, which revealed that half of the sales managers questioned reported that 30 per cent of the salesmen they had recruited in the last three years were unsatisfactory.

In the case of one office equipment firm, the situation was even worse. Not only were they concerned whether they were attracting and picking the right kind of candidate, but also they were losing a significant percentage of those selected within the first year of employment, i.e. at a time when they had not begun to produce sufficient revenue to cover the costs of recruitment, training and employment.

A research exercise was carried out to identify the basic causes of this unsatisfactory performance. It became clear that both the recruitment and induction system and the skills of those administering it were lacking. The company was organised on a branch basis and each of the over 30 branch managers recruited for his own needs, but because this meant employing only two or three each per year, none of them had sufficient practice to develop effective selection skills. The company's systems were weak too in that the branch managers were given no real guidance in, for example, how to write advertisements; the company's application form did not collect sufficient data and there were no defined standards or procedures for interviewing. Furthermore, the induction training was left almost entirely to the local branch (apart from centralised product knowledge training) and discussions with salesmen who had left or were leaving demonstrated that their reasons for quitting centred around how they had been treated in the early weeks with the company. For example many branch managers, largely for their own administrative convenience, set the same sales targets for all their salesmen, although of course they recognised that a new man could not possibly achieve them. Despite this recognition, however, many of the new salesmen found it extremely demotivating to be set targets that were impossible, particularly in the busy branches where they also felt they were given insufficient guidance and local training in the early months. These kinds of factor were the root cause of good men leaving during the first year of employment.

It was obviously important therefore to redefine the whole process of recruiting, selection and induction in much more detail, laying down standards of performance for branch managers at each stage. The Application Form was expanded, reference checking systems installed, interview structures designed, induction programmes established and the new system written up in detail in an operating manual which took the branch manager step by step from the moment he had a vacancy he needed to fill to the end of the first year of employment of the new salesman.

Although this solved the problem of the lack of common and detailed procedures, no manual by itself can inculcate skills. A training programme was therefore designed using the new manual as the basic structure. The main focus of the programme, however, was on skill development at each stage of the selection process; for example, exercises were constructed on the interpretation of application forms. The heart of any selection procedure is the interviewing stage and although some skills can be developed by roleplaying it is difficult to make such roleplaying realistic as the participants know each other too well. It was decided therefore to use real candidates, timing the training programme after a recruitment campaign. The shortlisted applicants were told that they would be interviewed by the relevant manager in the normal way, but for management training purposes, the interview would be video taped for analysis. Applicants were of course given the right to refuse to participate; in fact none did and the majority were impressed that the company was so concerned about recruitment that they went to such lengths.

After the interview, the video tape was then discussed with the manager concerned and his colleagues and all felt significant benefit from this real-life training situation. More importantly, evaluation some months after the installation of the procedures manual and the training programme showed that all managers felt that better candidates were being attracted and selected and later checking demonstrated a significant fall in staff turnover in the first critical year.

Case History No. 8: The computer and the sales activity

Most studies of sales force time utilisation show that only around 25 per cent at best is spent selling face to face with the customer. Much of the rest is occupied by tasks such as filling in orders, sales reporting, merchandising and of course travel. An increasing number of companies concerned about improving productivity are using the rapidly developing technology of computers to help reduce the time taken particularly in paper-work handling and, even more positively, to provide better information and tools for their sales force.

One food company, for example, has provided its sales force with hand-held micro-terminals which can be connected via an acoustic couple and a telephone to the company computer. Thus when the salesman is with the buyer he can check directly stock availability and when the order is agreed enter it immediately into the computer. This avoids lengthy checking on supply and filling out order forms. The sales manager can also access the computer for immediate sales data by product, customer and salesman, thus obviating the need for written sales reports. Furthermore, by closed circuit TV links, the same data can be made available to the area managers at home via their own domestic TV receivers. A great deal of time on paperwork is saved and, because of the rapidity with which the information is available, faster, more specific management direction can be given to take advantage of local demand, etc. This whole system was paid for in one year from the cash flow improvement of direct order entry from the point of sale, replacing the traditional time-consuming method of working out the order on paper, posting it and manually entering it into the computer.

A variation on this system in a toiletries company again employs hand-held terminals into which the salesman enters orders during the day where they are stored. At night he connects his terminal to his home telephone and the computer calls each in turn automatically during the night to collect the previous day's orders.

Another use of computerisation to reduce order handling time is employed in a Swedish tool company where the manufacturer's computer is directly connected with those of his major distributors. When sales are made by a distributor and entered into his own computer, thus reducing his stock, his computer orders direct replenishment without involving the salesman in this routine task. Again all unnecessary sales analyses are printed out without the salesman having to fill in forms.

One task that takes up a considerable amount of sales force time, particularly in the consumer goods trades, is that of merchandising. Often the salesman has the extremely difficult and time-consuming problem of designing an attractive display using products of different shapes, sizes, demand, prices and margins to fit into the space allocated by the retailer. Some companies provide their salesmen with photographs or plans of typical displays to guide them, but as each outlet is different, even such examples have often to be severely modified to fit the individual retailer.

A toy company found itself in this situation which was being exacerbated by the ever increasing cost of sales time and the introduction of large numbers of new products. It was taking typically up to two full days for a salesman working in the company showroom to design a display which would attractively show the products ordered by the retailer within the limitations of the space allocated. Having developed a solution the salesman had then to draw it, dismantle the display and take it to the outlet concerned.

Working with the company we developed a computer based merchandising system designed to achieve seven objectives:

1   provide a lay-out plan from which the display could be built easily;
2   ensure that the most profitable lines were stocked and sales and/or profits maximised;
3   utilise as much as possible of the available shelf space;

4   equalise the rate of depletion of all products thus reducing out of stock situations;
5   determine stock levels and the cost of fully merchandising the display at preset intervals;
6   be simple enough for non-technical people (salesmen or store staff) to use;
7   be cheap enough for use in small as well as large retail outlets.

To operate the system the salesman inputs certain basic information via a computer terminal; such terminals are portable and can be taken to the customers' premises and linked to the main computer by telephone. The salesman enters the expected rate of sale, price, cost and dimensions of the products involved and the dimensions of the space to be used (i.e. number of shelves, length, width, etc). The computer program then calculates the sales and profit per product line over a given period, the quantity of each product that can be placed on the shelves, the stock required and a scale diagram of the layout as well as the order details.

The total time of designing a display has been reduced to well under an hour and the computer costs are only about 50p per outlet. Perhaps even more important than this dramatic reduction in time and cost is the fact that the sales force now has available a powerful sales tool unique in its industry to help persuade retailers to buy and display its products.

The computer has made its presence felt in other areas of sales activity. The management and negotiation of major customers' business is being facilitated by the provision of computerised profit and loss accounting by customer. The modern sales office is typified by visual display units giving instant access to key data for sales office personnel dealing with telephone enquiries. New approaches to sales force incentive schemes can be developed on micro-computers which have the capability to handle the many different factors involved such as area potential, past sales results, sales targets, effect of promotion campaigns, etc.

It is often said that technology has the answers to the future; perhaps the problem is that management does not know the questions to ask! For the sales manager, the best approach to identifying areas where computerisation may be helpful is not to focus on the technical aspects of the equipment. It is to analyse in more detail using research where necessary the activities that he controls. Indubitably costs of all kinds will continue to rise, some faster than others, most for reasons beyond his control like inflation, energy price escalation etc. All that the sales manager can do is understand his own responsibilities better and search for more productive ways of discharging them. With each salesman currently costing up to £20000 p.a. to keep on the road, it is an expensive way to collect routine orders or fill out forms.

Those companies who have positively sought ways in which computerisation can help have generally done so not to replace salesmen with machines, but to release the scarce and valuable time of the sales force to be concentrated on those things which only the sales force can do – finding new customers, introducing new products, arranging new promotions. With the increasing simplification and miniaturisation of computing and the dramatic reduction in its costs, its benefits are within the reach of any sales manager; the challenge is to take these benefits and use them to support the efforts of the sales force to the ultimate benefit of the company and all who work in it.

Bibliography

As the sales manager is always desperately short of time there seems little point in offering voluminous booklists. For those who wish to expand beyond the limitations of this volume, a few books that the author has found particularly valuable have been selected.

MARKETING
P. Kotler, *Marketing Management*, Prentice-Hall, 1980
J. Stapleton, *How to Prepare a Marketing Plan*, Gower, Third edition, 1982
M. T. Wilson, *The Management of Marketing*, Gower, 1980

MANAGEMENT
P. Drucker, *Managing for Results*, Heinemann, 1964, Pan, 1967
P. Drucker, *The Effective Executive*, Heinemann, 1967, Pan, 1970
J. Humble, *Improving Business Results*, McGraw-Hill, 1968

SPECIFIC ASPECTS OF SALES MANAGEMENT
J. B. J. Lidstone, *How to Recruit and Select Successful Salesmen,* Gower, Second edition, forthcoming
J. B. J. Lidstone, *Training Salesmen on the Job*, Gower, 1975
J. B. J. Lidstone, *Motivating Your Sales Force*, Gower, 1978
J. B. J. Lidstone, *Negotiating Profitable Sales*, Gower, 1977
A. V. Melkman, *How to Handle Major Customers Profitably*, Gower, 1979
P. Forsyth, *Running an Effective Sales Office*, Gower, 1980
National Training Systems/Marketing Improvements, *Creating Major Sales*, 1981

Index

Conclusion

Practical Follow-up

The nature of sales management has changed dramatically in the last two or three decades; in many firms even the last few years have seen a complete re-orientation of the function. As markets became increasingly competitive and competition increasingly international, this process of change will not simply continue. It will accelerate as the margins of error become even finer. No longer will finger in the wind management be precise enough to generate profits.

Sales management in particular and marketing management in general must become more professional and more scientific to survive in the future. The great barrier to progress at the moment is the lack of proven theory. To overcome this hurdle, the sales manager must be prepared to hypothesise about better operating methods, not simply perpetuate techniques because they are traditionally accepted. He must experiment with innovative approaches and most important of all, he must attempt to validate his hypotheses by rigorous assessment.

It is by such procedures that the body of scientific knowledge has been painfully compiled over the years. If marketing is to grow as a discipline it too must be prepared to undergo similar evaluation.

If all this book has achieved is to encourage sales management to take a more systematic approach to its vital task, it will have succeeded. The attempt has been made to construct this volume in such a form that any manager can take its ideas, translate them into action and assess their effectiveness. It is believed that this is something of a new concept in business communication. Unless the gap is bridged between what is written and what is practised, there is little value in business literature.

As was said in the Introduction, the onus of responsibility for translating words into deeds lies heavily on the reader. However, business authors should take their own medicine if they believe in it sufficiently to prescribe it for others. This book represents a series of hypotheses about the methods and techniques necessary to the sophisticated sales manager. In particular it postulates a concept of how to communicate more effectively with him. In itself it is an experiment in business communications. It must now be validated in true marketing terms. Does it provide the appropriate need satisfactions to its consumers?

The questionnaire is aimed at assessing this. Please complete it and return it. It will be studied and analysed with great interest. Most important of all it will help contribute to the development of a proven body of marketing theory which should be the prime interest of us all.

Appendix

Reader's Questionnaire

Please detach or copy and, when completed, return to:

> M T Wilson
> Marketing Improvements Ltd
> Ulster House
> 17 Ulster Terrace
> Regents Park Outer Circle
> London NW1
>
> 01-487 5811

1 *Do you consider that the objectives of the book were defined?*

VERY CLEARLY	QUITE CLEARLY	SOMEWHAT UNCLEARLY	NOT AT ALL CLEARLY

Comments on answer

....
....
....

2 *Does the material of the book achieve the objectives?*

COM-PLETELY	IN THE MAIN	NOT VERY WELL	NOT AT ALL

Comments on answer

....
....
....

3   *Does the method of approach*
     enable the techniques
     described to be translated
     into action?

VERY EASILY	QUITE EASILY	WITH SOME DIFFI-CULTY	NOT AT ALL

Comments on answer

....
....
....

4   *Is the level of the book*
     appropriate to the practising
     sales manager?

COM-PLETELY	IN THE MAIN	ONLY IN A FEW PARTS	NOT AT ALL

Comments on answer

....
....
....

5   *Does the book achieve its*
     intended balance between
     consumer and industrial
     selling and product and
     service selling?

COM-PLETELY	IN THE MAIN	ONLY IN A FEW PARTS	NOT AT ALL

Comments on answer

....
....
....

6   *Has the book improved your*
     managerial practices?

TO A LARGE DEGREE	TO SOME DEGREE	TO A SMALL DEGREE	NOT AT ALL

Comments on answer

....
....
....

Other comments – for example, omissions, sections lacking clarity, topics that should have been included, examples of how it has helped you, etc

....

....

....

....

....

....

Name..

Position..

Company...

Address...

....

....

....